Department Head's
SURVIVAL GUIDE

Department Head's

SURVIVAL GUIDE

Ready-to-Use Techniques and Materials for Effective Leadership

MICHAEL D. KOEHLER

PRENTICE HALL
Englewood Cliffs, New Jersey 07632

Prentice-Hall International (UK) Limited, *London*
Prentice-Hall of Australia Pty. Limited, *Sydney*
Prentice-Hall Canada, Inc., *Toronto*
Prentice-Hall Hispanoamericana, S.A., *Mexico*
Prentice-Hall of India Private Limited, *New Delhi*
Prentice-Hall of Japan, Inc., *Tokyo*
Simon & Schuster Asia Pte. Ltd., *Singapore*
Editora Prentice-Hall do Brasil, *Rio de Janeiro*

10 9 8 7 6 5 4 3 2

Library of Congress Cataloging-in-Publication Data

Koehler, Michael D.
    Department head's survival guide : ready-to-use techniques and
materials for effective leadership / by Michael D. Koehler.
        p.   cm.
    ISBN 0-13-015165-3 :
    1. Departmental chairmen (High schools)—Handbooks, manuals, etc.
2. Educational leadership—Handbooks, manuals, etc.   3. High
schools—Administration—Handbooks, manuals, etc.   I. Title.
LB2822.K64   1993
373.12'013—dc20   93-5829
                                                                            CIP

ISBN 0-13-015165-3

PRENTICE HALL
Career and Personal Development
Englewood Cliffs, NJ 07632

Simon & Schuster, A Paramount Communications Company

PRINTED IN THE UNITED STATES OF AMERICA

DEDICATION

To my father-in-law, Bud Sexmith, for living the principles in this book and for sharing them so sensitively with his family and with me.

ACKNOWLEDGMENTS

I am grateful to the following people for the special assistance they provided in the development of this book:

Pat Moorhead, Jan Jordan, Vince Malek, John Heerman, and Dave Ritter for the benefit of their experience. Sue Hutchison for her initial editorial help. John Scornavacco for permission to use his school's forms. Jim Warren for setting a positive and creative tone. Al Cohen for his professional growth program. Greg Royer for his information on hiring and for being such a willing sounding board. Dorothy Michno and the Deerfield High School Curriculum Committee for the forms on curriculum change. Win Huppuch for his continuing willingness to take the high road. Dick Moore for his materials on the Early Bird Tutoring Program. John Woodward for many of his ideas. And Connie Kallback for doing the lion's share of the editorial work and for being so available and supportive.

And especially to my wife, Pat, for tolerating my absences during the composition of the manuscript and for sharing her special brand of good humor the rest of the time.

ABOUT THE AUTHOR

Mike Koehler has been teaching both educational administration and supervision at the university level for almost 20 years. A Ph.D. in administration, he is the author of seven books, an education series for Sears, a nationally syndicated radio show, and a videotape distributed nationwide by the College Board. Dr. Koehler has written a wide range of articles for professional journals, a nationally syndicated radio show, even the Dial Santa Claus series for Illinois, New York, and Pennsylvania Bell Telephone. Dr. Koehler has lectured nationwide on different aspects of education and has been a department chair, an administrative assistant to the principal, and the administrative assistant to the superintendent of a large school district in Northern Illinois. He has been happily married to wife Pat for 31 years and is the father of three daughters, Kathleen, Carrie, and Peggy.

ABOUT THIS SURVIVAL GUIDE

Department chairs are neither teachers nor administrators. They perform a range of "administrative" duties and in some schools may regularly attend building "administrator" meetings, but at best they are lower-case versions of principals and assistant principals and must maintain their focus on *departmental* rather than building and district issues. This neither fish-nor-fowl position is unique in schools, and it requires considerable skill. Department chairs walk a tightrope between the maintenance and survival needs of the school and the human and professional needs of the people within it.

Being intermediaries, they come in frequent contact with both elements and must at times deal with controversial issues that pit one against the other. Resolving such conflicts requires strong interpersonal skills and a working knowledge of organizational dynamics. Above all, it requires professionals who are well-liked by the members of their departments.

This Survival Guide provides ways for department chairs to engender such acceptance and, in the process, to increase their power within the school. It

- identifies ways to establish processes of classroom observation that are nonthreatening and that result in teacher growth,
- engages teachers in their own evaluation and in the evaluation of their programs,
- provides processes for the cooperative development of relevant in-service training activities, and
- identifies a format for hiring the best teachers, motivating them, and building departmental teams that work cooperatively to educate all students.

The Guide also identifies strategies for resolving conflict and for dealing constructively with the problem teacher. It provides sections on teacher dismissal, student discipline, the budget as a planning document, and ideas for dealing collaboratively with other departments, the district building, and the

Board of Education. Additional sections acknowledge the importance of maintaining relationships with the parent community, of making intelligent use of the school's support services, even of working closely with the custodial staff.

The Guide provides sections on the need for department chairs to maintain their own professional growth and self-revitalization and to make the best use of current research. A concluding section suggests ways to establish priorities, avoid teacher burnout, and set personal and professional limits.

The author acknowledges that the responsibilities and duties of department chairs may vary from school to school. They may have the primary responsibility for teacher evaluation in one building and none in another. They may plan and coordinate the department's budget in one school and operate within a preplanned budget in another. The functions and tasks as identified and discussed in this book, therefore, although they may not be characteristic of every department chair, do describe the range of potential responsibilities for all department chairs.

The *Survival Guide* contains step-by-step procedures and a wealth of reproducible forms conveniently located at the end of each chapter. These include observation forms, letters, handouts, and memos. The variety of sample pre- and postconferencing strategies, observation reports, needs assessment techniques, sample budget documents, and curriculum and other materials are included as valuable time-savers. In short, the Guide provides everything the practicing department chair needs to control departmental activities without making all the decisions that affect those activities.

Controlling the process without making all the terminal decisions is the key to effective leadership. It results not only in an increase in power but in personal popularity among staff members. Department chairs who use the materials contained within this guide, then, guarantee not only their survival but their personal and professional effectiveness within the school system. They will realize that the *authority* to work with teachers is conferred by the administration and the Board of Education but that the *power* to influence student learning and teacher morale is granted by the teachers themselves. This book provides the key for securing such power.

With such knowledge, department chairs will reduce teacher anxiety during classroom observations, increase the involvement of staff in departmental activities, improve the professional competencies of teachers, consolidate their own power base, and foster a climate of mutual trust within the school. Most importantly, because the process encourages teacher investment in their own professional growth as well as in departmental activities, it results in improved learning experiences for students—the ultimate goal of any successful department chair.

Michael Koehler, Ph.D.

CONTENTS

What Are Curriculum and Instruction? (2) • Influences on a Changing Curriculum (3) • Other Influences (3) • Problems Resulting from These Influences (4) • How Do We Respond? (5) • Let's Be Proactive (5) • The Need for Process (7) • A Suggested Process (7) • More About the Department's Curriculum Committee (9) • Process Doesn't Stop (10) • A Word about Scope and Sequence (10) • We're All in This Together (11) • Textbook Adoption (12) • Let's Wrap It Up (13)

Section 2   HELPING TEACHERS GROW PROFESSIONALLY 39

The Department Chair as Teacher Aide (40) • Five Critical Questions about Classroom Observation (40) • Defining Mirrors of Performance (41) • Giving Objective Feedback (42) • How Video Technology Helps (42) • Feedback from Peers (43) • Evaluation for All Styles and Abilities (44) • The "Willing-and-Able" Teacher (45) • The "Willing-but-Unable" Teacher (45) • The "Able-but-Unwilling" Teacher (45) • Keeping Feedback Objective (46) • Asking the Right Questions (46) • When Answers are Needed (47) • Trust = Power (48) • Let's Wrap It Up (48)

Section 3   EVALUATING TEACHERS: A LITTLE QUALITY CONTROL 63

What is Evaluation? (64) • More on Evaluation (65) • Six Principles of Effective Teacher Evaluation (65) • Evaluation for What? (67) • Who Evaluates? (69) • Who Is the Audience? (70) • So What's the Difference Between Evaluation and Supervision? (71) • When Evaluation Doesn't Work (72) • Books, Mirrors, and Red Pencils

(Training, Evaluation, and Supervision) (73) • Strategies that Promote Trust (73) • Checklists? There's a Better Way! (74) • Evaluation and Video Technology (75) • Beyond Evaluation (76) • Let's Wrap It Up (76)

Section 4 MAKING IN-SERVICE TRAINING RELEVANT 95

What Is In-Service Training? (96) • Why In-Service Training? (97) • Relating In-Service Training to Supervision and Evaluation (97) • In-Service Training and Needs Assessment (99) • The Needs Assessment Process (99) • A Complementary Option (101) • In-Service Training and Video Technology (102) • Supplementary Sources of Information (102) • For the Records (103) • Coming Full Circle (103) • Let's Wrap It Up (104)

Section 5   HOW TO HIRE THE BEST TEACHERS... 121

Establishing the Criteria (122) • Setting the Scene (123) •
Setting up the Process (123) • The Initial Screening (125)
• Reference Checks (126) • The Interview Process (127) •
Guaranteeing the Process (129) • Avoiding Legal Pitfalls
(130) • Keeping Written Records (130) • Hiring the Best
Candidate (131) • Let's Wrap It Up (132)

Section 5 Figures:

Section 6   TEACHER MOTIVATION 147

Intrinsic Motivation (148) • Extrinsic Motivation (148) •
Maslow's Hierarchy of Needs (150) • Physiological Needs
(151) • Security Needs (152) • Psychological Security (153)
• Rapport (154) • The Hierarchy (155) • Team Building
(156) • Social Needs (156) • New Teacher Orientation (157)
• Esteem Needs (158) • Self-Actualization Needs (160) •
Let's Wrap It Up (160)

Section 6 Figures:

Section 7   MEETING THE CHANGING NEEDS OF STUDENTS 171

What Are the Needs? (172) • Reducing Competition (173) • Adjusting Standards (174) • Eliminating Punitive Control Models (176) • Increasing Affective Learning Experiences (179) • Developing Support Systems (180) • Special Classes (184) • Maintaining Contact With the Home (184) • What Else Does the Future Hold? (185) • Let's Wrap It Up (185)

Section 7 Figures:

Section 8   PLANNING FOR SUCCESS.............. 223

Identifying the Problem (224) • Focusing on Values (225) •
The Mission Statement (226) • Problems within the System
(226) • Focus on "What" for Problem Identification (227) •
Where Do We Want to Be? (228) • How Do We Get There?
(229) • Monitoring Solutions (230) • The Budget as a
Planning Document (233) • The Art of Grants (235) •
General Guidelines for Proposal Writing (236) • General
Planning Procedures (237) • Let's Wrap It Up (239)

Section 8 Figures:

Section 9   MANAGING AND AVOIDING CONFLICT 265

Managing Conflict (266) • Conflict Resolution Strategies
(266) • The Conflict Resolution Process (268) • The Need

On Being a Good Department Chair (301) • Teacher Burnout (302) • Delegation as a Key to Sanity (304) • You and the Job (305) • The Ten Suggestions (305) • Let's Wrap It Up (306)

Promoting Curriculum Development and Effective Instruction

Before 1910, fewer than 6% of our nation's teenagers graduated from secondary schools. The "relevancy" of curriculum wasn't an issue; a wide range of offerings wasn't necessary. The majority of adolescents were in the work force and learned more from job experience than school curricula. A few decades later, the majority of the nation's jobs were still blue-collar; the economic demands on a high school education were yet to be felt.

By 1950, approximately 50% of the nation's youth were graduating from high school, and 60% of the nation's jobs remained blue-collar. But much had changed in forty years. We had experienced two world wars, an accompanying explosion of knowledge, changing social perspectives, television, random access retrieval systems, the acceptance of protest, even the reconstruction of time-sanctioned theories of learning. Rote learning was giving way to discovery learning, the scientific method, and varying problem-solving approaches. The need to think and to relate schooling to the changing world of work, the importance of resolving increasingly complex social and personal problems, and the demand for relevancy had arrived. With their arrival, education was challenged to promote curriculum development and improved instruction.

Education responded with vocational education, career counselors, media centers, individualized instruction, team teaching, multiple grouping patterns, learning labs, computerized instruction, variable modular scheduling, Head Start, and continuous progress curricula. Today, only 6 to 10% of the nation's jobs are blue-collar, and approximately 25% of our high school students are still dropping out. Many graduates and nongraduates still can't read. Recent reports from the government indicate that 3.6 million adults are involved in literacy programs. Education has responded with elective courses, "pay to stay" in school, cooperative learning, the open classroom, values education, student-centered curricula, higher order thought process, the voucher system, and the use of recent technological innovations such as fiber optics and interactive computer technology.

But the demands persist—as they should and will. Society continues to change and critics of education continue to take potshots at us when we seem unable or unwilling to keep pace. Fortunately, our schools are filled with good people who are constantly seeking alternatives and refinements to current practice. The purpose of this section, however, is not to agree or disagree with the chorus of critics who challenge today's schools. Our purpose is to identify the processes of curriculum development and instructional improvement that will enable you to make the most of what you have in your school and to foster whatever changes are necessary within your department.

Such changes are impossible without well-regarded processes that promote the ongoing collaboration of the persons that affect and are affected by the school. Only such processes are capable of satisfying continuing demands for relevancy and change. Add to all this the predictions of futurists that high school students within the next ten to twenty years may experience a 100% increase in knowledge every month and a half, more or less in certain fields. The implications for the recording and transmitting of knowledge are obvious. High schools require processes that provide for the study of such implications. This section outlines such processes for you.

WHAT ARE CURRICULUM AND INSTRUCTION?

Let's define our terms. What are curriculum and instruction and how do they interrelate? Perhaps the best way to define each is to identify curriculum as the "what" of learning and instruction, the "how." *Curriculum* is the *content* of the learning experience. Generally, it's divided into content *elements*—facts, concepts, laws, rules, values, and attitudes; and content *packages*—courses, units, lessons, programs, modules, and the like.

The process of curriculum development must acknowledge both the elements and the packages of content in order to result in purposeful and relevant learning experiences for students. Department chairs must be the resident experts. They must understand these characteristics of curriculum and promote processes that accommodate them. They also must understand the relationship of instruction to curriculum.

Instruction is curriculum's Siamese twin, each existing individually but inseparably from the other. Curriculum is the content of learning, *instruction* the *process*. Like any process, it consists of operational and situational elements. The operational elements involve the method of learning: discovery, scientific, verbal, and so on. The situational elements involve the circumstances of the learning: self-contained classroom, open classroom, large-group/small-group, and so forth.

Distinctions between curriculum and instruction, the content and process of learning, are important for discussion but misleading in application. Only the effective combination of the two results in student learning. The best-conceived curriculum depends on instruction to promote learning. Every student enters the learning experience with a perceptual window that opens wide to good instruction. The more effective the instruction, the wider the perceptual opening; the wider the opening, the more curricula learned.

It is safe to say, then, that every school has at least 3 different curricula; the one found in the curriculum guides, the one the teacher teaches, and the one the learner learns. An optimal school experience for students requires that all three be equivalent. Department chairs, therefore, promote not only the development of curriculum but an adherence to it. This will be the focus of another section in the Guide.

The point to emphasize now is that curriculum is a living thing, constantly growing and changing. Elements within it are born, while others die; most grow to be strong, if the environment is nurturing. It is one of the jobs of the department chair to provide that environment. A friend and long-time department chair once told me: "We never arrive at a best course in our curriculum. Our courses are always getting better. They are constantly changing."

Influences on a Changing Curriculum

The most obvious influence on a changing curriculum is the experience gained by the teacher each time he or she teaches a course. If the content elements remain the same, if the "facts" within the course reflect current perceptions of reality, only the content packaging may need to be changed. To accommodate the changing needs of students and the influence of current research, it may, for example, promote more "hands-on" activities, emphasizing student sensory experience. "Modality learning" is this operational element of instruction that brings curriculum to life for students and suggests further how a change in instruction affects curriculum.

Such changes are unlikely, however, without a process to secure student and teacher feedback about course content. At the end of each final grading period, use the ***Student Input/Curriculum*** reproducible in Figure 1–1 to secure student feedback and ***Faculty Input/Curriculum*** in Figure 1–2 for teacher feedback. Remember to use the student feedback to evaluate only the curriculum, not the teacher. Be sure the teacher sees it before filling out the form in Figure 1–2. When the teacher form is completed, save it for future planning and for discussion at the end of the year. That's also a good time to discuss student feedback.

This process also suggests the need to have teachers responsible for different courses every two to three years. You may have one or two teachers who are best suited for the Advanced Placement senior English class in American Literature, but most teachers, especially in curricula like math, English, and social studies, can be rotated to bring a fresh perspective to the course and an unbiased opinion about its place in the curriculum.

Obviously, not all departments can rotate teachers. Foreign language, science, and a few others are too specialized to permit rotation. The forms can still be used, however, to receive evaluations of the *course*. Be sure never to use such evaluations to judge the *teacher*. Once you start using everything you can get your hands on to evaluate teachers, you will lose your credibility, trust, and power with the staff. As a rural, wise man once said, "It just ain't worth it."

Other Influences

At a recent IBM Educational Systems Conference, the president of the National Urban League urged business and school professionals to eliminate the educational gap between white and minority students. He suggested that such an effort would involve structural changes in schools, funding adjustments, and improvements in teacher education and training. He also advocated the elimination of tracking in order to force schools to raise their expectations for black and poor children.

Just a couple of years ago, the Urban League's position on tracking was supported by the Center for Social Organization of Schools at Johns Hopkins University. The Center reported that tracking is common in all parts of the United States and that it becomes more inflexible as students progress through school. The study also indicated that tracking has some advantages but that it can harm minority and poor students by isolating them and lowering expectations of their achievement.

Also consider the educational reform plan passed by Oregon legislators: All tenth graders will be expected to pass a series of basic exams resulting in a "Certificate of Initial Mastery." Students who fail the exams will be held back until they pass, at which time they will have the option of selecting either a college-prep or a job-training track. With the passage of this law, Oregon has become the first state to develop a formalized tracking system.

What does all this mean? Well, it suggests that I'm not going to try to convince you one way or the other about the relative advantages and disadvantages of tracking, but it seems obvious that schools continue to be affected by sometimes conflicting federal and state mandates, sociological and psychological studies, trends resulting from research, and parental and community expectations. Consider too the recent changes in college admissions requirements, which have increased academic preparation in secondary schools and have virtually eliminated fine and applied arts courses in some of them.

The challenges confronting department chairs and curriculum experts are staggering. Equally disturbing is the evident inability of recent trends to respond to such challenges. Professional journals bubble each month with hot new ideas: restructuring, teacher empowerment, hemisphericity, questioning technique, student self-esteem, reflective teaching, modality learning, and higher order thought process. They are all well-researched and generally sound.

Why then, do they arrive on the educational scene in such a whirlwind of expectation, flourish so enthusiastically, and disappear so indifferently? It must have something to do with the persistence of the problems confronting education and the inability of many schools to respond to them.

Problems Resulting from These Influences

Ask fine and applied arts teachers if an increased emphasis on academic courses does much for their job security. See how they feel about changes in the curriculum mandated by colleges and universities. And when fine and applied arts courses are dropped from the curriculum, ask the counselors how they feel about the limited courses available for special-needs or limited kids. For further illustration, assume that you had the power to eliminate tracking or ability grouping in the nation's schools. After you did it, imagine the teachers' reactions when confronted with truly heterogeneous groupings of students and with the need to expand their instructional repertoires to teach them.

It would be an interesting picture. Change occurs slowly in education, if at all, and the reason is amazingly consistent with theory. Don't worry, I'm not seeking sanctuary in the ivory tower. Neither am I denying the value of theory. Strip the ivy off system theory, and it emphasizes one basic point: All systems, by definition, are resistant to change.

Systems don't like surprises, and they don't want to change. They establish self-regulatory and feedback processes that enable a "steady state." My body, for example, seeks to maintain a steady temperature; my car, a steady gas/air mixture; my home, a steady budget; my wife and I, steady relationships with our children; and my dog, a steady supply of treats. Education, like all social institutions, establishes a method of organization and operation—and then strives to maintain it, as is, with few changes. The self-contained classroom, tracking and ability grouping, teacher training, even the structure of education have all come under fire, and each has yet to change significantly.

The changes we experience, therefore, tend to come from outside the school, unless we have developed internal processes that promote them, at least that respond to the array of social issues confronting education. Consider, for example, the impact of television. The average high school graduate has spent 12,000 hours in classrooms—and 18,000 in front of television sets.

The average consumption of books by kids in the country has decreased over 300% within the past 20 years; and within a recent five-year period, remedial math courses in college have increased by over 50%. According to the results of international achievement tests, U. S. students lag behind several other countries in math and science skills. Proportionally fewer minority students are going to college, and only about 46% of all students entering a four-year college will graduate in 4 years.

How Do We Respond?

Department chairs have an important, if less visible, role in the response to these problems and influences. Our most obvious response is to prove to legislators, pressure groups, and the parent community that sweeping change may be unnecessary in a school/department that already has a solid curriculum and a valid process for making needed changes. Invite such people into the school, talk to them, and ask them if their mandated change is really in the best interests of the students. A mutual look at what already exists is sometimes the best response to outside influences.

The best way to guarantee the strength of such a response is to have processes and products in operation that are vital, growing, and relevant to the changing needs of teachers and students. In effect, they should be proactive, not reactive. They should anticipate problems, not simply respond to them.

Let's Be Proactive

Prominent educator Art Costa once said, "Intelligent people know what to do—when they don't know what to do." He reminds us of at least two important considerations. One, students must learn how to learn. Certainly, this often-repeated expectation of classrooms comes as no startling revelation to most teachers. What might be surprising to some of us is the claim by genetic engineers that a child born today could live to be 125 years old. In our society, such a child may have to retool 6 or 7 times to maintain a career or to find a new one. "Learning how to learn" then, is critical.

The second consideration suggested by Costa's comment involves the processes established by department chairs to make the right decisions when "*they don't know what to do.*" Sometimes the most unlikely curriculum change, whether it be an addition, deletion, or revision, results in the best learning experience for students. It does so because it benefits from the synergy of a worthwhile process.

Synergy occurs when the combined output of two or more agents is greater than the sum of their individual outputs. Synergy can be bad, as when two drugs, harmless individually, become deadly when combined. And it can be good, as when teachers engage in a process that benefits from the best each has to offer, when separate, yet excellent ideas combine to form superior ideas. In essence, mutual cooperation produces high synergy; mutual antagonism produces low synergy. I'm sure you can think of scores of examples in your personal and professional life that produce high and low synergy.

The point is, department chairs who have a strong belief in process establish such activities for themselves and their teachers. They recognize that the synergy that results really does provide "something to do when they don't know what to do." They also recognize that the teachers require learning experiences to guide their thinking. In-service training activities—the focus of a future section— provides such experiences; so do college courses, workshops, journals, conventions, consultants, and visits to other schools.

Teachers, especially those on departmental curriculum committees, should use such experiences as a measuring stick to assess the need for curriculum change. Curriculum committees are excellent for making departmental decisions. To assure "enlightened" decisions, however, the teachers involved require a knowledge of the principles to guide their thinking.

Teachers can gain such knowledge by requesting a "professional leave day" to attend a workshop or to visit another school. The reproducible **Prearranged Absence Request Form**, Figure 1–3, opens the door to such opportunities and provides documentation for future reference. The department chair might need such documentation for budget purposes and monthly or annual reports. These topics are the focus of future sections. Also, if your school has difficulty finding substitutes when teachers leave, you might fill in for them as your schedule permits. There is no quicker way for a department chair to be well-liked than to extend these kinds of favors.

Members of the curriculum committee also require some conceptual ground rules, some basic principles that complement the knowledge and common sense they bring to the task of making decisions about curriculum. The **Curriculum Committee** reproducible in Figure 1–4 provides a way to welcome new members to the committee. A copy or a modification should be given to each new teacher at the first meeting. It can be used by the teacher for future reference, and it will help set the tone for committee activities.

The handout is an abstraction of the concepts of Ralph Tyler and other curriculum experts. It is purposely general. It provides only a conceptual framework for the committee to ask the kinds of questions that lead ultimately to sound decisions. Too often, committee decisions bog down in the absence of a common understanding of the basic tenets that fashion the thought about a subject. This handout provides these essentials. As such, it precludes the dominance of one or two knowledgeable people on the committee, and it provides a common starting point for discussions.

The Need for Process

What is process? Well, it's movement, generally constant movement, movement with a direction. Professionals never *arrive* at anything they do. Teachers can always improve their teaching, department chairs can always refine their supervisory skills, and curriculum can always get better. As one department chair told me: "Our curriculum planning activities are simply opportunities to formalize what has been happening informally every day." Her teachers frequently attend workshops, have access to the most recent literature, are encouraged to visit other schools, and have discussions about curriculum in the lunchroom as well as in committee sessions and department meetings. For her and them, curriculum planning is not a once-a-year, even a once-a-month proposition. It is ongoing.

Her teachers realize that curriculum is a tool and that their role is to *make* as well as use it. If the tool no longer satisfies a particular purpose, it should be changed by the people who best know how to use it. Once asked whom he talks to when a car model has a performance problem, the engineers or the designers, Lee Iacocca responded: "The guy on the line, the person putting it together. He knows better than anyone else what the problem is. He sees it every day."

The same is true of teachers. It is also true of students. Who is more sensitive to an improperly used instrument than the patient on whom it is used? Any good doctor understandably disregards a patient's advice about operating procedure, but welcomes any feedback about the patient's condition after the operation. American education is receiving its share of criticism about the "condition" of our high school graduates; periodic feedback from "the patients" might provide some of the information that helps improve the quality of our operation. Figure 1–1 secures such information.

Students, therefore, are not just the passive recipients of curriculum. They may not shape it, but they can provide the information that helps the "shapers." Provide the processes within your department, then, that foster influence on the curriculum *for* students and, later, *by* students.

A Suggested Process

Figures 1–1 and 1–2 are administered easily at the end of each final grading period and provide useful information to departmental and school curriculum committees. The department chair, therefore, should keep the originals but provide copies to appropriate committees and other persons in the building and district. The information will be helpful to curriculum developers and to the department chair, who may need the information for monthly or annual reports, or other written documents required by the administration.

Whether the curriculum committee is departmental or all-school, the process is fundamentally the same. The committee's primary mission is to develop or examine curriculum proposals according to the criteria in Figure 1–4. In addition, there are several other questions that must be asked in judging the merits of the proposed change. Here are a few:

- How strong are the reasons for the change?
- What factors provide the impetus for the change?
- To what group or groups of students is this change directed?
- How will these students—and others—be affected by this change?
- What are the possible negative implications for other courses in the curriculum?
- Are the suggested purposes and content of the course appropriate?
- Does the proposal provide ways to determine if the purposes are being realized?

Obviously, other questions will be asked as the proposal is considered by the committee and other reviewers. They will be answered easily if the proposed form is complete in its requests for information. Figure 1–5, *Curriculum Change Proposal*, provides a 4-page proposal form that requests most of the information required by curriculum planners and administrators. It requests information regarding:

- The type of change
- The purpose of the change
- Relevant explanations involving the change
- A course description as it might appear in a curriculum book
- The objectives of the course and a tentative outline of its content
- Routing information
- Financial considerations such as materials, equipment, and location
- Personnel considerations
- Additional planning considerations such as summer workshops.

Once the proposal has been discussed by the committee and all questions have been answered—a process that includes dialogue with the initiator of the proposal—it is voted upon by the committee and forwarded to the department chair for his or her approval. The department chair may either sign the routing slip and forward the proposal to the next review level or meet with the committee to discuss concerns or additional questions.

This is a process used by many department chairs. Others prefer to be members of the committee itself, some as chairs of the committee, others as nonvoting members, many as members with one vote. Obviously, the department chair's involvement with the committee is a factor of his or her leadership style. My purpose in the section is not to influence your administrative style but to outline a process that engages your staff and creates purposeful curriculum change.

You may give the committee in your department complete decisional authority to recommend changes to the administration, or you may make them advisory to you. Whatever you decide, the process should be consistent with your philosophical style and encourage the kind of synergy that results in enlightened decisions. No one way is best. Administrative policy, the union contract, or personal style may even rule out the use of a committee. If such is the case, you can still use the reproducibles in this section and throughout the book. They are still appropriate.

If you decide to use a committee, follow this procedure when the committee has made its decisions. Attach a form such as the *Disposition of Proposal* in Figure 1–6 to the proposal and forward it to the next review level, whatever it may be. Figure 1–7 provides a sample of what this form might look like when it's completed. Depending upon the size of your school, the next level could be you, the all-school curriculum committee, the building administration, or the district administration.

At this point, the proposal will be judged by its financial and personnel requirements. Even the most desirable curriculum change is sometimes delayed until additional funds are found or the right teacher hired. Good administrators become surprisingly creative when a solid curriculum change is proposed. Even the best and most creative among them, however, must at times surrender to the inadequacy of funds or personnel.

Whatever the ultimate decision, however, it should be communicated to the initiator(s) of the proposal. Nothing destroys morale in a school faster than inadequate feedback about hard work. It follows, then, that feedback should be immediate and complete. It should thank the initiators for their hard work and for their investment in the department, and it should provide the final decision regarding the proposal and the rationale behind it.

More About the Department's Curriculum Committee

Appropriate feedback and periodic notes of appreciation from the department chair will do much to sustain the energy levels of the committee members. They are likely to meet after school and to receive little compensation for their efforts other than the gratitude of their department chair. In most instances, if the department chair enjoys positive relationships with his or her staff, periodic recognition of the committee's efforts is all that's required.

This is especially true if the committee is organized thoughtfully. First, it should represent the natural divisions of courses within the department. The English department, for example, might have teachers representing the courses by year and by elective, the social studies department by graduation requirements and electives, the math department by clusters of courses, and the applied arts department by divisions such as home economics, industrial arts, and business education.

The actual representation will be determined by your department and the nature of the curriculum within your school. In a small school, the "committee" might consist of the department chair and one or two other teachers. Whatever the composition of the committee, the teachers on it should possess several important characteristics:

- An ability to see the Big Picture
- Intellectual flexibility and open-mindedness
- Professional and personal integrity

- The ability to disagree and to say *No* sensitively
- A basic knowledge of the principles of curriculum (*see* Figure 1–4)
- A commitment to the goals of the department.

A group of such people contributes much to the department and probably learns a lot in the process. The professional growth experienced suggests another characteristic of the process of curriculum development.

Process Doesn't Stop

A good process provides as much for the participants as for the needs of the department. During a discussion in my supervision class of Abraham Maslow's metavalues (truth, justice, honesty, beauty, etc.), a department chair once told me that she has encouraged some of her staff to volunteer for the department's curriculum committee for the professional growth it provides.

New teachers can benefit from the honesty and fair play that characterize discussions about curriculum. They also learn to see the Big Picture, to understand the many factors that affect decisions about curriculum, and to accept the compromise and occasional disappointment that result from inadequate resources. As young members of the committee, they contribute a fresh, unbiased perspective to discussions, energy to committee activities, and a willingness to learn from their veteran colleagues.

Like these colleagues, they discover that much of what happens in the school provides valuable information about the program. Consider, for example, the P–ACT scores that are available to high school personnel. The tests are designed by the American College Testing Program to provide students a preliminary experience with the ACT and to give schools insights into their curricula. Figure 1–8, *Curriculum Analysis*, provides a reproducible that encourages teachers to consider the results of an item analysis of student performance on specific areas of the test.

Such analyses are provided by the ACT and can be used by schools to judge the effectiveness of certain areas of the curriculum. The Advanced Placement tests provided by the College Board can be used the same way. The College Board has gone several steps further recently by developing a program called Pacesetter. It provides states, school districts, and schools with a comprehensive approach for setting higher academic standards, improving instruction, and assessing student achievement. It's a good idea, therefore, to maintain contact with groups like the College Board and to encourage students in the appropriate courses to take the AP exams. The results may be helpful not only to them but to the school.

A Word About Scope and Sequence

Perhaps the most complete picture of the curriculum is provided on a series of scope and sequence charts. Related to the principles of continuity, sequence, and integration presented in Figure 1–4, scope and sequence charts reveal the courses within a curriculum and their relationship to the district's philosophy, the department's objectives, such specifics as thinking skills, and other courses within the curriculum.

Scope and sequence charts serve several purposes. They enable the department/school:

- To provide graphic representation of the curriculum to relevant populations within the community: parent groups, the Board of Education, the district administration, etc.
- To give curriculum planners a big picture of course sequences.
- To relate the specifics of the curriculum to the sometimes obscure goals and philosophy of the district.
- To provide a ready reference for teachers as they plan instructional activities for units or specific courses.
- To enable department chairs and administrators to assess the relationship between instruction and curriculum.
- To offer a format for the periodic evaluation of curriculum.

Schools will discover a variety of uses for scope and sequence charts. A reproducible **Scope and Sequence Chart** blank is provided in Figure 1–9. Figures 1–10 and 1–11 provide examples of two possible stages of development. Department chairs will find that the periodic development of such charts, perhaps every five to six years, will be seen by teachers as either tedious, perfunctory, or professionally stimulating. Their reactions to the task will reflect the department chair's perception of it.

If the department chair reacts to use of the charts as a perfunctory task that must be done every five to six years, the staff will see it as more useless paperwork that requires periodic shuffling. If the department chair accepts the responsibility as a necessary and revealing stage in the development of an outstanding curriculum, the staff will be stimulated and satisfied by their efforts, particularly if the final product is shared with them and used frequently in professional growth conferences and other departmental activities.

Nothing is more disturbing to teachers than to work on a committee, submit their findings, and hear nothing about them. Committee reports and completed scope and sequence charts that gather dust until the next accreditation evaluation sustain a facade of professionalism in a department or school. More than anything else, teachers realize the pretense of such activity. The delusion that follows affects their investment in future such activities and even in the performance of their daily responsibilities.

We're All in This Together

If educational planning seeks more than the completion of perfunctory tasks, teachers and administrators alike must share the same sense of purpose. The department chair's role in this regard is critical. He or she must sustain a focus on the department's shared values and reach beyond the department to project the same values as well as the willingness to work with others in the building.

Some schools, particularly high schools, become compartmentalized. Departments become provinces preoccupied with their self-interests: generous budgets, community and administrative recognition, teaching security as reflected in high enrollment/registration figures, and a sense of autonomy. An effect is the school's occasional failure to coordinate planning activities that result in complementary learning experiences for students.

Curriculum planners, for example, whether they be on departmental or all-school committees, must ask themselves about the conceptual relationships between social studies and science, math and rhetoric, social studies and foreign language, literature and history, and literature and fine arts. The combinations are endless, and they involve such specifics as study habits and the completion of term papers.

Will social studies require a term paper format substantively different from English or science? If so, why? Is the difference defensible or does it reflect an absence of cooperative planning and the synergy that results from it? Does English encourage students to outline reading materials and social studies to emphasize the highlighting of significant passages? Are their recommendations to students regarding effective reading and study complementary or mutually exclusive? More to the point, have they worked cooperatively with each other, perhaps with a reading specialist, to encourage similar reading and study habits in students?

To promote cooperative planning, department chairs are encouraged to use the *Curriculum Planning* form in Figure 1–12. It identifies the results of departmental curriculum planning and invites one or more other departments to share in the development of curriculum and/or materials. As such, the form promotes a process that:

- Results in complementary experiences for students.
- Promotes high synergy-planning activities.
- Broadens the base of support for proposals.
- Increases the likelihood of administrative approval for costs and personnel requirements.

Textbook Adoption

Finally, department chairs must promote a process that evaluates the appropriateness of current texts in relation to a changing curriculum. New or modified courses usually require different textbooks. The adoption process, therefore, usually is a responsibility of the curriculum committee or one of its subcommittees.

In many schools, however, because department chairs are the first and sometimes the only people to meet textbook salespeople, they often circulate desk copies among teachers for reaction and approval. The *Textbook Review* form in Figure 1–13 promotes the process. Regardless of the specifics of the process, department chairs must provide forms like the *Textbook Adoption* in Figure 1–14 for teachers to recommend texts.

Their workshops, in-service, and convention activities often introduce them to new materials. They require a process to suggest such materials for adoption. Throughout all this, however, department chairs must guard against an ever-present tendency in schools. They must guarantee that the curriculum, not one or more textbooks, determines the learning experiences of students.

Current theories of instruction regard textbooks as supplements to curriculum. The textbook model of curriculum started in this country before 1920 has since been challenged repeatedly but continues to direct the learning experiences of a significant number of students. Generally, it permits only passive learning, fails to adapt to the individual differences of students, and often involves content that is dated. For these reasons, it's a good idea to engage the curriculum committee is an assessment of proposed textbooks to assure their complementary relationship with the curriculum.

Finally, Figure 1–15, ***Bookstore Notification,*** provides a form for departments to notify bookstores of specific texts for the current school year. Even in schools without bookstores, the form is appropriate to notify persons responsible for the sale and purchase of books.

Let's Wrap It Up

The primary purpose of this section is to emphasize the value of *process* in designing curriculum, not to identify "the curricular imperatives for the year 2000." The vigor of your curriculum, that is, the relevance and appropriateness of courses and sequencing, depends upon the quality of the process that creates or modifies it. As one department chair told me recently: "I don't worry about the products if I have the right process operating. The products will take care of themselves."

The comment summarizes the focus of this section. Because curriculum preferences are based on a belief in what is worth learning and how learning occurs, the process must engage and/or cultivate knowledgeable people to make enlightened decisions about the needs of students. The forces for change are many; they come from cultural movements, research studies, social dissatisfaction, trends, staff creativity, parental pressure, or from any of several authoritative opinions.

Curriculum designers must operate within a conceptual framework that enables them to consider these forces and to distinguish the superficial from the substantive and the whimsical from the well-conceived. Many educational trends are at best ephemeral. Others hold promise. They must be considered by knowledgeable curriculum designers, then accepted, discarded, or adopted, based on their merits. Figure 1–16, ***Curriculum Change,*** provides a reproducible that explains the process to teachers and others interested in curriculum change. It is appropriate for inclusion in teacher handbooks or for distribution during department meetings.

No matter how effective the process, no school's curriculum can accommodate the needs of every student. For that reason, department chairs are well-advised to include independent study options for students who have interests that extend beyond departmental offerings. The form ***Request for Independent Study*** in Figure 1–17 meets those interests. Students are asked to identify their goals for the program, the content and methods by which they will be evaluated, and are to find a teacher to sponsor them. The forms are then returned to the department chair who files them for future reference. The independent study option is appropriate for students who are interested in courses not offered in the curriculum or in areas of study that extend beyond current course offerings. This is a very important part of this section.

A form such as the ***English Department Course Offerings*** in Figure 1–18 provides a quick reference of all the courses offered in the department, in this instance, the English department. Because the form also identifies the levels available, the credits, and the prerequisites for each course, it is equally appropriate for inclusion in a curriculum book for registration and posthigh-school planning. Figure 1–19, ***Suggested English Course Sequences***, can be adapted in format for other courses as well.

Finally, this section emphasized that department chairs are the "resident experts" in their fields. The power they enjoy within the school should be a function of their knowledge and ability to relate to people, not their hierarchical positions. A dependence on hierarchical authority when knowledge is needed is the quickest way for department chairs to lose the trust and respect of their colleagues—and sometimes to become laughable.

Be reminded, then, to study your academic discipline, to read the research and sift the opinion, to attend conferences and workshops to share information with knowledgeable colleagues, and to discuss with your teachers the most recent thinking in your field. The processes you establish for your teachers will result in enlightened decisions for students. The learning processes you establish for yourself will result in *your* enlightenment, a quality that will enhance your value to your students and staff.

STUDENT INPUT/CURRICULUM

Purpose: The continuing relevance and effectiveness of our department's curriculum depend upon the reactions of those who are most closely associated with it. We have discovered that students often provide the best recommendations for change. On that basis, please take a few moments to answer the following questions. And remember, please, that we are asking for your reactions to *what* is in the curriculum, not to *how* it was taught. Your comments are very important to us, so please respond as thoughtfully as possible. Thanks for your help.

Think about this past semester. You were provided a great deal of material in this course. We'd like you to react to it in two ways:

1. Which part of the course was most interesting to you? Why was it interesting? Should it be expanded in some way? If so, how might we expand on it? In other words, what specific elements should be added?

2. Which parts of the course were least interesting to you? Exactly why were they uninteresting? How might they be changed?

Thanks for your help. Your comments will be judged carefully as we consider possible curriculum revisions. We can't guarantee that we'll make the revisions you suggest, but we certainly will look at them.

Figure 1–2

FACULTY INPUT/CURRICULUM

Purpose: Because we believe that curriculum revision is ongoing, our department benefits each semester from the reactions of teachers to the courses they teach. Please take a moment to answer the following questions about each of your courses. I will use the information as input when curriculum decisions are made. If, in addition, you would like to discuss one or more of the questions, be sure to stop by at your convenience. In advance, thanks for your help.

---

1. What elements within the curriculum are the strongest and must *not* be changed? Should they be expanded? Why? If so, what specifically should be included?

2. What elements are missing in the curriculum and must be added? Please provide a sentence or two of rationale.

3. What elements within the curriculum must be changed or eliminated? Again, please provide a brief statement of rationale. At this time, you might also make a statement about the appropriateness of the textbook(s) for the course. Are any changes necessary?

Thanks for your help. Positive curriculum change is not possible without your help. Again, if you want to discuss any of this, be sure to stop by.

Figure 1–3

PREARRANGED ABSENCE REQUEST FORM

Staff Member's Name: _____ **Department:** _____

I request a prearranged absence for the following date(s) _____

I will need a substitute: _____ yes _____ no

     Circle periods for which sub is needed   1 2 3 4 5 6 7 8 9

Please be reminded that lesson plans must be in the hands of department chairperson or designate.

Check reason for absence below: (When possible, submit a minimum of two weeks in advance)

_____ Personal Day

_____ Death in Immediate Family or Family Illness

_____ Civic Duty (e.g. Jury Service)

_____ Religious Holiday

_____ Field Trip

_____ Other (Please Specify)

_____

_____ Professional Activity:

    _____ Collegial Observation

    _____ Conference/Convention (Please Specify)

    _____

    _____

    _____ Other (Please Specify)

    _____

Expenses (fees, travel, etc.) are being paid by:

_____ Dept.   _____ District   _____ Personal

Procedures for Professional Activity

1. Use this form to obtain approval for professional activity time *before* filling out conference registration, etc.
2. Once approval for time is granted, forward copy of this form with your travel request to department chairman if you seek reimbursement for professional activity expenses.

Chairperson's Signature _____ **Date** _____

Special Requests _____

Asst. Principal Approval: _____

Figure 1–4

CURRICULUM COMMITTEE

Welcome to the Curriculum Committee. You are a very important part of a process that guarantees relevant and purposeful learning experiences for our students. As a member of this committee, you will be asked to meet many times during the school year to discuss our department's curriculum and to consider specific proposals for change. To help you during your considerations, we are providing a brief and very general framework to guide your thinking. The concepts are the work of Ralph Tyler, a leader in the field of curriculum development.

Six Important Questions to Ask of Each Proposal

1. Will the learners interact with the content? Will they have a chance to practice the behaviors that express it?

2. Will the learners have the chance to challenge and extend the content?

3. Will the learner realize satisfaction from his or her involvement with the course content?

4. Are the desired outcomes within the capabilities of the learners?

5. Are several different experiences provided for obtaining particular behaviors? Will all the modalities of the students be encouraged?

6. Will the experiences lead to additional learning?

Three Important Concepts regarding Organization

1. *Continuity*—This involves the vertical repetition of major curriculum elements (Basic sentence syntax, for example, repeated throughout four years of English).

2. *Sequence*—This involves successively higher levels of treatment (Movement, for example, from the simple sentence to the compound/complex sentence).

3. *Integration*—This includes a unification of concepts across subject lines (Writing skills, for example, emphasized in science and social studies as well as in English).

We will be discussing a great many other considerations as well. These basic guidelines, however, will help you get started. We hope you have a good year, and we look forward to working with you on this very important committee.

Figure 1–5

CURRICULUM CHANGE PROPOSAL

Dept. _____

Date _____

A. **Type of Change:**

_____ Addition of new course

_____ Deletion of existing course

_____ Name change

_____ Course reorganization in terms of sequence, etc.

_____ Other (Please specify)

B. **Brief Statement of the Purpose of the Proposal**

C. **Explain the Proposal** (address the following issues):

Describe

1. The evolution of the proposal;
2. The relationship of the proposed course or change to other courses in the curriculum;
3. The perceived student need for the course;
4. The place of the course in a sequence;
5. The support for the proposal by reasoning from "best practice" or current research.

Figure 1–5, continued

D. **Preliminary Course Description** (as it might be quoted in the *Program of Studies*)

E. **Course Objectives and Tentative Course Outline** (Be as detailed as possible.)

Objectives	Possible Content

Figure 1–5, continued

Routing

A. **Signatures**

_____ _____
Proposal Initiator (Departmental Committee)   Date

_____ _____
Department Chair   Date

Comments (Dept. Chair) _____

_____

_____

B. **Recommendation**

_____ _____
Chair, Curriculum Committee   Date

Comments/Vote _____

_____

_____

_____ _____
Building Administrators   Date

Comments/Vote _____

_____

_____

C. **Decision**   _____ Approved   _____ Not Approved

_____ _____
Principal   Date

_____ _____
District Executive Council   Date

Figure 1–5, continued

Curriculum Proposal Appendix

A. **Fiscal Considerations**

1. Nonconsumable materials/equipment costs
   (Please specify)

$\overline{\hspace{3cm}}$
$ \hspace{2.5cm}

2. Consumable materials
   (Please specify)

Subtotal $\overline{\hspace{3cm}}$
$ \hspace{2.5cm}

3. Room, space, or location requirements

B. **Personnel Considerations**

1. Please comment on FTE considerations. Does this change suggest an increase in current departmental allocations? _____ Is a teacher in the department able to teach this course? _____ If not, which employee in the school or in the district is available for this assignment?

2. Summer Workshop Requirements (Estimated)

   a. Number of teachers   _____

   b. Number of working hours   _____

   c. Materials/xeroxing   Yes/No

   d. Secretarial time   Yes/No

Figure 1–6

DISPOSITION OF PROPOSAL

To:

Title of Proposal:

Type of Proposal:

Observations from Committee:

Vote: In Favor: _____   Opposed: _____

Additional voting information:

Figure 1–7

DISPOSITION OF PROPOSAL
(Completed Sample)

To: Tom Frederichs, English department head

Title of Proposal: Creative Writing–Fine Arts

Type of Proposal: Change of credit

Observations from Committee:

Many members of the committee agreed that Creative Writing would be a legitimate course for fine art credit. Increasing academic requirements for college have seriously depleted the fine arts course offerings, and Creative Writing could expand the options available to students to meet the Fine Arts graduation requirement of one-semester credit.

The problem, however, is the impact such a change of credit would have on the Fine Arts department, which is already losing student registrations to academic departments. Obviously, we had mixed feelings about this proposal, but the consensus opinion seems to be that the Creative Writing I course should continue to be offered by the English department but that it should *not* receive fine arts credit.

Vote: In Favor: __0__   Opposed: __5__

Additional voting information: None

Figure 1–8

CURRICULUM ANALYSIS

Attached to this form is an item analysis of our students' performance on the most recent P-ACT. I have had the opportunity to review the results already and have made a couple of observations. This year's results seem to be significant in the following areas:

I am interested in your observations. Are we pretty much in agreement about the areas of significance? Have you spotted additional areas that warrant our attention? Obviously, much of this information is appropriate for curriculum planning. It might also have some PR value, so I am interested in your reactions. Try to get them to me within the next couple weeks. As usual, thanks for your help.

Figure 1–9

SCOPE AND SEQUENCE CHART

FOR: _____ _____
     (course)   (semester)

Instructional Strand

Figure 1–10

ENGLISH DEPARTMENT
SCOPE AND SEQUENCE CHART
(Completed Sample A)

FOR: ___ E 1–2, II ___ ___ (semester)
(course)

Instructional Strand

Thinking Skills (DHS)

I. Analytical thinking	
1. Grasp the literal and the implied meaning of a statement.	1.1 Homework assignments and class discussions of literature will focus on key passages from the material which students must recall on a literal level and interpret on an inferential level to understand the writer's meaning.
	1.2 Students use contextual analysis to define vocabulary words.
2. Formulate the problem.	Students formulate a problem: when creating a topic sentence, when analyzing a character's problem in literature, when drawing inferences about literature, and when developing successful personal management strategies (both for behavior and for study skills).
3. Establish adequate operational definition.	Know or define terms referring to short story, novel, and grammar. Literary terms for poetry and drama.
4. Determine the factual accuracy of a statement.	4.1 Determine a character's credibility.
	4.2 Recognize hyperbole and irony.
	4.3 Locate and use accurate and factual information to support topic sentence.
5. Distinguish between verifiable facts and value claims.	In class discussion, students evaluate each other's contribution based on whether statements are verified by the material under discussion.

Figure 1–11

Page 1 of

ENGLISH DEPARTMENT
SCOPE AND SEQUENCE CHART
(Completed Sample B)

FOR: _____E 1–2, II_____
(course)

E 2, II

_____(semester)

Instructional Strand	E 1, II	E 1–2, II / E 2, II
English Department Philosophy and Objectives (DHS)		
I. Activities for students:		
1.1 The study of language which includes grammar, usage, vocabulary, semantics, and logic.	A. No Excuse Spelling List, and other spelling rules. B. Organized review of mechanics and usage in *English Writing and Skills* and in teacher materials. C. Vocabulary skills via contextual analysis.	A. Students are responsible for the spelling of vocabulary words. B. Continuation of grammar in textbook. C. Continue vocabulary skills.
1.2 The study of imaginative literature of all types which portrays a broad variety of human conditions.	A. Novel: *Of Mice and Men* B. Short Stories: *Arrangement in Literature* and *Short Stories: Characters in Conflict*	A. Poetry: *Arrangement in Literature* B. *Romeo and Juliet* C. *A Tale of Two Cities*
1.3 Writing experiences in description, narration, exposition, and argumentation, ranging from the single paragraph to the documented research paper.	A. Narrative paragraphs B. Descriptive paragraphs C. Expository paragraphs D. Journal Writing (optional)	A. Emphasis on writing expository paragraphs based on literature B. Short research project utilizing IMC

Figure 1–12

CURRICULUM PLANNING

To:

Fr: Phyllis Thomas, English Department

Curriculum Changes

Our department is in the process of making changes in our curriculum. You and your department may be interested in one or more of them. After reviewing them, if you have any questions, give me a call or stop in:

I have been thinking that it might be wise for us to work cooperatively on these topics. Our curricula share a lot of common ground. Think about it; I'll give you a call in a week or two to discuss your reactions. Thanks for taking the time to look it over.

Figure 1–13

TEXTBOOK REVIEW

The attached textbook has just been brought to my attention. I'm interested in your reaction to it. When you get the time, look through it and give me your reactions. Does it have merit? It is a possible replacement for the current text in your course? Should we consider it further? Please try to get back to me by _____. Thanks for your help.

Figure 1–14

TEXTBOOK ADOPTION

School: _____   **Date:** _____

Department: _____

Course: _____   _____ Replacement

Course # _____   _____ New

Ability Level _____ **Grade Level** _____   _____ Required _____ Optional

Recommended Text:

Author(s): _____

Title: _____

Publisher: _____   Copyright _____ Price _____

Total Cost for Course: Previous _____ New _____

Reading Level: _____   According to: _____

   Strengths: Weaknesses:

   _____   _____

   _____   _____

   _____   _____

   _____   _____

Reason for New Adoption: _____

_____

_____

_____

Brief Description of Selection Process: _____

_____

_____

_____

Recommended Text replaces:

   Author(s): _____

   Title: _____

   Publisher: _____   Copyright _____ Price _____

   Date of Adoption: _____

Figure 1–14, continued

Disposition
Submission:

Chairperson: _____ Date:_____

Committee: _____ _____

_____ _____

_____ _____

Approvals:

Department Chair: _____ Date: _____

Principal: _____ Date: _____

Executive Director: _____ Date: _____

Board of Education accepted _____ adoption on _____

rejected _____

Notification to: Initiator

Dept. Chair

Principal

Bookstore

Figure 1–15

BOOKSTORE NOTIFICATION

To: The Bookstore

Fr: Janet Frederichs, English department

Re: This year's books

Please be advised that the English department will be using the following books for the current school year:

Course	Cost	Publisher

If you require additional information, please contact me at your convenience.

Figure 1–16

CURRICULUM CHANGE

The following is our department's process for curriculum change. The explanation section at the bottom of the page provides additional information about the process. Proposals are available in the department office.

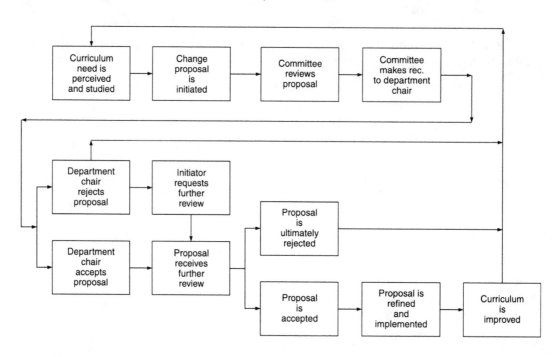

Explanation: A need within the curriculum is perceived and studied by a teacher, student, department chair, the curriculum committee, or another qualified party. A change proposal is initiated, reviewed by the curriculum committee, and forwarded to the appropriate department chair for a decision. If the department chair rejects the proposal, the initiator can request further review or change the proposal. If the department chair accepts the proposal or the initiator requests further review, the proposal is forwarded to the building and then the district for ultimate approval or rejection. If rejected at either level, the proposal is returned to the initiator for further study. If approved, the proposal is refined as needed and implemented. Once implemented, the curriculum is improved. Further improvement awaits the perception and study of the next curriculum need.

Figure 1–17

REQUEST FOR INDEPENDENT STUDY
1st SEMESTER _____

Date _____

Student: _____ Phone _____

Year: Freshman   Sophomore   Junior   Senior

Counselor: _____ Homeroom (1st period) _____

Subject: _____ (4th or 5th–*Circle One*)

Reason for Request: _____

_____

Written Proposal: (Attach to this page a statement describing the objectives, the mechanics of the meeting time, the nature of the final product, and the evaluation procedures related to the independent study project.)

This subject will be added to your schedule.

Is any other change necessary?   _____ Yes   _____ No

If yes, please see your counselor.

Signatures:

_____   _____
Teacher   Student

_____   _____
Department Chairperson   Parent

_____   _____
Administrative Approval   Counselor

School Routing: Teacher
　　　　　　　　　　　Department Chairperson
　　　　　　　　　　　Counselor

Deadline date is September _____ .

Figure 1–18

ENGLISH DEPARTMENT COURSE OFFERINGS

The English Department is committed to helping every student attain maximum effectiveness as both a sender and receiver of language communication. Our commitment is based on the premise that language is the key which unlocks a student's potential. Challenging reading and writing experiences are an integral part of every course; in addition to these, formal speaking, discussion, research, and organizational skills are developed throughout the English program.

Students interested in taking Level I or AP courses must meet the placement criteria described in the listings below. Level III courses are offered at every grade level, and students are recommended for Level III on the basis of teacher recommendations, standardized test scores, and prior grades in English. Questions about leveling and placement should be directed to the department chair. Any student or parent who needs assistance with their child's English course selection—either required courses or electives—should contact the department chair. **Currently enrolled students interested in courses for which they must have a recommendation by their English teacher should contact their present English teacher and ask for this recommendation.**

Course Title	Levels Available	Credit per Semester	Open to Grades	Prerequisite(s)
Required English Courses				
Freshman English 1,2	II, III	1	9	None
Sophomore English 1,2				
Sophomore English 1	II, III	1	10	Freshman English
Sophomore English 2	II, III	1	10	Freshman English
Sophomore English 2 (Honors)	I	1	10	Recommendation of present English teacher
Junior English 1,2	II, III	1	11	Freshman English and Sophomore English
Advanced Placement Junior English 1,2	I	1	11	Freshman and Sophomore English, Qualifying Exam, and recommendation of present English teacher
Elective English Courses				
Senior English 1,2	II, III	1	12	Freshman, Sophomore and Junior English
Advanced Placement Senior English 1,2	I	1	12	Freshman, Sophomore, Junior English, Qualifying Exam, and recommendation of present English teacher
Freshman Reading	II	1	9	None
Power Reading (Honors)	I	½	9,10	Recommendation of present English teacher or Junior High counselor/Strong CTBS scores
Study Strategies	II	See Course Desc.	10,11,12	None
(s) Great Books 1 (Honors)	I	1	9,10 (Offered in summer school only)	Recommendation of Junior High or present English teacher and strong CTBS scores
(s) Etymology	II	1	10,11,12	None
(s) Creative Writing	II	1	11,12	Recommendation of present English teacher
Newspaper Production	II	1	9,10,11,12	Permission of sponsor
(s) Television Production	II	1	10,11,12	None

(s) Denotes a semester course.

Figure 1–19

SUGGESTED ENGLISH COURSE SEQUENCES

Freshman Year	Sophomore Year	Junior Year	Senior Year
Freshman English 1,2 Level II or Level III (required)	*Sophomore English 1* Level II or Level III (required) and *Sophomore English 2* Level II (required) or *Sophomore English 2* Level I (elective)	*Junior English 1,2* Level II or Level III (required) or *AP Junior English 1,2* Level I (elective)	*Senior English 1,2* Level II or Level III (elective) or *AP Senior English 1,2* Level I (elective)

Enrichment Courses

Freshman Year	Sophomore Year	Junior Year	Senior Year
Freshman Reading (Level II)			
Power Reading (Level I)	*Power Reading* (Level I)		
Great Books 1 (Level I–Summer)	*Great Books 1* (Level I–Summer)		
	Study Strategies (Level II)	*Study Strategies* (Level II)	*Study Strategies* (Level II)
	Etymology (Level II)	*Etymology* (Level II)	*Etymology* (Level II)
Newspaper Production (Level II)	*Newspaper Production* (Level II)	*Newspaper Production* (Level II)	*Newspaper Production* (Level II)
	TV Production (Level II)	*TV Production* (Level II)	*TV Production* (Level II)
		Creative Writing (Level II)	*Creative Writing* (Level II)

HELPING TEACHERS GROW PROFESSIONALLY

Any educator worth his or her salt knows that the "action" in any school is found in the classroom. Students learn indirectly from the decisions made by the Board of Education and the administration. They learn directly from teacher interactions, which deserve a lot more attention than they seem to be receiving in most schools. Department chairs can provide the attention and support such interactions deserve; they have a powerful influence when they do their jobs well.

The first step is to climb down from the hierarchy to work with the teachers as colleagues. One of the essential characteristics of a good department chair is the ability to engender trust in his or her colleagues. The next step is to develop processes of professional growth that are nonthreatening and relevant. This is no easy task, but it's a whole lot easier when department chairs build the process on a solid philosophical base. The foundation is strongest if it includes an awareness of what teachers want and need. One of the things they want is a working relationship with a department chair who is quick to promote and slow to judge teacher performance; they need someone who "catches 'em being good." They relate much more comfortably to a process of supervision, not "snoopervision."

Consider the words of Woodrow Wilson: "Judgment should provide light, not heat." Although he didn't realize it at the time, the one-time president of Princeton University made a powerful statement about supervision in education. It may not have been strong enough, however, to dent a tradition that still regards teacher evaluation as more bonfire than beacon, directing rather than revealing, heating rather than lighting the way. This may not be all bad. As we will see in the next section, teacher evaluation is essential in a total program of professional growth.

When a school's emphasis on evaluation, however, crowds out opportunities for teachers to help each other or to self-evaluate, it tends to become more threatening and less relevant to them. Carl Glickman, one of this country's foremost theorists in the field of supervision, indicated a few years ago that approximately half of all teachers claim that they have never been observed for purposes of instructional improvement. They perceive observation as a judgment of their teaching, sometimes suggesting improvements, rarely providing processes to help make such improvement possible.

As such, classroom observation continues to emphasize heat over light and may not provide the elements teachers require to improve their teaching. To improve, teachers must see and accept what they are doing wrong and then have the opportunity to practice the right way. Periodic and infrequent evaluation has failed to provide such opportunities.

What is needed is ongoing supervision, the kind that gives teachers a systematic chance to see what they do, to make decisions regarding improvement, and to practice such improvement. Obviously, such a program takes time; it also requires good organization. The materials in this section will help with both.

THE DEPARTMENT CHAIR AS TEACHER AIDE

Classroom teachers have one of the toughest jobs in the community. Even the best need all the support they can get. Focusing 20 or 30 young minds on something other than soap operas, sports, or shopping malls is challenge enough. Add the school's expectation of superior knowledge of the subject matter, awareness of educational research, interpersonal skills, competence in one or more extracurricular activities, and a cascade of paperwork, and it's evident that teachers deserve a little help from their friends.

The department chair should be the closest of these friends. Good ones realize that education's hierarchy is at times more an obstacle than a stepping stone to such friendships. They behave less as "the boss" and more as a "teacher aide," especially when classroom observation is the focus. Teacher aides complement and support the work of teachers; so do department chairs. They provide maximum support during classroom observations when they acknowledge the importance of the following five questions.

Five Critical Questions About Classroom Observation

Figure 2–1, *Classroom Observation,* outlines five questions that must be answered before any classroom observation. The form sets the stage for the three kinds of formative activities provided by the department, all of which are discussed later in this section. It is provided in reproducible form because you may want to distribute copies to your staff each year to explain your department's observation process and to assure them that their input and involvement are valued by you.

During discussion of the questions, indicate to your staff that if the answers to questions 2, 4, and 5 are "the department chair" or "an administrator," the observation will be *administratively-directed,* and the results are likely to be placed in the teacher's file. If the answer is "a colleague" or a "colleague group," the observation is *peer-directed* and is designed to use the skills and experience of fellow teachers. Any comments, evaluative or otherwise, will remain with the group.

If the answer is "the teacher," the observation is *self-directed* and is controlled by the teacher exclusively. Any data collected from the observation are analyzed by the teacher, and any of the value judgments that result from the analysis are made by the teacher. Nothing goes in the teacher's file; nothing is even said after the observation unless it is requested by the teacher.

This is a whole lot different from the way it used to be, and maybe still is in some schools. The peer-directed and self-directed elements in this observation/ professional growth process are significant departures from traditional evaluation in the classroom. They're also healthy because they give the teacher a sense of ownership in the analysis and evaluation of his or her teaching. The responsibility for growth rests squarely on the teacher's shoulders and identifies others in the building, even those in hierarchically superior positions, as "teacher aides" who are available to provide "mirrors of performance" for the teacher.

DEFINING MIRRORS OF PERFORMANCE

Most obviously, a mirror of performance lets the teacher see what he or she is doing during the act of teaching. Excuse the pun, but it promotes teacher reflection. The better and the closer the look, the better the mirror and the more the teacher is likely to gain from the experience. Traditional checklists like the partial form, *Teacher Evaluation*, in Figure 2–2 don't get the job done. Even with this limited but detailed example, it is too general, covers too much territory, and doesn't target the specifics of what the teacher hopes to accomplish during the class. There is very little "formative" about it.

Contrast the checklist with the data-gathering form, *Critical Question Tally Sheet*, in Figure 2–3. The form collects information about a specific teaching behavior and provides data the teacher can use to analyze and evaluate that behavior in order to decide if more work is needed to improve it. This particular form instructs the teacher to do some preliminary planning regarding the purposes of the lesson, then asks him or her to identify the focus of the observation, in this case the critical questions he or she will be asking of the students.

The form then tells the observer what to do. In this case, the observer will be putting a checkmark next to the name of each student that has been asked one of the critical questions. The teacher can then use the information to identify the number of times a particular question was asked, of whom it was asked, and if all questions were asked.

Obviously, such a mirror can be used by an administrator to evaluate a teacher. A particular teacher may be having problems sticking to daily objectives and may need such a focus to keep him or her on track. In such a case the form is useful. It is also useful, however, for teacher self-evaluation. Sometimes teachers want to self-direct their observations to check on themselves, to work on suggestions from earlier evaluations, or to practice what someone preached during an in-service training program.

The point is, such a form provides specific information that the administrator, the colleague, or the individual teacher can use to analyze and evaluate classroom teaching. That's why it's a mirror. Most often, such a form is used by the teacher to self-evaluate. In such cases, a colleague or the department chair visits the class, uses the form to collect information, gives it to the teacher after the class, and leaves the room. Whatever happens to the information is then up to the teacher.

Giving Objective Feedback

Let's look at it this way. Some golfers, folks like me, spray their shots into every hazard on the course. They do it without any knowledge of what they're doing wrong. At such times, they are desperate for help—any kind of help—in answer to the question: "What am I doing wrong?" Many teachers ask the same question. When the kids are bouncing off the walls every period and teachers leave school each day questioning their sanity, they're asking the same question. Evaluation from a knowledgeable and trusted someone provides a way to get answers.

Other golfers can diagnose their own mistakes, or they simply want to try a new technique or to get a look at what they're doing. They just want someone to watch them, to see if the backswing is too fast or the follow-through too short. They want objective feedback to make sure they are doing what they planned to do: a mirror of their performance. They will do the rest. Teachers want the same kind of feedback, much more often than they want evaluation.

How Video Technology Helps

Video technology can provide some of the best feedback. The video camera is a very objective observer. Any evaluation of the feedback must come from the viewer, whether this be the teacher, colleague, or administrator. This, in fact, is one of the big advantages of videotaped supervision. It doesn't have to be done in the classroom. Colleagues or administrators can evaluate or supervise the teacher's performance in the comfort of their own family rooms on a Saturday morning. The only tools they need are the videotape, perhaps the teacher's self-evaluation as a guide, and a cup of coffee.

As helpful as videotaped observation is to department chairs and administrators, it is perhaps more helpful to teachers. It takes only a few sessions for the teacher and the students to forget that the videocamera is in the front (or the back) of the classroom. Once this happens, the videotape provides an objective and revealing look at what really occurs during the class period. This "look" gives teachers a range of insights into their teaching behaviors.

To structure that look, department chairs are advised to provide a series of questions that enable teachers to focus on the important elements of their teaching. Figure 2–4, *A Mirror of Performance (General Self-Evaluation)*, provides an excellent reproducible for this purpose. We use it extensively and, in the words of one of our teachers: "This self-evaluation is a very thorough self-study, and has touched upon every aspect of teaching objectives, class dynamics, and teaching style. It should be reviewed after watching the video so that teachers can process the entire teaching episode more thoroughly."

Notice that the reproducible encourages a general self-assessment. It encourages considerations such as what the teacher did well, what he or she may have forgotten, what techniques were successful, whether or not the purpose of the lesson was realized, what might have to be changed for the future, which students listened attentively and which were distracted, and what teacher mannerisms may warrant some changing.

Obviously, there are many more considerations that can emerge from such an experience. The point is, when they emerge, the videocamera is available to provide a series of looks at this specific teaching behavior. The reproducible form in Figure 2–5, *A Mirror of Performance (Specific Teaching Behavior)*, takes that specific look. As with the general form, it can be used by department chairs and administrators to review when using the videotape for purposes of teacher evaluation.

It is used most often, however, by teachers who are looking at a specific element of their teaching. When given the chance to review their teaching in the comfort and security of their homes, even the intractable veteran finds a moment or two to accommodate the camera and to review one or more teaching behaviors. The process is facilitated by the reproducible form in Figure 2–6, *Request for AV Services*, which instructs the AV department/personnel about the particulars of the teachers' needs.

Feedback from Peers

Another enlightening experience available to some teachers is the program of peer-directed supervision. It's been called many things in education within the past several years: peer coaching, collegial teaming, cognitive coaching, peer mentoring, and collegial consultation. All of these programs have one common element, friends helping friends. The help comes in the form of feedback, sometimes evaluative, along with the sharing of the accumulated knowledge and experience of two or more peers.

Collegial programs are as difficult to implement and maintain as they are helpful to the participants. Teachers involved in such programs must learn appropriate observation techniques and conferencing strategies. If simply thrown together without an introduction to the skills required for such a program, teachers can actually alienate rather than help each other. Expecting a helping hand, they sometimes find a clenched fist.

It's wise, therefore, to engage interested teachers in in-service programs that spell out and give them time to practice needed skills and expectations. It's also wise to foster coordination of team activities by providing materials that outline the specifics. The *Peer-Directed Observation* form in Figure 2–7 accommodates several of these specifics. It requires the teacher to identify the purposes of the lesson and its relationship to the long-range goals of the course.

It also identifies the teaching behaviors that the teacher wants the group to observe. Some colleague groups provide a general reaction to the teacher after the observation; others, like this one, focus on specific teaching behaviors, most always identified by the teacher.

Obviously, when the group focus is on specific behaviors, particularly when they have been identified by the teacher, any group discussion about other behaviors is inappropriate—no matter how such behaviors may seem to need the group's attention. Trust among team members is critical if colleague groups are to be successful. Trust will suffer if members of the group bump into too many surprises. Their expectations should be respected during the actual observation. Other behaviors that seem to require the group's attention may be identified later during one or more administratively-directed observations. Such is the complementary relationship among the three modes of classroom observation.

EVALUATION FOR ALL STYLES AND ABILITIES _____

The same is true when teachers are involved in self-directed supervision. Because the teacher determines the focus of the observation and expects to make all the value judgments regarding the feedback he or she receives, comments from the group should be specific to the focus identified by the teacher. By occupational expectation, teachers are evaluative. They evaluate debates, student behavior, cheerleader tryouts, pop quizzes, semester exams, and each other.

Fortunately, programs of peer-directed and self-directed supervision allow such evaluation; they just discourage sharing it. Any evaluation in self-directed supervision is made by the individual teacher, unless he or she requests it from one or more colleagues, just as any evaluation in peer-directed supervision should be specific to the focus identified by the teacher. Only administratively-directed observation involves "unrequested" evaluation.

The distinctions among the three kinds of classroom observations provide several advantages:

- They acknowledge the importance of occasional evaluation from administrators.
- They provide a broad base of participation within the school. Any collegial program underscores the fact that persons other than administrators can help teachers with their professional growth experiences.
- They reflect the school's awareness that teachers are capable of controlling their own growth activities.
- They provide alternative ways for teachers to realize professional growth within a given school year.

This particular point deserves additional mention. Every school is composed of different levels of teacher competence. Much of the literature indicates that 15 to 20 percent of any staff are the very competent—in essence the "willing-and-able." The next 50 to 60 percent represent some combination of the "willing-but-unable" and the "unwilling-but-able" teachers. These teachers constitute the majority in the school and are the ones who can benefit most from programs of ongoing observation/supervision.

In effect, they require less evaluation. This is less true for the final group, the "unwilling and unable." They usually constitute only 5 to 10 percent of the teachers in the school and require special attention. A future section is devoted to them.

The "Willing-and-Able" Teacher

This group of teachers is capable of a great deal of self-reflection. If given adequate feedback about their teaching, they will self-evaluate and adjust their teaching accordingly. The self-directed mode of classroom observation is fine for them. Although they may warrant administratively-directed observation once or twice every two to three years, they can be involved in self-directed programs most of the time.

The willing-and-able teacher is capable of integrating in-service themes within his or her teaching and requires only the practice time of a self-directed mode to continue performing at a high level. Such teachers should be encouraged to tandem with another willing-and-able teacher to develop periodic activities for themselves that provide the feedback so necessary for self-evaluation and growth.

The "Willing-but-Unable" Teacher

These teachers, generally young and eager, are motivated to perform at a high level but lack the strategies, techniques, and experience of superior teachers. They require periodic contact with the "willing-and-able" teachers who can make assessments of performance, suggest needed strategies and techniques, and provide feedback regarding progress.

Some of the "willing-but-unable" teachers in the building are veterans who have discovered successful survival strategies but have never had the supervision needed to transform such strategies into effective teaching. They, too, are motivated to learn and will benefit from periodic contact with the willing-and-able.

All willing-but-unable teachers are potentially superior performers. What they require is periodic contact with a competent and trusted someone who can help them grow professionally. That someone may be another teacher, an administrator, or department chair—anyone who expresses a willingness and is available to help. Forms should be provided early in the year to give staff the opportunity to select a mode. See Figure 2–8, ***Professional Growth Alternatives,*** for a reproducible. You might attach the reproducible in Figure 2–1 at this time to discuss the options available to the staff.

The "Able-but-Unwilling" Teacher

The first section in Figure 2–8 explains the three modes of observation. It then relates supervision to the teacher's annual goals and paves the way for a discussion with the department chair. The process, therefore, provides a way for the teacher to select an observation mode or to be assigned one. Assignment of a mode may be based on school or district policy. For example, policy may require every staff member to be involved in administratively-directed supervision once every three or four years.

Superior teachers might be asked to select one in order to be available to colleagues; other teachers might be assigned based exclusively on their performance as documented by previous evaluation reports. The able-but-unwilling teacher won't benefit from peer-directed or self-directed activity as much as others in the building. He or she probably will require frequent administratively-directed observation in order to improve or to decide that teaching is no longer a viable career alternative.

Such a teacher may be burned out and in need of some kind of revitalization, or he or she may be too far gone to benefit from any kind of remediation. The persistently unwilling teacher eventually falls into the pool of the bottom 5 to 10 percent who are best described as problem teachers. They require much different treatment. Section Nine of this book provides some suggestions.

KEEPING FEEDBACK OBJECTIVE _____

Some of our earliest school experiences as students involved "Show and Tell." We generally showed our classmates something that was important to us and then explained it. Department chairs and others involved in the supervisory process do the same thing when they observe a classroom teacher. They "show" the teacher what he or she did during the class period.

"Telling" is a different issue. If the observer's comments are restricted to a description of what happened during the observation and to encouragement for the teacher to analyze and evaluate the information for him- or herself, the experience will be of most value for the teacher. If the "telling" involves the supervisor's value judgments and specific suggestions for improvement, the experience is more an affirmation of the supervisor's authority than a learning experience for the teacher.

Show them and tell them, therefore, but be careful to do more showing than telling. The more you evaluate your staff, the less chance they have to self-evaluate. Self-evaluation encourages ownership of behavior. It makes sense that if I evaluate you, I own the evaluation. If *you* evaluate you, you own it. I want you to own it.

Asking the Right Questions

Showing and telling must give way to showing and asking—or showing and helping. Supervision, particularly in the peer-directed and self-directed modes, should emphasize as much teacher self-evaluation as possible, a practice which is consistent with Wilson's idea that judgment should provide light, not heat. The light resulting from self-evaluation shines brighter and longer than the few glimmers sparked by evaluation from others.

As soon as possible after the observation, the information gathered by the observer(s) should be provided to the teacher. Discussion of the information depends upon the teacher's mode of professional growth. If the teacher's program is self-directed, the observer might simply collect the information, give it to the teacher, and await the teacher's next request for help.

If the mode is peer-directed or administratively-directed, the observer(s) are likely to have a follow-up conference with the teacher to promote his or her analysis and evaluation of the information. In some instances, value judgments may come from the observer(s), but the conference is most valuable for the teacher when observers choose to ask questions instead of give answers.

Questions such as the following encourage teachers to self-evaluate:

- What are your feelings about the lesson? How do you think it went?
- Do you think the objectives were achieved?
- What did you observe in your students' behavior that leads you to believe this?
- What did you do to make them behave that way?
- How did your actual behavior compare with your intentions?

- What about their behavior? Was it what you expected?
- Will you do anything differently in future lessons?

Figure 2–9, **Form A**, provides an example of another variation on the General Observation Form. This one relates to Madeline Hunter's concept of checking for understanding. It may have been devised for or by a teacher who wanted to improve his or her awareness of student progress toward an understanding of the day's lesson. It provides very specific information about the teacher's interaction with individual students.

The point is, it can be used by an administrator to evaluate a teacher, or by a colleague or the teacher to facilitate teacher self-evaluation. As such, most of the aforementioned questions can be asked in reference to this particular form, or others like it. Figure 2–10, **General Observation Form B**, provides a reproducible of the basic form. It can be used to create variations, such as the one in Figure 2–9 or the earlier example in Figure 2–3.

The questions can also be asked after the observer provides a general picture of what happened during the class period. Such a picture can be provided by a videotape or a written record of teacher and student behavior during the class period. Whatever the focus, general or specific, and whatever the mode of professional growth, the observer's desire to ask the right questions should always take immediate priority over volunteering answers.

When Answers Are Needed

Naturally, right answers are warranted in certain instances. However, answers (recommended teaching strategies, suggestions for improvement, et al.) are best received by teachers when they *ask* for them. Reconsider the golfing example. When I slice every drive into the nearby timber, I want all the evaluation I can get, from anyone who is willing to give it. The key is my awareness that I am doing something wrong and that I have a trusted someone nearby who can help me.

Usually, incorrect performance is not as immediately obvious to teachers as it is to golfers. That's where good department chairs come in. They should be as available as possible to teachers, and they should have the skills needed to help teachers with their professional growth. Good ones generally reject the "I-know-more-than-you" notion; they accept the competencies of their teachers. Instead, they focus their skills on helping teachers to self-evaluate.

A major result of this process is a written observation report that reflects the teacher's perceptions and opinions, not the observer's. Consider Figure 2–11, an example of a concept I used a while back in an article for the National Association of Secondary School Principals' (NASSP) *Bulletin*. The first report reflects the opinions of the observer; the second reflects the teacher's comments and analyses. The second is less threatening to the teacher and probably more likely to provoke a needed change in his or her teaching.

The second also assumes considerable skill on the part of the observer. He or she must establish the right kind of atmosphere and ask the right kinds of questions to lead the teacher into effective self-analysis. Such a skill is not difficult to learn. Generally it requires a department chair who accepts the philosophy of teacher self-evaluation and who practices the technique with every member of his or her staff.

Figure 2–11, *One Way to Write an Observation Report*, is provided as a reproducible. It might be useful in department chair in-service training programs to highlight the value and feasibility of teacher self-evaluation in the observation process. It also shows how observation reports can be written to increase the light and reduce the "heat" of a classroom observation. This important difference between the right way and the wrong way to write observation reports will be discussed at greater length in the next section. The difference also suggests another big advantage.

Trust = Power

Which of the two observation reports would you as a teacher rather receive? I know that I would rather work with a skillful someone who could lead me through an analysis of the information gathered during the observation and encourage me to evaluate my own performance. Professor Daniel Griffiths indicated years ago that people who control the process by which decisions are made and don't make all the decisions have most of the power in the organization and are accepted by everyone in it.

It follows, then, that the department chair who avoids making the value judgments in the first section of Figure 2–11 and follows the process in the second section will be more well-liked by the teachers in his or her department. Such acceptance implies trust, and trust equals power. Teachers give power to people they trust. It's that simple. The more inclined we are to step down from the hierarchy and acknowledge that we don't have all the answers, the more power we will have in the department and school.

Such a statement seems to contradict much of what we have learned or heard about organizational power. The more we think about it, however, the more sense it makes. The Board of Education and the administration give department chairs the authority to observe teachers, but teachers give department chairs the power to make a difference in their teaching. This is a critical point, one that presupposes your competence and that increases your effectiveness in the school. It also assures your survival. And that's what this book is all about.

Let's Wrap It Up

The literature reminds us that 85% of all classroom observations should be designed to help teachers grow professionally, not to simply evaluate them. Some department chairs and administrators across the country have reacted enthusiastically to this suggestion. Most haven't. They claim they have an insufficient amount of time to do their yearly evaluations, much less to provide such a large commitment to professional growth. Such a reaction is a cop-out.

The involvement of peers in the supervisory process and the growth of programs like self-directed supervision have relieved department chairs and administrators of the responsibility to do all the observations in the school. They can still do their evaluations—as refined by the suggestions here and in the next section—and oversee a process that engages teachers in their own professional growth. In addition, video technology now provides the opportunity for department chairs to observe teachers on Saturday morning, in their own homes.

Let me emphasize the point once more. The need to evaluate staff is as important as ever, but it doesn't have to be the only focus of classroom observation. In fact, the desirability of evaluation probably is in direct relation to the teacher's level of competence in the classroom. The following graph gives a visual representation of this. Highly competent teachers don't need evaluation; at least they don't need it as often as others may. In fact, they usually don't like it because few people in the administrative hierarchy can teach as well as they do.

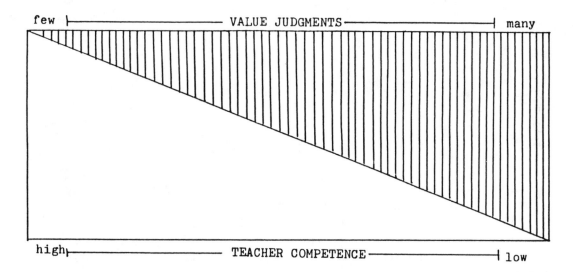

Good department chairs, however, and other knowledgeable persons involved in the supervisory process may not be better teachers than everyone else in the building, but they do have the ability to help even the best become better. Save ongoing and frequent evaluation for the rest of the staff. Poor teachers require it, whether they like it or not. How to make it work for them—and for the competent others—is the focus of the next section.

To conclude this one, however, let's look at a flowchart that shows the relationships among in-service training, evaluation, and the different components of supervision, specifically peer and self-directed supervision. This flowchart shows that the process begins with either an observation by an administrator or a peer (both of which can be evaluative) or with in-service information. The teacher can incorporate the information without help immediately or initiate a self-directed program with a colleague to practice and refine it. As indicated already, the colleague can be anyone who is willing to observe the teacher and provide information as directed by him or her.

During the self-directed practice time, the teacher works to incorporate the earlier recommendations or the in-service input into his or her teaching. Subsequent self-directed experiences or the next administratively-directed observation can assess his or her success in doing so. As indicated at the end of the flowchart, if the teacher has been unsuccessful, other alternatives will have to be identified, one of which might be to increase the number of administratively-

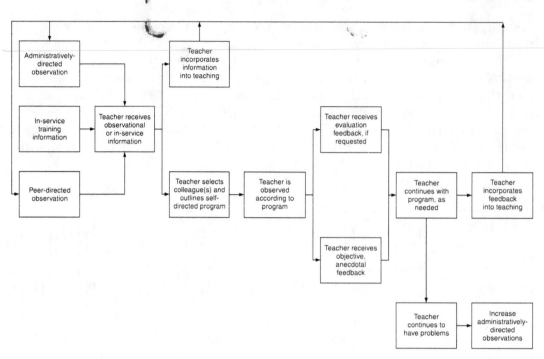

directed observations (evaluations). If successful, the teacher begins the process anew, emphasizing a different competency.

The link to the evaluative elements in the professional growth program, therefore, is clear. Evaluations from supervisors, even peers, provide direction for teachers. Such evaluations, if well-conceived and carefully communicated, need not be frequent, unless the teacher clearly requires them. The frequency of *nonevaluative* observations is the key. The next section will cover more of this.

Figure 2–1

CLASSROOM OBSERVATION
(Five Critical Questions)

This department encourages a three-part program of teacher observation. No part is more important than any of the others. All are designed to complement each other in order to provide worthwhile professional growth experiences for each staff member. Each of us, therefore, is able to ask the following five questions before a classroom observation. The answers will identify the focus of the observation:

1. *What is the purpose of this observation?* Is it to provide objective, anecdotal feedback to the teacher for purposes of self-evaluation, or is it to document teacher performance for evaluative/employment purposes?

2. *Who is to conduct the observation and what kinds of data are to be gathered?* Who will make such determinations?

3. *How will these data be gathered?* Instrumentation? Script-taping? Video or audio taping?

4. *Who will analyze these data to determine implications for teaching?* Myself? An administrator? The department chair? A colleague?

5. *Who will use the analyses to make value judgments about the quality of teacher performance?*

The answers to each of the above questions determine the focus of any observation. The answers to the last two in particular determine if the observation is directed by an administrator/department chair, a teaching colleague, or you. You probably will experience all three within any two- or three-year period. See me any time I can be of assistance with any one of them.

Figure 2–2

TEACHER EVALUATION

Teacher: _____

Subject: _____

Period: _____

Date: _____

Observer: _____

Classroom Instruction

Classroom instruction is the heart of the school program. The instructional competencies teachers bring to the classroom determine the quality and scope of student learning.

Knowledge and Training	Strength	Weakness	NA
1. Has demonstrated knowledge of subject area.	_____	_____	_____
2. Reflects in teaching a knowledge of learning theory, educational psychology, and curriculum development.	_____	_____	_____
3. Advances own knowledge by studying and applying new techniques and expanding own mastery of subject matter.	_____	_____	_____

Classroom Management			
1. Provides a relaxed and comfortable classroom atmosphere and interacts in a friendly manner with students.	_____	_____	_____
2. Applies standards of appropriate behavior consistently and fairly.	_____	_____	_____
3. Provides well-structured classroom activities and provides sufficient time on task to promote student learning.	_____	_____	_____

Figure 2–3

CRITICAL QUESTION TALLY SHEET

To the Teacher: Indicate in the space below specifically what you want your students to be able to do by the end of this lesson. What purposes have you established for them, and how will you know they have been realized?

Next, list the four, five, or six questions that you absolutely must ask during the period to be assured that your students are progressing toward your purposes. The questions may be asked several different ways; generalize them for now:

1.

2.

3.

4.

5.

6.

To the Observer: Each time one of the above questions is asked of a student, place its number next to the name of that student.

Figure 2–4

A MIRROR OF PERFORMANCE
(General Self-Evaluation)

A Suggestion: The following is a checklist of ten questions to help guide your self-analysis. The checklist is offered only as a reminder of what you already know. The questions are general and will be helpful if you are analyzing the everyday characteristics of your teaching. If you are looking at one or more specifics, you may want to share the tape with a colleague for another perspective.

Did You:

1. Maintain a *focus* on the day's objective?

   Feel that the *objective* was clear to you and your students?

   Feel that the objective *related clearly* to the lessons which preceded and will follow it?

2. Establish a *comfortable atmosphere* in the class?

   Feel that *exchanges* with students were *positive*, sometimes *humorous*, and unaffected?

   Feel that they promoted *positive self-images* in the students and involved appropriate rewards?

   Feel that needed disciplinary comments *influenced* students without *embarrassing* them?

Did You:

3. Observe any *distracting mannerisms* in your behavior?

   Observe any *distracting verbalizations* in your behavior?

4. *Move freely* about the room and call on as many students as possible?

   Did you establish a *physical* as well as verbal relationship with the students?

5. Ask a *variety* of questions, emphasizing, as appropriate, *higher order* as well as memory-level thought processes?

   Probe student thinking and ask students to *elaborate* on interesting and well-conceived ideas?

   Provide *sufficient wait time* after you asked questions and received answers?

6. *Model* the "how to" elements in the material?

   Give *concrete examples* of general information?

7. Appeal to the different *modalities* of your students?

   Enable them to have a chance to *look, listen, and do?*

Did You:

8. Provide enough *guided practice* for students to integrate the material?

9. *Check* periodically to see if the students *understood* the material?

   Feel comfortable after reviewing the tape, that the students seemed to *understand* the material?

   Decide to *reteach* any of the lesson or teach it *differently* next time?

10. *Summarize* the lesson?

    Feel that your students could *have summarized* the lesson and related it to the objective?

Figure 2–5

A MIRROR OF PERFORMANCE
(Specific Teaching Behavior)

This form is designed for *your* use! The questions encourage a reflective look at the specific characteristics of your teaching. Answer the questions before and after you watch the tape to structure the experience, then save the completed form to compare with future videotapes. Share the tape and/or the form with others as you see fit.

Questions to Ask Yourself:

1. What changes will improve my students' learning?

> *EXAMPLES:*
>
> ☐ More questions and answers
> ☐ More higher order thought questions
> ☐ More active involvement in the learning process

2. What must I do to encourage such changes in my students? What specific behavior(s) in my teaching must I change?

> *EXAMPLES:*
>
> ☐ Develop more "critical" questions
> ☐ Ask higher order thought questions
> ☐ Provide more activities for students during class

3. What evidence will I accept from the videotape as proof that I have made the appropriate changes?

> *EXAMPLES:*
>
> ☐ An increasing number of higher order thought questions
> ☐ Less lecture and more student activity

4. After viewing the tape do I still want to focus on the original change? Would another change be more effective? If yes, what would it be?

Notes:

Figure 2–6

REQUEST FOR AV SERVICES

Teacher's name: _____

Department: _____

Please provide a videocamera _____ and an operator _____ to videotape my

class on _____, period _____.
            [Day(s) and Date(s)]

The focus of the observation will be:

Myself _____   My students _____   Both _____

I will require all _____ / part _____ of the class period taped.

Comments:

Thanks for your help.

Figure 2–7

PEER-DIRECTED OBSERVATION

Teacher's name: _____ **Room no.:** _____

Name of class: _____ **Level:** _____ **Period:** _____

Please complete the following information and give copies to each of your team members before your observation.

1. *What are your purposes for this lesson?*

2. *How do these purposes fit into your long-range goals for this course?*

3. *What teaching/learning activities do you want the team to observe? How do you want them to collect information for you?*

4. *What particular teaching behaviors do you want observed? Be as specific as possible and clarify how you want them observed.*

Figure 2–8

PROFESSIONAL GROWTH ALTERNATIVES

Administratively-Directed Observation

The department encourages a range of professional growth alternatives in order to provide the best possible experience for individual staff members. Administratively-directed observation provides periodic evaluation from an administrator or department chair. You may request the times of such evaluations, or they may be determined by the administrator. The evaluations will follow some kind of observation of your performance and will be provided in writing after a postobservation conference, one copy to be given to you, another to be placed in your file.

Peer-Directed Observation

Peer-directed observation provides evaluation and/or feedback from a group of peers who will join you in the analysis of your/their teaching behaviors. You will observe each other's classes on a regular basis and share feedback and recommendations, all of which will be given to you. Nothing will be placed in your file. Someone will contact you regarding the specifics of your involvement should you select or be assigned to this mode of professional growth.

Self-Directed Observation

Self-directed observation provides the opportunity to develop and control your own professional growth program. You may work with one or more colleagues, but only at your direction. You may request feedback only from them, occasional evaluation, or specific suggestions regarding your teaching. The information they collect is to be given to you for purposes of self-evaluation; nothing will be placed in your file.

Goals

On a separate sheet of paper, please identify your goals for the current school year. One or two will be sufficient. Our upcoming discussion of them will identify what I can do to help you realize them and how they relate to one or all of the alternative professional growth processes in the department.

Professional Growth Preference

Finally, please select the professional growth alternative that you would like to emphasize during the current school year. We will discuss both your selection and your goals when we meet.

_____ Administratively-directed observation

_____ Peer-directed observation

_____ Self-directed observation

I'll be in touch soon regarding a meeting.

Figure 2–9

GENERAL OBSERVATION FORM A

To the Teacher: Using the symbols below, identify on the seating chart the students who are your best indicators of progress toward lesson objectives. In essence, their answers to questions have influenced your decision to reteach certain parts of the lesson or to continue as planned.

K—*most* knowledgeable   M—*moderately* knowledgeable   L—*least* knowledgeable

After the Lesson: Did you decide to reteach any part of the lesson during class? Did you decide to reteach any or all of it tomorrow? Briefly, what in the lesson influenced your decision to reteach or not to reteach?

To the observer: Place a tally next to the names of the students the teacher has questioned.

Seating Chart

Figure 2–10

GENERAL OBSERVATION FORM B

To the Teacher:

To the Observer:

Seating Chart

Figure 2–11

ONE WAY TO WRITE AN OBSERVATION REPORT

Mr. Bestor's class was very interesting. His insights into Hamlet's character held the attention of the class very well. They even provoked occasional spontaneous remarks from the class such as, "He was a pretty confused guy, wasn't he?" and "Wow, I didn't know that." But his questions remained largely at the memory level and did little to provoke higher order thought process in the students. As interesting as his lecture was, it spoon-fed a great deal of the material and didn't leave much room for the students' analysis of Hamlet's character. I would recommend that Mr. Bestor and I meet once or twice before his next evaluation to discuss some of Harvey Silver's materials on higher order thought process and question-and-answer technique in the classroom.

A Better Way

I must admit that I share your excitement about the enthusiasm of your students. They do, in fact, seem to be very interested in their current reading assignment. I was also quite impressed by your self-analysis of the class period, particularly about your comment that you have always had the tendency to "give" everything to your students rather than to promote their analysis of the material with appropriate questions. You also indicated that you have the tendency to ask too many memory-level questions and not enough analysis, synthesis, and evaluation-level questions. If you would like to explore this concern further, I have some of Harvey Silver's materials on hand and would enjoy sharing them and perhaps discussing them with you.

Let me know if I can help further.

EVALUATING TEACHERS: A LITTLE QUALITY CONTROL

Frederick Taylor, the father of "The Principles of Scientific Management," is recognized in most textbooks as a pioneer in management theory. Many writers acknowledge his early contributions as provident stages in the evolution of school administration. Taylor was born near the end of the Civil War and published his most significant work, *Shop Management,* with Harper in 1911.

Here is a quote from that book: ". . . it is important that workmen should not be very much overpaid, as it is that they should not be underpaid. If overpaid, many will work irregularly and tend to become more or less shiftless, extravagant, and dissipated. . . . Most men tend to become more instead of less thrifty when they receive the proper increase for an extra hard day's work. They live rather better, begin to save money, become more sober, and work more steadily."

Taylor was the theorist who gave administration the Separation-of-Planning-from-Performance principle; "Managers should plan; workers should work." He also gave us the Functional-Management principle: "The strict application of military principles should be reconsidered and used to coordinate the activities of various specialists." Taylor was a spokesman of his times and did much to influence the future development and design of educational administration. Surprising? Not really.

Remember, this was a time in our history when "mechanics, artisans, and laborers" were considered professional athletes, primarily because Gentlemen Amateurs preferred never to associate with the lower classes, least of all on the playing field. It was a time of social elitism, when hierarchical organization not only patterned work relationships but reflected the class consciousness of our society.

Because the current organizational design of most schools has been shaped by such thinking, it isn't too surprising that most of them continue to regard administrators as evaluators, not simply the keepers of the organizational flame, but the most knowledgeable people in the building about teaching. I have taught educational administration at the university level for almost 20 years and, before that, had served in varying administrative jobs at the school and district levels. Within that time, I learned much.

One of my earliest and most important lessons taught me that I was *not* the building's most knowledgeable person about teaching. I knew a great deal about it and have since learned more, but I realized early in the game that there were several teachers in the building who were better than I. In fact, several could teach circles around me. Such an awareness introduced me to one of my first administrative dilemmas.

The hierarchy gave me a considerable amount of authority. I wondered if I should use it to enter teachers' classrooms and exercise my organizational *right* to evaluate their performance—then suggest areas of improvement. Or I thought I might do what some of my administrative colleagues were doing. They watched these same teachers for a full class period, then wrote glowing "evaluations" of their teaching. They most always used checklists, so the evaluations were general enough to allow for a variety of interpretations.

I recall opting temporarily for this latter practice. It got me off the hook and seemed to please the teachers. I thought it made them feel closer to me. Only later did I realize that the practice failed everyone. Although the "evaluation" was complimentary to teachers, they paid little attention to it and learned nothing from it. What some of them learned was that I didn't know what I was doing, that I was relying more on my organizational position than my knowledge of effective teaching.

Does this sound a bit extreme? Maybe, but I don't think so. I say "maybe" because many of our schools are blessed with knowledgeable and competent administrators who have the ability to promote relevant learning experiences for their staffs. My question to you is, do they provide these experiences by assuming that the hierarchy has invested them with sufficient knowledge to tell everyone else in the building how to teach? Experience has taught me that the answer to this question is No.

If you as a practicing or potential department chair, therefore, cannot claim to tell *all* your teachers how to teach, you had better reconsider the issue of teacher evaluation. Even if you feel you *can* tell them all how to teach or if you would rather ask most of the right questions than give all the answers, you'll benefit from this section.

WHAT IS EVALUATION?

First of all, it's important to recognize that evaluation is merely a description of "what is." It successfully identifies problems with performance only if both parties involved in the evaluation agree on the description of "what is" and the expectation of "what should be." If the person being evaluated or the evaluator disagree on the wording of either, both will disagree on the extent and the characteristics of the problem, whatever it may be.

For our purposes, let's define a problem as a measurable or observable discrepancy between "what is" and "what should be." If I disagree with your description of "what is," and/or you disagree with my expectations of "what should be," we probably see different problems, or one of us sees none at all. At this point, the evaluation is useless. It has created an adversarial rather than a trusting relationship between the teacher and the evaluator.

More on Evaluation

There are other problems as well. My experience indicates that too many supervisors are unaware of the specific elements of teaching that determine "what should be." I refer to such teaching essentials as Madeline Hunter's 7-step lesson design, the fundamental principles of modality learning, the simple psychology of classroom management, the importance of disciplining with dignity, a basic understanding of higher order thought process, and the principles of effective questioning technique.

There are more, not a lot more, but enough to form the substance of worthwhile professional growth experiences for teachers. They are uncomplicated and revealing, unless wrapped in jargon. The department chair's job is to know them, communicate them in the simplest terms possible, underscore them as the "what should be" of evaluation, and relate them to the "what is" of classroom observation.

This suggests another problem. Many supervisors rely too much on general checklists and too little on specific data-gathering techniques that provide a revealing picture of "what is." As indicated in the previous section, *every* classroom observation should *show* before it *tells*. In fact, the less it tells, the more likely it will encourage teacher self-evaluation, the only sure-fire way to promote improved teaching.

Teachers need "mirrors" to reflect and help analyze their specific performance, not checklists that assess and prescribe general teaching behaviors. We'll discuss the relationship of mirrors to checklists in a few minutes. First, let's consider six additional principles of teacher evaluation. Use them as guidelines to organize your process.

Six Principles of Effective Teacher Evaluation

1. Evaluation considers the purposes of the teacher and the conditions of the teaching experience. I recall learning early in the game the importance of student/teacher interaction in the classroom. The Flander's Interaction Analysis Technique and the Guilford Technique were (and are still) just two of the observation tools that supervisors/evaluators used to determine levels of teacher and student talk during the class.

They became so popular with some administrators that teachers began to feel guilty if they lectured during most of the class period. Fortunately, people like Madeline Hunter were quick to point out that the *purposes* of the lesson should be considered when observing a teacher. If the purpose of the lesson is instructional input, lecture may be perfectly appropriate. Ask the teacher *before* the observation. If lecture is the primary/exclusive methodology and you want to help assess interaction, visit the class another time—which suggests the second principle.

2. Evaluation aims at agreement between observer and observee *before* the observation. If the purpose of the observation is to help assess teacher/student interaction, don't focus exclusively on classroom management. Some discussion of

student behavior may be appropriate as it relates to interaction, but don't focus on it to the exclusion of interaction.

If you observe that student behavior is an issue, schedule another observation, this time with a focus on classroom management. Every baseball player knows that a curve ball is designed to trick him. Don't throw curve balls at teachers; they don't like to be tricked. That's why it's wise to meet before the observation to agree on the focus and the method of gathering information. No tricks, no surprises, no misunderstandings. Figure 3–1, **Classroom Observation**, helps accommodate these last two principles.

3. Evaluation provides documented and objective proof of teacher performance. You may be familiar with the old bromide about teacher observation, but it bears repeating: "If you didn't write it down, you didn't see it. And if you didn't see it, it didn't happen." Don't try to convince a teacher about an element of his or her teaching if you didn't somehow document that behavior. Effective documentation doesn't require a video camera; your written anecdotal record is sufficient, if you have recorded the behavior objectively. See Figures 3–2, **Observation Record**, and 3–3, a completed sample of that form, for examples.

4. Evaluation describes growth in comparison to previous observations. Observations should build upon one another. The discussion of one behavior should identify specific areas for improvement, hopefully *by* the teacher. Subsequent observations should focus on those areas of improvement, new areas to be identified only after the original behaviors are performed to the satisfaction of the teacher and the observer.

5. It follows, then, that evaluation doesn't overwhelm the teacher with a wide range of topics to discuss. Too many department chairs, particularly rookies, spend a great deal of time proving to everyone within earshot how much they know. It's sometimes a fine line to consider, but the observation process is not the opportunity for you to reveal all you know about teaching. It is designed to provide opportunities for teachers to learn, and, most often, the impetus for such learning can be found within the teacher.

It's wise, therefore, to discuss one or two, sometimes three different areas of teacher performance that emerge from a mutual analysis of the information you have gathered. The identification of four, five, six, or more areas of teacher performance provides a series of hurdles that can overwhelm even the best, most confident teacher. In addition, such an overwhelming experience can cause anger and alienation and eventually compromise your ability to work with the teacher in the future.

6. Finally, and perhaps most importantly, evaluation should encourage teacher self-evaluation before, during, and after the discussion of the information you have gathered during the observation. Figure 3–4, **Your Self-Analysis**, provides a set of questions to accompany the observation record. These help guide the teacher's self-analysis. They are the same kinds of questions, phrased differently, that you will ask the teacher later during the postobservation conference.

Certainly, there are times when the department chair must *tell* a teacher what his or her observation notes seem to reveal about the teacher's performance. Some teachers, usually inexperienced or incompetent, are unable or unwilling to take an objective look at themselves and even less willing to identify behaviors needing improvement.

Such teachers require direction, probably ongoing supervision until they gain a sense of autonomy. Most teachers, however, probably a significant majority, are capable of reviewing their teaching and identifying one or more areas that need some work. Their ability to do that will depend on their sense of self-esteem, their relationship with you, and any help you can provide them.

Rudolph Dreikurs once said: "Until I can risk appearing imperfect in your eyes, without fear that it will cost me something, I can't really learn from you." The quote is true of the relationships between parent and child, student and teacher, and teacher and department chair. If the focus of teacher evaluation is to "catch 'em being bad," teachers will never learn from the experience. That's another reason why self-evaluation is so important for them.

Evaluation for What?

This brings us to a discussion of what we hope to accomplish when we observe/evaluate a teacher. Our purposes will vary, depending upon the competence of the teacher and the expectations of district or school policy. The following five forms of teacher evaluation are the most prevalent:

1. *Summative Evaluation.* This is an end-of-the-year assessment of the teacher's total contribution to the school and department. It may involve the discussion of specifics from earlier observations and affirmations of teacher progress toward "what should be." It will also include mention of the teacher's involvement with departmental committees, community activities, extracurricular activities, all-school committees, awards and other accomplishments, publications, workshops attended, presentations at conventions, and any of several other yearly activities. The **Summative Evaluation** in Figure 3–5 provides a reproducible. It provides enough categories to include everything the teacher did during the school year.

Summative evaluations are the school's annual attempts at quality control. They guarantee effective education for the community. As such, a summative evaluation is very important within the total program of professional growth for teachers. The only time it becomes a problem is when it violates one or more of the principles discussed in this section or when it is used to the exclusion of other, more frequent forms of professional growth.

Because summative evaluation covers the teacher's total contribution for the year, it provides an excellent starting point next year for the planning of follow-up professional growth activities. See the form for **Annual Goals** in Figure 3–6. Without such follow-up, summative evaluation seems to exist for its own sake and affirms Carl Glickman's observation that most teachers feel they are observed for purposes *other than* instructional improvement. When linked with activities described in Section Two, summative evaluation becomes a necessary part of the department's total professional growth program.

2. *Periodic Monitoring.* The periodic monitoring of teachers provides frequent opportunities to "catch 'em being good." Normally, the observation is unexpected by the teacher, short (usually only ten minutes), and unconcerned with

follow-up, unless the department chair observes something extraordinary. Monitoring provides four important advantages:

- It increases the visibility of department chairs and the school's administrators.
- It provides opportunities for department chairs to continually reinforce excellent teaching.
- It reinforces the department chair's commitment to the instructional program.
- It keeps the "heat" on poor teachers informally and subtly.

A friend of mine, a very successful administrator, makes a point of visiting/monitoring at least 3 and usually 5 teachers a day. He then uses the form, *Informal Visit,* in Figure 3–7 to tell them how pleasant it is working with them and to reaffirm his willingness to assist them whenever possible. He makes only positive comments after such visits, feeling that he can find something good in the classroom of even the building's poorest teacher.

Needless to say, his teaching staff is crazy about him. I should mention, however, that he doesn't have many poor teachers. If he did, he probably would use monitoring a bit differently—the way you may have to.

3. *Teacher-Initiated Evaluation.* Rare though it may be in most schools, teacher-initiated evaluation is alive and well in some. It is an excellent format for the teacher experimenting with a new teaching strategy. What he or she needs from a knowledgeable and trusted someone is an answer to the question: "How am I doing?" The "someone" can be the department chair or a teaching colleague who has mastered the strategy. See Figure 3–8 *Teacher-Directed Evaluation* for a reproducible that promotes the process.

Teacher-initiated evaluation also provides a couple of unique ways to look at your professional growth program and the department chair's place in it. Feedback (*Teacher-Directed Observation*) in Figure 3–9 provides an example of a form returned to the teacher after an observation. Notice the pronoun "you" throughout. Many schools prefer the third person pronouns "he" and "she." We will discuss the issue later in this section.

Back to the department chair's place in the process. The easiest way for you to conduct a quick "trust check" is to determine how often you are asked to assist a teacher with a teacher-initiated evaluation. If your staff comes to you often, you have established trust with them and can feel confident that their professional growth is ongoing. If they are going to each other or to one particular teacher, you had better take a quick look in the mirror.

I discovered a long time ago that the mirror was the first place to look when my expectations weren't being met. It's easy to look someplace else when things don't go as expected; it's wise to look first at yourself. Always ask yourself if you're doing something wrong. You can make corrections in yourself a whole lot easier and faster than in someone else. If you can honestly say that it's not you, then look somewhere else.

4. *Routine Evaluation.* This kind of evaluation usually is conducted with non-tenure teachers, teachers coming up for triennial conferences, or teachers having

professional problems. Unlike summative evaluation, which occurs at the end of the school year, routine evaluation may occur every two or three months, in some instances even more often. The frequency of routine evaluation is proportionate to the intensity of the problem.

Teachers with upcoming triennial or quadrennial conferences may have only two or three observations throughout the year. Nontenure or problem teachers may be observed every month, sometimes more. Figure 3–2 is also appropriate for routine evaluation. The postobservation conference may require more direct interpretation from you, depending upon the competencies of the teacher.

5. *Intensive Evaluation.* Intensive evaluation occurs infrequently within most schools. It probably should occur more often, but it's so time-consuming, threatening to both the teacher and the evaluator, and fraught with such a wide range of legal implications that most schools avoid it, except in the most extreme cases.

Intensive evaluation is usually for the tenured teacher who simply isn't doing the job. He or she may be burned out, purposely out of touch with new knowledge in his or her field, uncooperative, insubordinate, or abusive with students and parents. Whatever his or her problem, it has been recurrent, to the point of requiring a program of remediation and possible dismissal.

Intensive evaluation, if used thoughtfully and skillfully, can remediate the problems of even the most intransigent teacher. For the highly uncooperative teacher, intensive evaluation provides the documentation that is so necessary for the legal consequences of teacher dismissal. I know schools that visit every class of some teachers on intensive evaluation for weeks on end to document the teacher's problem and his or her unwillingness to help correct it.

Tenured teachers can be dismissed, even those who came with the building. The process, however, is time-consuming and requires thorough documentation, which, in turn, requires instructional experts who can identify professional problems, develop reasonable programs of remediation, and prove the teacher's failure to improve. It is a difficult process but usually is in the best interests of the teacher, always of the students.

Who Evaluates?

Tradition dictates that administrators evaluate teachers, but current thinking suggests that others in the department can do as well, if not better. Persons other than administrators certainly provide different perspectives. That alone sanctions their involvement. In addition, the involvement of others broadens the base of participation, expanding the helping relationships available to teachers and underscoring the expert power of persons in nonhierarchical positions.

Teachers. Teaching colleagues are significant in this regard. Whereas administrators may still evaluate for purposes of quality control, teaching colleagues can evaluate fellow teachers to recommend needed changes in methodology, specific teaching strategies, elements of classroom management, and approaches to innovative techniques. This kind of evaluation is particularly effective if it is requested by the teacher, as in the teacher-initiated evaluation.

Students. Student reactions can provide significant insights to teachers if information is requested and treated thoughtfully. Some students will use the opportunity to "get even" or "be cute," but most will accept the task reasonably, especially if it is presented to them the right way. That's why most department chairs use forms like **Student Evaluation** in Figure 3–10 and distribute them personally to each class.

The procedure is fast and efficient and provides valuable information to the teacher. Some department chairs use student evaluations to supplement their own. Others give the forms to the teacher for his or her use directly. Neither practice is better than the other. If your staff trusts you, they will accept either.

***Administrators.**   To repeat, administrators are generally responsible for many summative evaluations and for all evaluations involving employment decisions. In most instances, state law, district policy, or union contract mandates their involvement.

***Department Chairs.**   I will continue to make distinctions between department chairs and administrators throughout this book. Department chairs must not be perceived exclusively or predominately as evaluators. They will do their share, especially in the summative, routine, and teacher-initiated modes, but their primary responsibility is to serve as intermediaries between the survival and maintenance needs of the school and the personal and professional needs of the teachers.

As such, much of their classroom observation involves the nonevaluative collection and mutual interpretation of data. Their primary task is to help teachers self-evaluate in order to grow professionally. That's why the department chair always seeks teacher self-evaluation in even a routine evaluation. More of this will be discussed later in this section.

Who Is the Audience?

The answer to this question affects the entire process of teacher evaluation. Most schools tend to write evaluation reports in the third person, describing teacher activities in terms of "he" or "she" and addressing the document not to the teacher but to some unidentified "they." As a result, many teachers feel that supervision/evaluation is a process done *to* them, instead of *with* them, emphasizing a focus created *by* them.

It is important to recognize that for the department chair this is as true for evaluation as for supervision. The process, therefore, emphasizes the pronoun "you" and usually consists of four steps. I outlined each of these steps in an article for the *NASSP Bulletin,* the journal of the National Association of Secondary Schools Principals:

1. The first step requires the department chair *to analyze the data collected* during the observation but avoid sharing any conclusions with the teacher. Nothing should interfere with the teacher's initial self-assessment.

2. The second step involves *giving the data to the teacher.* Remember, the data can be your notes, one of several forms you might use, even video- or audiotapes. Whatever the observation record is, it should be cleaned up and given to the teacher at least 24 hours before the postobservation conference. The teacher should review the materials and be prepared to discuss them during the conference with the department chair. Review Figure 3–2.

3. The third step involves *the meeting,* a time when the department chair promotes analyses from the teacher, discusses reactions, and helps identify implications for future teaching. This meeting is not much different from those described so completely in the literature.

4. The final step involves the *supervisor's written record* of the teacher's self-evaluation. **Observation Report**, Figure 3–11, provides a reproducible. In the case of a summative evaluation, the record will be signed by the teacher and placed in his or her file. A completed sample of that form in Figure 3–12 represents the wording in a typical evaluation report. Figure 3–13, another completed sample, on the other hand, represents the kind of wording I have been emphasizing in this section.

Notice that the evaluation report in Figure 3–13 emphasizes the word "you" and reflects the self-evaluative comments of the teacher. As such, it suggests that the department chair perceived his or her job as that of the "asker" of questions instead of the "giver" of answers. Such a perception is less cumbersome for both the teacher and the department chair. As important, the evaluation report in Figure 3–13 belongs to the teacher; the report in Figure 3–12 belongs to the department chair or administrator.

When the teacher "owns" the report, he or she is likely to accept what it says and seek improvement. The teacher also is likely to regard the department chair as a helpmate throughout the evaluative process, thereby increasing the department chair's power to promote behavioral change. Remember Dreikur's comment: "Until I can appear imperfect in your eyes. . . , I can't really learn from you."

I learn to trust you when you don't throw value judgments at me. And when I trust you, I can risk imperfection in your eyes, especially if I can identify my own imperfections.

SO WHAT'S THE DIFFERENCE BETWEEN EVALUATION AND SUPERVISION? ___

In the first place, supervision *never* involves value judgments from the department chair, unless requested by the teacher. Evaluation sometimes involves value judgments, especially when teachers prove themselves, for whatever reasons, incapable of self-evaluation. Some just don't understand the characteristics of good teaching; some are incapable of self-reflection; some are too insecure; and others are just too perverse to acknowledge shortcomings.

These are the kinds of teachers who require evaluation from the department chair. The mope who simply refuses to break bad habits and seeks sanctuary in tenure laws needs a lot of outside evaluation and maybe a good psychological ear-twisting. My suggestions so far in this section should not be interpreted as a myopic disregard for the realities of working with the poor teacher.

On the contrary, I would be the first to grab a consistently lousy performer by his or her proverbial ear and evaluate him or her right out the door. The point is, most teachers—the vast majority—don't require such treatment and benefit from processes that emphasize self-evaluation. This is not to say that department chairs never make value judgments, even with superior teachers.

The whole process of summative evaluation involves very important value judgments. Often, the comments made by a discerning department chair about a teacher's performance during the year provide the focus for the teacher's professional growth the following year. On that basis alone, summative evaluation is absolutely essential to any teacher's growth as a professional. Problems arise when evaluation becomes the exclusive focus of teacher/department chair relationships.

Let's put it this way. Value judgments are unavoidable in any kind of relationship. We are always measuring ourselves and others against standards that are important to us. *What we do* with those value judgments, however, is critical. If our relationships are too value-oriented, they fail. Perhaps that's why nature gave us two ears and one mouth: to hear twice as much as we say.

When Evaluation Doesn't Work

Hopefully, you have accepted the importance of teacher self-evaluation and the possible interference of persistent value judgments made by observers. Well, schools are full of administrators so tempered by tradition that, to them, teacher evaluation is a series of value judgments gathered, written, and filed according to the expectations of the state and district. And this may not be all bad, if such administrators provide supervisory experiences for the teachers to complement the evaluations. Unfortunately, many of these administrators see evaluation as just another responsibility involving a deadline and are disinterested or unable to provide follow-up activities to remedy problems.

They use evaluation to the exclusion of other forms of professional growth. That's when problems develop, when the teacher perception of "we-they" emerges and they see evaluation as something that happens for its own sake. It is a perception easily avoided by department chairs. The *Follow-Up to Observation* form provided in Figure 3–14 provides a link between summative evaluation and ongoing supervision. Then the form already referred to in Figure 3–6 promotes planning early the following year to engage whatever collegial or self-directed activities are available to the teacher.

The flowchart for *Professional Growth Relationships* in Figure 3–15 provides a look at the process and the linkages within it. Notice that in-service activities and administratively-directed observation (evaluation) both feed into peer-directed and self-directed follow-up activities. These are the activities that enable teachers to "practice what someone else has preached." In-service training activities, for example, may have involved lectures emphasizing new teaching strategies; administratively-directed observation may have involved "lectures" of a different type. Both, however, provide substance for the follow-up activities in the peer and self-directed modes.

Without these follow-up modes, we can eliminate the three boxes in the middle of the flowchart, the ones enclosed in the dotted lines. What happens without them? We have evaluation on one level and teacher in-service training on the other, and neither affects the ongoing formative growth of teachers. As a matter of fact, they have little connection with each other. As such point, evaluation exists for its own sake, and in-service training programs have little relevance for the day-to-day activities of the staff.

Does this happen in schools across the country? Of course it does; we would be short-sighted to deny it. Is it changing in some schools? Absolutely. Can you change it in yours? You bet. All you require are an awareness of the needs of teachers and the development of processes to meet those needs.

BOOKS, MIRRORS, AND RED PENCILS
(TRAINING, EVALUATION, AND SUPERVISION)

Let's look at it another way. All the research on learning indicates that images stimulate long-term memory. So let's apply one image to in-service training, one to evaluation, and another to supervision. Recognizing that each of us needs some help with just about everything we do, let's say that the first form of help comes as information, well-structured and interesting. Such information may provide better ways to think or to perform certain tasks. Let's refer to such information as a *Book*.

The help we require may also come in the form of feedback regarding our performance of a task. Such feedback is either self-perceived or provided by someone else. Usually practice is involved, often by using the information (Book) that was provided earlier. Let's refer to this feedback as a *Mirror*. To further develop this image, consider the characteristics of mirrors: reflective, objective, nonverbal, uncomplicated, specific in focus, provocative of change, and so forth.

Finally, the help may come in the form of advice, suggestions, encouragement, even directives that push us in a certain direction. Such advice always involves an emphasis on external criteria and/or the perceived inability of someone to meet these criteria. Let's call this kind of help a *Red Pencil*. To develop this image, let's consider some of the characteristics of a teacher's red pencil: subjective, imposed, infrequent, suggestive of an inferiority/superiority relationship, dependency-oriented, and reactive.

These three images, *Books, Mirrors,* and *Red Pencils* comprise the ideal professional growth program for teachers. *Books* constitute in-service training; more will be said of this image in the next section. *Mirrors* constitute the reflection that takes place in supervision, especially in the peer and self-directed modes. And *Red Pencils* constitute evaluation, in the sense that they correct and often *direct*.

Operating together and complementing each other with information, feedback, and opportunities to practice, they provide teachers with ongoing opportunities to refine their professional skills. The absence of any one of them compromises the effectiveness of the other two. Without *Mirrors,* therefore, evaluation doesn't work. It may satisfy an administrative responsibility, but, when used without adequate supervisory follow-up, cannot improve the quality of teaching in your department.

Strategies that Promote Trust

What about a few specific strategies? Obviously, the best practice is to heed the principles mentioned earlier in this section and to adopt the philosophy and behavior of the administrator who visits 3 to 5 teachers a day to "catch 'em being good." He has transformed Periodic Monitoring from "snoopervision" to supervision and, as a result, enjoys a very positive relationship with his staff.

Another friend of mine provides two "wave-offs" during the year to each staff member. Assume he has scheduled a routine evaluation with a teacher. When he arrives at the door to the teacher's classroom, he may see only a smile and a wave of the teacher's hand. The signal indicates that something has gone wrong; the teacher doesn't want to be evaluated. Without asking about the problem, the department chair simply schedules another observation/evaluation with the teacher.

He has discovered that his staff uses the wave-off infrequently; rarely does anyone use it twice. But it gives his staff confidence to know that if they're having a bad day, they have a way out of the observation. They also appreciate the fact that their department chair understands their situations and has the flexibility to meet their needs.

He has another strategy that's every bit as good. Every time he conducts a routine classroom evaluation, he asks the teacher if he or she wants to identify one element of his or her teaching that he will not write up as a part of the evaluation to put in the teacher's file. He reminds the teacher that the element will become a focus of their future discussions and maybe for future supervisory experiences—*Mirrors*.

The strategy encourages teachers to take risks with the department chair. They are helped to appear "imperfect in his eyes in order to learn from him." By way of contrast, consider the reactions of most teachers to a classroom evaluation. They want to put on their best face and do whatever they can to *hide* their imperfections.

This strategy actually highlights imperfections and devises a way for teachers to get the help they need to eliminate them. Teachers having a problem with classroom management, for example, simply identify it as the element they don't want written up for their files. Then they work with the department chair to improve their classroom management skills.

Obviously, if the teacher continues to identify classroom management as the element to be excluded from the evaluation report and shows no signs of improvement, the department chair eventually has to write it up. That, however, happens infrequently because teacher needs are out in the open, and the trust that teachers feel for the department chair enables them to get the help they need to improve their teaching.

Checklists? There's a Better Way!

Now a quick word about checklists. Checklists are convenient ways to evaluate teacher performance. They assess the teacher's performance only generally, but are quick and easy and have gained acceptance in many schools across the country. Unfortunately, what may be most convenient for the observer is for the most part useless for the teacher.

We have discussed this topic at some length in Section Two, so we won't belabor the issue now. Just be reminded that some kind of written record is the best documentation for specific teaching behaviors. If administrative expedience is the goal, use checklists. If teacher growth is the goal, use audio-visual or written *Mirrors* to record the behaviors in order to identify and work on them.

Some administrative expedience is always permissible. It is the organizational equivalent of finding a shortcut to work: quicker, safer, and a whole lot easier. Without it, we may never get the job done. So we find ways to handle routine chores expediently.

Figure 3–16, *Department Evaluation of Substitute Teacher*, provides a reproducible for handling one of these chores, the evaluation of substitute teachers. Because department chairs assume little responsibility for the professional growth of substitute teachers and are concerned with quality control exclusively, the form is useful. I repeat, however, that it is one of the few times that such forms are effective with your staff.

Evaluation and Video Technology

Section Two discussed the use of video technology as an aid to productive supervision and evaluation. The *Classroom Observation* form in Figure 3–17 is a supplement to the ones mentioned earlier. It provides useful information to department chairs while they watch the tapes that teachers submit for evaluation.

Recognize that teachers are often reluctant to submit tapes for evaluation. "Supervision" and "Evaluation" are still bad words in some schools. Once trust is established, however, and teachers accept professional growth as an opportunity to improve their satisfactions as well as their skills, they will be more inclined to submit tapes for evaluation as well as supervision. At this point, the form in Figure 3–17 is useful.

Videotaped evaluations provide several important advantages:

- Teachers have the opportunity to submit what they think is their best work. My experience indicates that they will tape several class sessions before submitting one for evaluation. While reviewing each one for possible submission, they will be involved in self-evaluative situations that provide growth in their own right.

- The process is easy for the department chair. He or she need not worry about the difficulty of scheduling classroom observations during school hours.

- The videotape allows for review. If the teacher and department chair disagree on what they see, they can watch the tape together and reach agreement more easily.

- The videotape can be reviewed at a future date and compared to more recent tapes to reflect teacher progress.

- With the teacher's permission, excellent examples of teaching can be filed and used with new teachers for orientation or in-service training. Many schools have developed intravisitation schedules to encourage teachers to visit each other's classrooms. Most schools have not developed such schedules because of the difficulty of coordinating teacher time. A file of videotapes can relieve the problem and provide opportunities for everyone to share their best strategies and techniques. As such, it can provide for creative in-service programming. More of this will be addressed in Section Four.

Beyond Evaluation

Teachers want and need more than "evaluation for its own sake." They need the kinds of follow-up experiences that complement both evaluation and in-service training and develop competence and autonomy. Without a sense of competence, autonomy and self-satisfaction are impossible for teachers. Ben Franklin said it best: "I am lord of myself, accountable to no one."

Evaluation for its own sake makes teachers accountable to someone. It fosters dependence. A complement of self-directed and self-evaluative activities fosters autonomy. Without autonomous teachers, self-reliant students are an impossibility. A mutually complementary process of evaluation and supervision, therefore, is one of education's most fundamental needs.

Let's Wrap It Up

Evaluation is absolutely essential within a total program of professional growth for teachers. The frequency of such evaluation will be mandated by the state, board policy, and the competencies of the staff. Evaluation becomes destructive when it consists of value judgments imposed on teachers and when it is used to the exclusion of in-service training and appropriate follow-up opportunities for teachers to work on their improvement. To be effective, evaluation must accompany the kind of supervision discussed in Section Two, along with in-service training—the focus of the next section.

Figure 3–1

CLASSROOM OBSERVATION
(Preliminary Input)

Prior to your classroom observation, which is scheduled for _____, I would appreciate some information regarding the purposes of the lesson and the aspects of your teaching you want me to watch. In addition, prior to the observation, I will review previous evaluations to identify aspects that we may have discussed already. Both pieces of information should provide a focus for the observation and assure each of us that we share a common perception of what we hope to accomplish. With this thought in mind, please take a moment or two to answer each of the following questions. I will get back to you before the observation to discuss the need for a preobservation conference. Thanks for the help.

1. What is the purpose of the lesson and what methodology will you use to accomplish it? (The introduction of a new unit, for example, may require lecture; student understanding of poetic imagery may require a question-and-answer session.)

2. What recorded student/teacher behaviors will you accept as evidence that your purpose(s) was/were realized?

3. Do you have any suggestions as to how to document these behaviors? I can take notes, or we can develop an instrument to record the behaviors. Let me know your preference.

Figure 3–2

OBSERVATION RECORD

Teacher: _____

Period: _____

Date: _____

The following is an anecdotal account of the class I visited recently. Please review it when time permits and be prepared to discuss specifics when we meet to discuss the class.

Figure 3–3

OBSERVATION RECORD
(Completed Sample)

Teacher: _____ Tom Baxter _____

Period: _____ 3 _____

Date: _____ Oct. 5, 1993 _____

The following is an anecdotal account of the class I visited recently. Please review it when time permits and be prepared to discuss specifics when we meet to discuss the class.

The class started with your request for students to take their seats. You repeated the request two times and started the class five minutes into the period. You asked the students to open to page 37 of their books and indicated that you would be discussing with them a few of the significant passages in Hamlet, especially the "To be or not to be" soliloquy. You indicated to them that Hamlet already had learned of his father's murder, that the murderer probably was Hamlet's stepfather, and that Hamlet seemed unable to do anything about it.

You indicated next that his inaction was reflective of his procrastination, which "in all likelihood was his tragic flaw." Fred asked you what "procrastination" meant, and you told him that it meant "hesitation, inaction, the tendency to put things off." Then Fred asked, "O.K. what is a tragic flaw?" You referred Fred and the class to page 5 of the text and asked Sally to read the definition of "tragic flaw." Sally read the definition, and you asked Tom to paraphrase it for the rest of the class.

Tom summed it up in one sentence: "It is a character trait that leads to tragedy for the protagonist and usually others." You said "Nice job" to Tom and asked the class to turn back to page 37 of their books. You then asked several of them to read the play. You stopped them just before the "To be or not to be" soliloquy. At that point you said, "Pay special attention to these next passages, even underline them. They are among the most important in the play."

You then asked Bruce to read the passages, and you stopped him periodically to point out examples of Hamlet's procrastination. You next told the class that Hamlet was considering suicide because of the unhappiness that his inability to act was causing him. After you finished, Bob asked, "To be or not to be—what? What is he talking about?"

You then indicated that the class period was almost over and that the class should start on their homework assignment, which was to answer the first five questions on page 52 of the text. Seven minutes later, the bell rang, and you dismissed the class.

Figure 3–4

YOUR SELF-ANALYSIS

Process: These questions are provided with the observation record to assist you with your self-analysis. They are provided simply as a reminder of the kinds of questions that lead to a sound analysis of classroom teaching. We will be discussing similar questions when we meet during the postobservation conference.

1. Were student behaviors consistent with what you had expected of the lesson?

2. Do you think the objectives for the lesson were realized?

3. Why do you think the lessons were or were not realized?

4. In the future, would you teach this material differently?

5. What did you notice in my observation record or in your introspection of the lesson that caused you to conclude this?

6. What has your analysis of this lesson caused you to think about?

7. In the future, what can I do to be of more help to you?

Figure 3–5

SUMMATIVE EVALUATION

Final Report for: _____

Date: _____

Department: _____

Director of Learning:

Manager of Interpersonal Relations:

Member of the Staff:

Performance Objectives:

Extracurricular Activities:

Summary:

Figure 3–6

ANNUAL GOALS

Please review last year's summative evaluation and the observation records/ reports you received to identify your goals for this school year. Develop only two or three at the most. You'll want your focus for the school year to be specific. Be sure to describe how the goal will change you and identify any and all evidence that will reflect the change. Please have your goal statements to me by _____. We will meet on _____ to discuss them. Thanks for your help.

1. *Goal Statements:*

2. *Evidence of Change:*

Figure 3–7

INFORMAL VISIT

Teacher:

Class:

Period:

Date:

This is not a formal evaluation. It is an opportunity for me to visit teachers informally in order to stay abreast of what's happening in the building. I will be doing this frequently throughout the school year. This is the only copy of my visit.

Comments:

If you would like to discuss any of my comments, please feel free to stop by my office at your convenience.

Figure 3–8

TEACHER-DIRECTED EVALUATION

I am interested in receiving evaluative feedback from a colleague for one of my upcoming classes. The following information is relevant to the class and identifies the focus of the lesson and the specific feedback I need.

My Name: _____

Class: _____

Period: _____

Date: _____

1. *My purpose for the lesson is to enable students to:*

2. *My method of instruction will involve:*

3. *I need specific feedback on the following:*

4. *I suggest you gather the information I need by the following means:*

Figure 3–9

FEEDBACK
(Teacher-Directed Observation)

Teacher's Purpose:

To enable students to compute the volume of three-dimensional geometric figures. You indicated that you planned to use self-constructed models of three-dimensional figures during the class period to provide something visual for the learners.

Observational Focus:

You asked for feedback regarding the use of the figures. Did they enhance instruction? Did the students seem to benefit from the visual dimension they provided?

Method of Gathering Data:

You asked me simply to watch the students and to provide some subjective comments regarding the students' reactions.

Feedback

The figures worked wonderfully! The students actually seemed to become even *more* attentive when you showed them the figures and then discussed the formulas for computing their volume. I would recommend that you continue the practice, especially as it engages the visual modalities of your students.

But might I make one suggestion? As I sat in class, I noticed that my right brain was screaming to *touch* the figures. If the next time you use them, you circulate them among the class, you will engage the auditory, visual, and kinesthetic modalities of the kids. Just a suggestion. Let me know if I can help some more. I'm going to need your help in a couple of weeks, too!

Observing teacher: _____

Date: _____

Figure 3–10

STUDENT EVALUATION

To the Student: Circle the appropriate number under each characteristic. Circle a 5 if exceptional, 4 if good, 3 if average, 2 if fair, and 1 if poor. Then indicate with two or three words your general evaluation of his/her performance.

1. Each session involved obvious preparation and planning.

    5   4   3   2   1

2. The teacher presented the material in a friendly and understanding manner.

    5   4   3   2   1

3. The teacher is knowledgeable in the subject area.

    5   4   3   2   1

4. The teacher provided a positive learning environment. Each student felt accepted and was encouraged to participate in class discussions.

    5   4   3   2   1

5. The teacher was intellectually stimulating and provoked thought sometimes beyond the scope of the material covered.

    5   4   3   2   1

6. The teacher involved the students in discussion, question-and-answer, and varying activities.

    5   4   3   2   1

7. The teacher draws on outside but related information to teach the material.

    5   4   3   2   1

8. List the two or three best words that describe this teacher:

OBSERVATION REPORT

Teacher: _____

Class: _____

Period: _____

Date: _____

The following is the report of our discussion about your most recent observation. Please read it carefully and sign it if you agree with the wording. If you disagree with the wording, please return the form to me unsigned, and I will arrange for a meeting to discuss it further. Once the form is signed and returned to me, I will see that you receive a copy to use for future reference. Thanks.

_____

(Teacher Signature)

_____

(Date)

The teacher's signature doesn't necessarily reflect agreement.

Figure 3–12

OBSERVATION REPORT
(Completed Sample A)

Teacher: _____ Mr. Tom Hamilton _____

Class: _____ Freshman English _____

Period: _____ Third _____

Date: _____ October 17, 1994 _____

    The following is the report of our discussion about your most recent observation. Please read it carefully and sign it if you agree with the wording. If you disagree with the wording, please return the form to me unsigned, and I will arrange for a meeting to discuss it further. Once the form is signed and returned to me, I will see that you receive a copy to use for future reference. Thanks.

    I've attached a copy of Madeline Hunter's observations about teaching toward an objective. Mr. Hamilton should take a look at it before we meet again. I've asked him to read it very carefully; it should be useful. At times this morning, I found Mr. Hamilton rambling and occasionally losing sight of his objective. The instructional input he provided regarding Wordsworth's background and how it influenced his writing was generally interesting, but at times I wondered where Mr. Hamilton was going with it. He would be well-advised next time to sustain a focus on the purpose of the lesson and to relate all the instruction to each of the purposes. How, for example, does "Tintern Abbey" provide examples of Wordsworth's love of nature developed during his youth?

    I've indicated my availability to Mr. Hamilton to discuss these issues further and hope that he will take advantage of the opportunity.

_____

(Teacher Signature)

_____

(Date)

The teacher's signature doesn't necessarily reflect agreement.

Figure 3–13

OBSERVATION REPORT
(Completed Sample B)

Teacher: _Mr. Tom Hamilton_

Class: _Freshman English_

Period: _Third_

Date: _October 17, 1994_

The following is the report of our discussion about your most recent observation. Please read it carefully and sign it if you agree with the wording. If you disagree with the wording, please return the form to me unsigned, and I will arrange for a meeting to discuss it further. Once the form is signed and returned to me, I will see that you receive a copy to use for future reference. Thanks.

When we discussed the purposes of this lesson, I was intrigued by your comment that you have always had a tendency to ramble. As we both thought about your comment, you decided that it might be wise to specify your objectives for each lesson and then to put five or six critical questions on note cards for periodic reference during class. I asked if I could help somehow, and you asked that I visit early next week to tally the number of times you ask the questions. Madeline Hunter has some thoughts on the subject, too.

I took a moment to xerox a few of her comments. They're attached. Maybe they'll provide another dimension for your thinking. Use the materials as you see fit. If I can help in any other way, stop by. I can always help, if only to gather information for you. At any rate, I'll be in early sometime next week to help out. Let me know beforehand exactly what you want.

_____

(Teacher Signature)

_____

(Date)

The teacher's signature doesn't necessarily reflect agreement.

Figure 3–14

FOLLOW-UP TO OBSERVATION

Classroom evaluation requires appropriate follow-up activity if it is to be successful. Therefore, please review your observation report and let me know if any of the following may or may not be helpful to you.

Self-Directed Observation:

I'm not interested in it at this particular time: _____

I would like to initiate the following activity:

Peer-Directed Observation:

I'm not interested in it at this particular time: _____

I would like to be involved, with the following people:

In-Service Training:

The following in-service training topics are very important to me:

Figure 3–15

PROFESSIONAL GROWTH RELATIONSHIPS

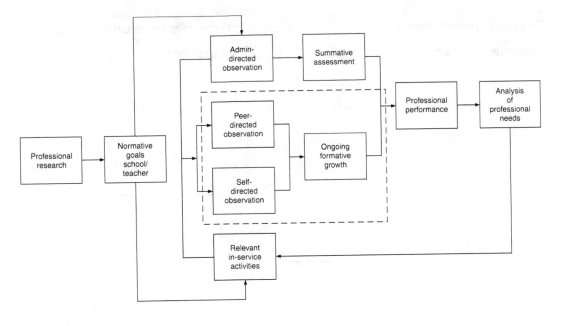

Figure 3–16

DEPARTMENT EVALUATION OF SUBSTITUTE TEACHER

Teacher substituted for: _____ **Date of substitution:** _____

Substitute teacher: _____ **Department:** _____

An evaluation of the substitute's performance should be completed by the absent teacher and department chairperson, and *returned promptly to Merle Monroe.*

Feedback from the classroom teacher:

	Excellent	Good	Satisfactory	Poor
1. Instructional competency:	_____	_____	_____	_____
2. Classroom management:	_____	_____	_____	_____
3. Follows requested procedures:	_____	_____	_____	_____
4. Comments:				

Teacher's signature _____

Feedback from the department chairman:

	Excellent	Good	Satisfactory	Poor
1. Promptness:	_____	_____	_____	_____
2. Ability to secure assistance when needed:	_____	_____	_____	_____
3. Comments:				

Dept. Chairperson's signature _____

Figure 3–17

CLASSROOM OBSERVATION*
(Videotape)

Directions: If you plan to use this videotape as part of your evaluation this year, please answer the following questions and forward them along with the tape to your department chair.

1. What objective(s) did you plan to accomplish during this lesson? Specifically, what student learnings were intended to result from your instruction?

2. Please provide information, *as appropriate,* about some or all of the following elements of your instructional strategy:

   Content:

   Methods of instruction:

   Materials of instruction:

3. What information should be shared about specific students or this class as a whole (LD issues, leveling considerations, behavioral problems, et al.)?

4. How do you plan to assess the outcomes of your instruction for this lesson?

5. As you view the tape, how would you describe the effectiveness of your instructional strategy?

*This is an optional activity.

Figure 3–17, continued

6. Did you check for student understanding during the lesson? How did you adjust your instructions as needed (*if* needed)?

7. To what extent did intended outcomes reflect the actual outcomes of the lesson?

8. Explain any causal relationships as to why the lesson objectives were or were not achieved.

9. Based upon your analysis and self-evaluation, what changes, if any, will you make the next time you teach this lesson?

10. Any additional comments?

Making In-Service Training Relevant

Let's admit it; in most schools "in-service" is a bad word. It's an occasion every two months when one or more "experts" manage to talk in someone else's sleep. At its best, in-service training is an entertaining and informative few hours that is enjoyed by teachers for the moment and all but forgotten several days later. At its worst, it's an interminable lecture that provides little more than "down time" to work furtively on grade books or openly on knitting.

Reconsider for the moment the three characteristics of your professional growth program: supervision, evaluation, and in-service training. Now consider them members of a family. We know, for example, that relationships among members are critical if the family unit is to help everyone grow positively—and equally. We also know that equal treatment among everyone is difficult and that inequality of treatment is not always intentional. Simple disregard often results in substantive neglect.

Perhaps that's why in-service training is professional growth's neglected child. It has been neglected for so long in most schools that its relationship with supervision and evaluation is almost nonexistent. While evaluation and supervision enjoy much of the family's attention, in-service training struggles for a nod of recognition.

Evaluation continues to be the favored son, with supervision growing in popularity, considering the recent emphasis in professional journals. In-service training, however, in spite of the state and district requirements that promote it, still doesn't receive the attention it deserves.

This section, therefore, emphasizes the importance of in-service training and further examines its relationship to supervision and evaluation. It acknowledges that the neglect of any one of these elements of the professional growth family inhibits staff development and jeopardizes the learning experiences of students.

WHAT IS IN-SERVICE TRAINING? _____

As mentioned in Section Three, I like the image of a *Book* because in-service training consists primarily of information and its uses; at least it should. The information it provides should be relevant to the lives of teachers and the work they do with students. Sometimes it isn't. Here's an example of what sometimes happens. I worked once with a district in-service committee that wanted to provide a range of alternative activities for its staff of 100+ teachers prior to a Thanksgiving break.

The committee had identified a series of workshops ranging from slides of the principal's recent fishing trip to hints on personal grooming. None of the topics related to classroom instruction. Please recognize that I've been known to wet my line with several of Wisconsin's most devout bass fishermen, but I've yet to understand its relationship to modality learning and higher order thought process.

Recognize also that I'm not opposed to watching the principal's slides. Just don't call it in-service training. When I asked the committee, which was composed mostly of teachers, why it had made such a decision, I was told that the staff needed something entertaining, something "fun." In-service training for them apparently had grown tedious, and the committee felt the need to revitalize the program with something unrelated to the complexities of instruction.

Wow! I had one response: "Are you telling me that learning can't be fun?" "What kind of message is *that* to send to a group of teachers?" Following a lengthy moment of silence, I asked another question: "Why do you suppose in-service training has become tedious for your staff?"

The discussion was immediate. Once we got beyond the quick-fix solution of irrelevant "fun" experiences for them and began identifying possible causes, we discovered that the teachers disliked in-service training because it had little meaning for them. The information provided at previous in-service programs may have been stimulating, but teachers had no follow-up opportunities to practice and eventually to incorporate it into their teaching.

I was reminded of the principal who once told me that his purpose for in-service training was to "excite" his staff, to stimulate them. His comment revived childhood memories of Saturday afternoons by my front window watching trucks drop piles of coal in our backyard and sensing the growing excitement of crawling to the top of each one, only to have my mother tell me it was time for my nap.

My friend apparently hadn't shared my childhood discovery that excitement without the opportunity for action lead inevitably to frustration. Excitement for its own sake is the emotional equivalent of hunger without food. I can think of scores of examples of stimulation leading to frustration, but prudence dictates I leave them alone.

The point is, the most exciting in-service information is likely to lead to the greatest frustration if the school provides no planned follow-up opportunities for teachers to integrate the material. In-service training as a series of "one-shot" deals doesn't work. Teachers require supervisory opportunities to use the information they hear, in essence "to practice what someone else has preached."

Remember the Chinese proverb: "I hear and I forget; I see and I remember; I do and I understand." It's true for students in the classroom and equally true for teachers involved in in-service training.

WHY IN-SERVICE TRAINING?

I wonder how many teachers know that divergent thought questions engage long-term memory in students? It may not be a startling revelation, particularly when one considers Madeline Hunter's advice over the years, but it is an important piece of information for teachers seeking ways to improve the retention rates of their students.

Such knowledge is popping up everywhere. The research manuals are full of it. Just page through *ERIC Clearinghouse, Dissertation Abstracts,* or any of several educational journals which share such information monthly. Then ask a teacher the last time he or she thumbed through *Dissertation Abstracts.* After lunging at you with a red pen, he or she'll probably shout that there isn't even time to read the mail!

That's one reason why we need in-service training for teachers. Many of them don't have the time to review all the research in their fields. And their time is becoming increasingly limited by the fact that knowledge is expanding at such a rapid rate. Futurists tell us that knowledge is expanding at a rate of 100% every five years, considerably more in some fields.

What are the implications for in-service training? For one thing, new knowledge is being created every day. There are new ways of looking at old ideas, new technologies in computer science, drafting, TV production, and health care, new "facts" in science, new ways of retrieving information, and new insights into the process of teaching. The school assumes a responsibility to incorporate such new knowledge into its curriculum and to refine the processes for imparting it to students.

Without opportunities for teachers to practice new techniques or to integrate new insights, however, such new knowledge remains a "trend" and never really finds its way into the classroom. It is soon replaced in the literature by another trend that enjoys its own exciting but ephemeral moment in the spotlight. One thing is for sure, however. If the idea behind the trend is good, it will be resurrected in ten to twenty years with a new name to enjoy another moment of popularity. And so it goes.

Good department chairs know how to break the cycle. They understand the complementary relationships among in-service training, supervision, and evaluation. They guarantee opportunities for teachers to practice the knowledge they gain during in-service activities and receive the expert help they need to integrate it effectively into their teaching. The following is an excellent example.

Relating In-Service Training to Supervision and Evaluation

Again, the *Book* provides the information; the *Mirror* promotes its practice; and the *Red Pencil* assures its effective use. All three are critical to growth. Here's what one school does to promote that growth.

The school is Caruso Junior High School in Deerfield, Illinois. Principal Al Cohen invites his staff to identify the issues within their classrooms that require attention annually. As a framework for their thinking, he provides an abstraction of some of the most recent research on effective schools. After two meetings with the staff and a written survey that explores several different issues, the school identifies five or six themes that become the focus for the following year's professional growth.

Teachers are then asked to organize themselves around a specific focus. During one representative year, one group selected "The Unmotivated Student," another "Cooperative Learning," a third "Questioning Techniques in the Classroom," and so on. Each group is then asked to explain how they plan to relate in-service training to their yearly goals and to the school's supervisory process. In other words, how they will, as a group, practice what they learn.

The growth component of the school's supervisory program, therefore, is handled in every instance by interaction among staff members between in-service presentations. The in-service training information provides the substance; the program of "teacher-helping-teacher" provides the practice time each needs to incorporate in-service strategies into their teaching. The insights provided by the in-service presentations, then, provide direction for the year's professional growth activities and promote positive teacher interaction.

Here's an example of how the program works. The group of 18 teachers who selected "Questioning Techniques in the Classroom" decided to meet with a local consultant to discuss higher order thought and its relationship to questioning techniques. Following the consultant's initial presentation, the teachers in the group were divided into tandems to provide nonjudgmental feedback to each other regarding the use of the strategies. During this interaction, the teachers shared ideas and evaluated themselves about the use of the strategies.

The consultant visited four to six weeks later to instruct the group again. This time, he analyzed and discussed the data they had collected, worked through the problems they had encountered, and explained additional strategies and techniques. Because each of his first four sessions lasted only an hour and a half to two hours and involved only 18 teachers, his fee was reasonable enough for the group to afford a third session. The six to eight weeks between the second and third sessions gave the teachers more practice time to use and discuss the strategies.

When the consultant returned for his final visit, he again helped interpret the teacher's experiences and shared information that reinforced their commitment to the questioning strategies he had introduced 18 weeks earlier. He also took time to remind them of their accomplishments. They had refined their questioning techniques, and they had worked together for 18 weeks to help improve each other's teaching.

Other groups of teachers in the school had been involved in similar experiences with consultants who charged reasonable fees, some even volunteering their time. In each instance, the consultant's in-service training information was followed by a 6 to 8 week period of practice time that required collegial interaction among the staff. Because the staff had chosen their topics and had selected the consultant to provide the information, each teacher felt a sense of ownership for the program.

The entire program for the school year proved to be less expensive than the four or five isolated presentations they usually offered. The consultants were not only less expensive but more effective as well because they worked with small groups of teachers, got to know them, and developed an informality that made everyone comfortable. In addition, principal Cohen had discovered that most of the expense for consultants could be covered by the funds that were available through state and federal grants. For more on grants, see Section Eight. More specific cost information is covered later in this section.

The important thing is that schools like Caruso have integrated in-service training with both supervision and evaluation. They are using it not only to introduce "exciting" and provocative information; they also are providing the kind of practice that, to Madeline Hunter and a great many other theorists, is so motivating to willing learners—if, like their students, the teachers' learning experiences are relevant and well-structured.

In-Service Training and Needs Assessment

Teachers are most invested in the activities of in-service training programs if they help develop them. When I suggest a Saturday night out with my wife and best friends at our favorite restaurant, my enthusiasm for the evening is evident. When she tells me that instead we're spending the evening with our neighbors and their four kids at a backyard barbecue, I may be less than enthusiastic. Don't get me wrong. I like our neighbors—sometimes even their kids. It's just that I had something else in mind for the evening.

So it is with teachers. When you determine the topics for the year's in-service training presentations, you might as well expect something less than an enthusiastic response from the staff, at least from most of them. Oh, you'll always find some guy who loves everything you do, and you'll also spend a good part of your time trying to avoid him.

Enjoy those independent thinkers on your staff; they're your best horses. When you ask them for input and accommodate most of it, they'll pitch in with a whole lot more than input. You'll never satisfy everyone, but you'll reach most of them if you genuinely involve them in the process. Again, process is the key. This piece of advice warrants the repetition. I know that repetition is like friction. It sometimes generates more heat than progress, but I'll take the chance. *Restrict your decisions to the process by which professional growth decisions are made and avoid making all the terminal decisions, and you are more acceptable to your staff—and more powerful.*

Consider for the moment the distinction between authority and power. Your position in the school's hierarchy gives you the authority to make decisions about in-service training. Such authority comes from the administration and the Board of Education. It can be coercive; it can push teachers and sometimes twist arms. But you want power, the kind your staff gives you. It locks arms in a common perception of purpose and gives you permission to enter their professional lives. Remember, authority comes from the administration; power comes from the teachers. Power accomplishes a whole lot more than authority.

The Needs Assessment Process

Here's how it works. Figure 4–1, *In-Service Training (A Needs Assessment)*, provides a reproducible to distribute to teachers. It asks them to identify their preferences for in-service training topics. First, it points out that teachers are guided by professional, not occupational, standards of performance. That is, teachers have no expected quota that signals "best" performance. Professionals can always get better; they are never "best."

The form lists the topics that currently are popular in the literature, followed by the topics that have emerged recurrently during the year's classroom observations. Hopefully, teachers will recognize these topics as conversation items during the year's postobservation conferences. Obviously, the lists will change as both the research and the classroom observations produce new ideas.

Finally, the form provides space for the staff to list their preferences for in-service training options. To assure some agreement between the teachers' preferences and their professional needs as evidenced in classroom observations, department chairs should distribute the packet of forms during one of the year's final department meetings. Talking about the forms is always preferable to pulling it out of a mailbox in the main office. When discussed at a department meeting, the process receives the importance it deserves.

The second form, as provided in *Categorization of Topics*, Figure 4–2, categorizes the preferences and requests and any additional topics that may have emerged from discussions among teachers. This form shows all the topics selected, indicates the number of teachers who identified each one, and provides a deadline for the return of the form.

Figure 4–3, *Topic Selection*, provides a reproducible of the third form, which asks teachers to select the topic that seems most appropriate for them. Most teachers tend to "bunch up" around the popular topics. It's likely they have discussed them and have already decided whom they want to team up with. For the few who have selected isolated topics, the department chair's meeting with each will help identify an appropriate topic.

In addition, the meeting will engage the teacher and the department chair in what might be a very helpful discussion of the teacher's professional growth needs. The teacher may be resisting a very important growth area for any of several reasons. The meeting might help overcome such resistance. Also, if the topic identified by the teacher *is* important for him or her, the meeting will help identify alternative ways to satisfy it, some of which may help enhance the supervisory relationship between the teacher and the department chair.

Finally, *Identification of Consultants* in Figure 4–4 provides the form on which teachers are asked to identify the names of persons inside or outside the school who can provide the expertise they need to learn more about their chosen topics. The form asks for the names of consultants and begins to pave the way for the collegial interaction that will occur between in-service training sessions.

It also begins to address financial issues, some of which may be prohibitive. Some consultants come with pretty big price tags. Fortunately, most are quite reasonable ($200 to $300 a session), particularly if the groups are workable in size (10–15). Obviously, the most reasonable consultant is someone in your school. Don't overlook this resource. Most schools have teachers who possess the expert power to help their colleagues grow. The right kind of nudge will give them some recognition, increase their sense of professional competence, and benefit several of their colleagues.

Also be aware of the many grants available through state and federal programs that can help pay for outside consultants. If your school or district is unwilling or unable to include the cost of such resources in your annual budget, you may be able to supplement it with grants from outside agencies. Each time you do, you enhance your expert power, the professional growth opportunities of your teachers, and your image within the school. Securing grants is the subject of a future section.

A Complementary Option

On occasion, individual teachers benefit from a one-on-one relationship with a consultant or colleague. The form in Figure 4–5, *Single-Teacher Consultations*, can foster such an opportunity for your staff. Again, the funds for such a program can be requested within the department's budget or secured through state or federal grants. Beyond financing, the process involves a couple of other important considerations:

- Whatever happens between the teacher and the consultant should be strictly confidential. Any "checking" that must be done can be handled through routine evaluations or periodic monitoring.
- All that is expected of the teacher is a brief evaluation of the experience, written after the final session with the consultant and submitted to the department chair.
- The meeting schedule with the consultant should be developed by the teacher in conjunction with the consultant and given to the department chair at least two weeks before their first meeting.
- Payment of consultant fees should be arranged after the final session, not after each individual session.
- Teachers should be encouraged to use in-house colleagues, including the department chair, as consultants throughout the process.

Figure 4–6 gives a completed sample of *Single-Teacher Consultations*. Figures 4–7 and 4–8 provide an Evaluation form for Single-Teacher Consultation, and a concluding evaluation, a completed sample. Neither the request for a single-teacher consultation or the concluding evaluation form need be long. They are designed simply to provide a reason for the teacher's involvement and some indication of the program's success. Expecting long narratives or too much paperwork from the staff is counterproductive to what you hope to accomplish with the program. If procedures are too detailed, teachers will reject the program as an opportunity for professional growth and perceive it as just another bureaucratic expectation.

Good department chairs always remember that organizations sometimes punish appropriate behavior. Think about it. You know as well as I do that the teachers who do a good job on lunchroom supervision invariably get more lunchroom supervision. Teachers who write good reports get more to write. Effective committee chairpersons get to chair more committees. Teachers who refer students for possible learning disabilities are rewarded with federal forms to complete. And so it goes. Keep the forms simple for your teachers, or the ones who really want it and who are most capable of modeling the benefits of the program will be punished by having to fill out lengthy forms. Believe me, they'll do it only once.

In-Service Training and Video Technology

Perhaps the most effective use of technology is the tapes that result from the videotaped observations as described in Sections Two and Three. ***In-Service Videotapes*** in Figure 4–9 provides a form to give each teacher who videotapes his or her classroom. The teacher may have used the tape to test out a new strategy or to evaluate an old one. It may have been evaluated exclusively by the teacher or by one or more colleagues or administrators.

The point is, veteran teachers have the confidence in themselves to share such tapes with colleagues, particularly those who are new to the department or school. The tapes can be catalogued according to teaching technique or purpose and viewed by other teachers as part of their professional growth goals for the year. In-service training, therefore, is not a one-shot presentation, nor is it necessarily group-oriented.

Videotapes of superior teachers are legitimate tools for in-service training. They are consistent with the informational image of a *Book,* and they are immediately accessible to teachers who are interested in the strategies of their respected colleagues. The process is a compliment to the videotaped teacher and a learning experience for the viewer.

SUPPLEMENTARY SOURCES OF INFORMATION _____

Files of videotaped observations are not the only examples of supplementary sources of information. Like curriculum revision, in-service training is a continuing process, facilitated by the department chair and nourished by a constant supply of information. Such information is found in journals, newsletters, and books that are published in the field periodically. It is shared routinely, circulated among members of the department and used for a variety of purposes.

Whenever the department chair receives such information, he or she may attach one of the forms in Figures 4–10, ***FYI***; 4–11, ***Help!***; 4–12, ***Want to Get Up and Go?***; or 4–13, ***We Need You***. The first is attached to materials that are circulated for information only. Such materials may be journal articles, newspaper columns, or letters from professional organizations. The second form requests a reaction from one or more of the members of the department. The reaction may be to journal or newspaper articles, in which case the department chair is most likely considering using the information in some way. Or it may be to administrative memos, letters from persons or organizations inside or outside of the school, or position papers developed by the chair or others in the department.

Form 4–12 asks members of the department if they are interested in traveling to certain educational functions, such as to another school for a workshop or to a local college or university for an informational meeting. Form 4–13 assesses one or more teachers' willingness to study a particular topic, such as those identified in administrative memos, needs statements, district priorities, departmental plans for improvement, curriculum proposals, or any of several provocative media items.

In a department that uses forms such as these, research is *Now*. It is the logical reaction to information that warrants additional study. The actual study can be conducted during the school year by one or more teachers or during a summer workshop, which also is an opportunity for in-service training, particularly if the workshop involves consultants or knowledgeable colleagues. The forms in Figure 4–14, ***Proposal for Project/Workshop—Summer***, provide the impetus for such an experience.

Another example of supplementary information involves sign-up sheets like ***Join the Computer Crowd*** in Figure 4–15 that invites teachers to learn the uses of computer technology. Computers are becoming commonplace in schools and are being used to coordinate student records, keep track of college applications, update class sizes, store registration information, and store and compute student grades by course. Anything that makes teachers more comfortable with computers increases the efficiency and, probably, the effectiveness of the school/department. It can also promote their use in lesson and unit planning.

For the Records

"Coloring outside the lines," those supplementary sources of information, may be innovative and courageous, but they can get pretty disorganized. Department chairs who encourage the practice must be careful to keep track of the professional advancement activities of teachers. Advancement activities differ from professional growth activities to the extent that they are specific, preapproved programs that satisfy the district's periodic requirements for professional progress.

Professional advancement activities fall under the more general heading of "professional growth," and, within many schools, have become increasingly comprehensive. At one time satisfied only by university coursework, professional advancement requirements are now satisfied by travel, publication, workshops, summer school activities, and a variety of programs. "Professional growth" encompasses these activities but combines the additional elements of classroom observation and specific in-service programming.

Figure 4–16, ***Professional Advancement***, provides a form that notifies staff members of professional advancement requirements and records individual activities. Figure 4–17, ***Professional Advancement Follow-Up***, provides a form to the teacher that specifies the actual activity and requests documented follow-up. Figure 4–18, ***Professional Advancement Requirements Approval***, indicates that his or her requirements have been approved by the school and/or district administration. Discrepancies between the teacher's intentions and the administration's interpretation of those intentions are explained in writing to the teacher. Obviously, the time frame will reflect the specific policies of the school.

Coming Full Circle

The forms provided in Figures 4–16 and 4–17 are one way of documenting professional advancement. In essence, they are a part of the summative evaluation that constitutes the needed "quality control" in the school. Department chairs use them not only to record teacher progress toward the completion of professional advancement requirements but to discuss with teachers the kinds of alternative activities that address comments made after observations.

If, for example, the teacher indicates after a particular lesson that he or she should have provoked more higher order thought in his or her students, he or she is likely to benefit from one or more activities that discuss questioning technique in the classroom. The department chair, then, can reasonably expect to see *something* on the form that addresses questioning technique and higher order thought process.

Look at it this way. Check the ***Professional Growth Relationships*** flowchart that was discussed in Section Three, Figure 3–15. Another look reaffirms the need to analyze the professional needs of the staff. Such an analysis, as described in the box farthest to the right, sustains the professional growth process in schools. The results of the analysis are fed back to the in-service box, where new information is generated and communicated to the staff.

The cycle, then, is complete. The entire process is driven by the normative goals of the school, its philosophy and objectives, its fundamental beliefs in the worth of knowledge and kids. The in-service training activities then combine with the input from an administratively-directed observation (evaluation) to give a sense of direction to the peer and self-directed activities (supervision) that provide the necessary practice, which leads to the professional growth of the staff. The cycle, therefore, is self-renewing.

Let's Wrap It Up

The *Reflection* provided by supervision and the occasional *Direction* resulting from evaluation are dependent upon the *Information* provided by in-service training. The three are necessarily interrelated. When one of them is missing, the process becomes disjointed, and fails to provide the complementary experiences that teachers need to improve their teaching.

The forms in this section may or may not be of use to you. They are provided as examples of desirable practice and as reproducibles you can use in your department. They may have to be modified somewhat to reflect the actual practices in your district or school. The important point, however, is that *some* materials be available to promote a process for teachers to practice what someone else has preached during in-service training activities.

Only with the opportunity to practice such information does it become useful. And without relevant information that responds to documented needs, supervision has little to practice. The two, then, are necessarily interdependent. And both depend upon the occasional direction provided by evaluation.

Unfortunately, many schools fail to acknowledge this interdependence among the three components of the professional growth program. One result is in-service programming that settles for the *appearance* of usefulness. Department chairs, therefore, must look beyond appearances to relevance. If they don't, they and the school will get the kinds of teachers they deserve. And though *they* may deserve them, the students don't. Our students require the best teachers we can provide.

Figure 4–1

IN-SERVICE TRAINING
(A Needs Assessment)

The Identification of Potential Topics

One of the values of our department is our desire to continually improve our program and our skills as teachers. The end of each year signals the opportunity for each of us to identify our professional needs and to outline an in-service format for next year that will provide the information and the practice we need to make our school even better than it is this year. Please take a few moments to think about topics that might constitute the substance of next year's in-service training program. In essence, what do we need and what might you learn to make our school more effective?

The following is a list of topics that are popular in much of the literature:

- Questioning Techniques
- Higher Order Thought Process
- Modality Learning
- Ability Grouping
- Collegial Coaching
- Student Self-Esteem
- Reflective Teaching
- Cooperative Learning

In addition, "classroom management" and "time on task" emerged repeatedly during postobservation conferences. Certainly, these topics are not exhaustive, nor are they intended to restrict your thinking. You may have topics of your own that are important to you. I would like to know what they are so that we can work together to accommodate them. An important result will be that you, our parents, and, most of all, our students will be more comfortable with our school's programs and processes.

Please take a moment to list your preferences in the space below:

Figure 4–2

CATEGORIZATION OF TOPICS

First of all, thanks for sharing the topics that you feel need our collective attention. They cover a range of responsibilities within the school. For that reason, I have listed the responses of the entire department within the following categories and have identified in the parentheses following each topic the number of teachers who have selected it. Please survey each list, give some thought, and decide if any more should be added to the list.

You may have given additional thought to the original request for information, or you may have discussed possible topics with one or more colleagues. Jot these down in the space provided within the appropriate categories and return the list to me by _____.

1. *Administration*

2. *Support Services*

3. *Instruction*

4. *Curriculum*

5. *Extracurricular and Other*

Thanks for your help!

Figure 4–3

TOPIC SELECTION

Thanks for your help with this final list. All the topics you have identified are listed within each category. To select the topic that you would like to study next year, please put a "1" next to the one that is most interesting to you and a "2" next to the one that is next most interesting. We will do our best to honor your requests. If we can't, we will be in touch to discuss alternatives with you.

1. *Administration*

2. *Support Services*

3. *Instruction*

4. *Curriculum*

5. *Extracurricular and Other*

Thanks for taking the time to do this.

Figure 4-4

IDENTIFICATION OF CONSULTANTS

Now that we have identified the topics we want to study next year, we should consider the names of persons who can help us. Please give me the names of the consultants or others who might be able to meet with your group to lead you in the study of your topic. They may be inside or outside consultants. If outside, I will contact them to determine their fees and availability. If everything works out, I will indicate that someone from your group will be calling to arrange a meeting schedule. I remind you to arrange for at least three meetings, with a 6- to 8-week period of time between each meeting to provide for practice.

Please provide the name of your group and the name or names of suggested consultants:

Name of group:

Name(s) of consultant(s):

Again, thanks for your help. I'll be in touch.

Figure 4–5

SINGLE-TEACHER CONSULTATIONS

Take a moment or two to answer the following question as concisely and completely as possible. You and I will be using the form to find the right consultant for you.

Name of Teacher: _____

Course Name: _____

I want to strengthen the following characteristic(s) of my teaching:

( ) I would like to work with the following consultant/colleague:

_____
      (Name)   *(Address)*   *(Phone No.)*

( ) I already have contacted the following colleague to assist me:

_____

( ) I need help finding a consultant.

Figure 4–6

SINGLE-TEACHER CONSULTATIONS
(Completed Sample)

Take a moment or two to answer the following question as concisely and completely as possible. You and I will be using the form to find the right consultant for you.

Name of Teacher: Tom Brown

Course Name: Freshman English—Third Period

I want to strengthen the following characteristic(s) of my teaching:

This is a lower-level class, my first in several years, and I am finding that I am having difficulty motivating the students to get their work done. I'm not even sure that it's a matter of motivation as much as it might be classroom management or my levels of expectation for them. I would like to be observed by Jeanne Baxter of Northeastern Illinois and then meet with her periodically to discuss strategies I might use with the students. I took a class from her a couple of years ago and am convinced that she can help.

(X) I would like to work with the following consultant/colleague:

Jeanne Baxter	UNI	312-794-2995
(Name)	*(Address)*	*(Phone No.)*

( ) I already have contacted the following colleague to assist me:

_____

( ) I need help finding a consultant.

Figure 4–7

EVALUATION
(Single-Teacher Consultation)

 Please write a *brief* evaluation of your experience with the consultant. Indicate the number of meetings and give some idea of the specifics you gained from the experience.

Your Name: _____

Figure 4–8

EVALUATION
(Completed Sample)

Please write a *brief* evaluation of your experience with the consultant. Indicate the number of meetings and give some idea of the specifics you gained from the experience.

I met with Dr. Baxter seven times, with two week intervals between each of the last five meetings. The first meeting was used strictly for observation, during which time she took notes regarding classroom interactions. We discussed notes immediately after the class during my free period. She asked a range of questions regarding the information she had collected, and I discovered, among other things, that the vocabulary I was using during lectures and later discussions was confusing to the students.

Dr. Baxter reminded me that most of the learners in the class are concrete and that my tendency to abstract is causing them some trouble. I am inclined to agree with her. The five meetings we had following the initial diagnosis confirm her suspicions. I have "toned down" my style somewhat, and I discovered almost immediately that the kids are much more attentive in class and inclined to do their homework afterward.

It's been a good experience.

Your Name: _____

Figure 4–9

IN-SERVICE VIDEOTAPES

We have discovered that a file of videotaped classroom observations is very helpful for informal in-service activities, particularly for new teachers. Examples of excellent teaching should be shared with other teachers in the department. Please consider volunteering your videotape for the department's file. If you decide to, take ten seconds to answer the following questions—maybe fifteen!

Course Content:

Lesson Content and Focus:

Primary Methodology:

Special Points to Consider:

Your Name: _____

Figure 4–10

FYI

To:

Fr:

I thought you might find the attached materials interesting.

- -

Figure 4–11

HELP!

To:

Fr:

Please review the attached materials. I'm interested in your reaction. I'll be in touch in a couple of days.

- -

Figure 4–12

WANT TO GET UP AND GO?

To:

Fr:

The information on the attached materials looks pretty interesting. Are you interested in going?

- -

Figure 4–13

WE NEED YOU

To:

Fr:

The attached materials could use some study. You seem to be the logical person for the job. It may require some time, so think about it for a couple of days. I'll be in touch. Thanks.

Figure 4–14

PROPOSAL FOR PROJECT/WORKSHOP—SUMMER

_____   _____
(Department)   (High School)

Short Title of Project: _____

Objectives of Project:

Time Needs		*Fiscal Needs*

Secretarial: _____
(flat rate: $8.75 per hour)

_____ Hours/teacher   _____ Hours   Materials: _____

× _____ Participants   × _____ Leader   Xeroxing: _____

_____ Total hours   _____ Total hours   Consultant: _____

- -

To Be Completed by Central Office

_____ + _____ (Stipend) =   *Salaries* _____

                                               Total   _____

- -

Meeting Dates: _____   _____

Names of Potential Participants:

_____   _____

_____   _____

_____   _____

_____   _____

_____   _____

Figure 4–14, continued

Personnel Responsible for:

    Initiating and Organizing _____

    Conducting and Reporting _____

    Fiscal (including timesheets) _____

Rationale for Project:

    Need:

    Implementation:

- -

Disposition

Initiator _____ **Date** _____

Approvals:

    Dept. Chair _____ Date _____

    Asst. Principal _____ Date _____

    Principal _____ Date _____

Action:

    Approved _____

    Rejected _____

    Reason:

    Revised _____

    Reason:

Figure 4–15

JOIN THE COMPUTER CROWD
(A Little Knowledge Can Be a Helpful Thing!)

As you certainly have observed by now, computers are becoming "commonplace in the workplace." And to some of us, they're a little scary, but they are as user-friendly as all those ads would have us believe. Want to learn more about them? Join us this semester as we spend a few moments after school to learn a few of the basics. If you're interested, give me some brief answers to the following questions and return the form to me at your convenience.

1. Give me a quick assessment of your knowledge of computers.

2. Do you own a computer?

3. Do you plan to buy one once you learn something about them?

4. Do you prefer before-school or after-school meetings?

Figure 4–16

PROFESSIONAL ADVANCEMENT

My records indicate that your professional advancement requirement must be satisfied within the following four-year period: _____. As you know, the district provides several ways to satisfy the requirement. Please give some thought to the one or more activities you prefer and give me a brief indication of your intentions in the space below. Thanks!

Teacher Signature: _____

Date: _____

Figure 4–17

PROFESSIONAL ADVANCEMENT FOLLOW-UP

(Follow-up activities are required for Professional Advancement recognition. Please complete this form and submit the appropriate documentation upon completion of your activity. The final due date is October 15 if any reimbursement is expected.)

Name: _____ **Date:** _____

Dept: _____

Effective Category (Check one):

Follow-Up Activity

1. Undergraduate Course Work (15 hours per unit) _____

_____ Submission of updated official transcript.

2. Graduate Course Work (15 hours per unit) (less than academic term; not offered in degree program; Credit Institutes/Workshops) _____

_____ Submission of updated official transcript. Description of activities, a statement related to meeting stated objectives, and a log of time spent (if appropriate).

3. District Workshop (30 hours per unit) _____

Description of activities, a statement related to meeting stated objectives, and a log of time spent.

4. Conference of Workshop Presentation _____

Description of activities, a statement related to meeting stated objectives, and a log of time spent.

5. Educational Travel (1 week per unit) _____

_____ Daily annotated log and summary paper related to meeting stated objectives (see sample in departmental office).

6. Work Experience (60 hours per unit) _____

_____ Description of activities, a statement related to meeting stated objectives, a log of time spent, and a sample of work (if appropriate).

7. Research (30 hours per unit) _____

8. Publication _____

_____ Description of activities, a sample of the publication, and a statement related to meeting stated objectives.

9. TV or Correspondence Course (15 hours per unit) _____

_____ Submission of updated transcript, a program outline, and a log of time spent.

Figure 4–18

PROFESSIONAL ADVANCEMENT
REQUIREMENTS APPROVAL

Signature of Applicant: _____

Routing Sequence

Dates	Signature	Reimbursement	Lane Change Credit
_____ Dept. Chpn. _____		Yes ___ No ___	Yes ___ No ___
_____ Asst. Princ. _____		Yes ___ No ___	Yes ___ No ___
_____ Principal _____		Yes ___ No ___	Yes ___ No ___
_____ Superintendent _____		Yes ___ No ___	Yes ___ No ___

If recommended units differ from requested units, reasons should be communicated in writing to the teacher with the returned form.

Complete information is available in your teacher's handbook.

SECTION FIVE

How to Hire the Best Teachers

We've already observed that intelligent people know what to do when they don't know what to do. Now let's add that they're the smartest people in the organization when they hire people who are smarter than they are. Aside from the apparent contradiction, this is a difficult task, much more difficult than most of us realize. Current statistics indicate that most college students deciding on education as a career are graduating in the bottom quartiles of their classes. This doesn't mean necessarily that they're not intelligent, but it does indicate that the most successful students are seeking careers outside education. Getting the best teachers, therefore, is one of the primary challenges facing any department chair.

It's important to recognize that all teachers, potential or otherwise, fall into a hierarchy of ability, talent, and work ethic. And it comes as no surprise that the best of them require little direct supervision. In fact, they are much like the superior students they teach; put them in the classroom and get out of their way. This may be one of the most important characteristics of a good department chair. The need to impress others with how much we know can become a significant interference to productive relationships.

Smart department chairs find good people and then turn them loose. I also spent a good many years coaching football and discovered early in my career that overcoaching turns people off. The more I facilitate and let effective processes engage good people in collaborative activity, the more effective the team—any kind of team. So how do we get good people? If "Process" is important to us in everything we do as department chairs, what process do we follow to bring in the best people available? And what criteria do we use to determine just how good they are? Both these issues will provide part of the focus for this section.

Many administrators readily admit that hiring and handling personnel is invariably the toughest part of their job. This may not be true for all administrators, but it does ring true for a good part of my experience "wearing the badge." Burned-out, disenfranchised, or otherwise poor teachers consume a great deal of time and energy. To bring in the best, therefore, and to orient them within the framework of your expectations will avoid a lot of potential problems.

The interviewing and selection processes, then, must not only assess candidates' current strengths and weaknesses but project their future growth. Do they have the brainpower needed to command the respect of bright secondary school students? Do they have the caring and sensitivity to work with special problems or with the significant issues that confront even the normally-adjusting teenager? Do they have the social skills to relate comfortably to classrooms full of adolescents, some of whom by definition are "developmentally confused?"

Do they evidence and project a willingness to grow? Are they interested in relationships *outside* the classroom? Will they *seek out* students to provide help? Do they have a presence and a demeanor that are consistent with the expectations of the community? Will they fit in with the "culture" of your department and school? There are many other questions as well, all of which must be anticipated by the effectiveness of processes you establish to find and hire the best candidates available. According to recent research, the *availability* of teachers is not the problem.

Some Recent Research. The *Occupational Outlook Quarterly* is one of the best publications available to determine job availability, the necessary qualifications, salary, even the conditions of the work experience. It also provides information about job outlook within a particular period of time. According to the *Quarterly,* the anticipated teacher shortage has not materialized and probably won't in the 90s. According to labor economist Daniel Hecker, the original data provided by the National Center for Educational Statistics may still be valid regarding the need for teachers in inner-city, rural, and even some suburban areas. He sees it, however, as an indication of supply and demand rather than a shortage.

The good news is that the surplus of college graduates is likely to increase the supply of teaching candidates. Further, increased salaries and educational reforms are likely to bring better-qualified people into the field. Given this expanding pool of candidates, what does the smart department chair look for in a prospective teacher, and how does he or she develop recruiting and hiring processes that secure them? Let's look first at selection criteria.

ESTABLISHING THE CRITERIA

A long-time friend of mine and a very successful department chair told me a story recently about a young science teacher he just hired. She was bright and had earned almost straight As in a very challenging university. She had personality; she had been involved extensively in sorority activities, even athletic and university administration programs. The department chair had remained somewhat concerned, however, as all department chairs do with a new teacher. Some new teachers can amaze us with behaviors that are virtually unpredictable.

A couple of days before he told me the story, he had left his office to attend an after-school meeting and as he turned a corner in the hallway, he spotted the teacher sitting on the floor with a student next to an open locker. They were discussing the student's chemistry assignment and apparently had been for quite some time because school had been over for almost an hour. The department chair told me from that moment on he stopped worrying about the teacher's qualifications. He admitted that she would need supervision and the periodic evaluation that all new teachers required but that he no longer wondered about her willingness to do *all* that teaching required.

Good story. The question is, how do we establish a process that eliminates as many of the question marks as possible? How do we hire people we don't have to worry about, who don't require that chance encounter in the corridor? The answer is not simple, but it can be found in processes that tap into the synergy we discussed in earlier sections. Involving department members and students in the interviewing and selection process provides two important advantages. One, it gives the people who are most affected by hiring decisions a chance to influence them; and, two, it gives interviewees the opportunity to meet prospective colleagues.

This second advantage suggests a related issue. Interviewers must realize that "buying" the right teacher for the department is one thing; "selling" the department to the right teacher is another. Good prospects come to an interview not only to put on a show but to see one. They're "good" because they are competent and have a sense of purpose. The really good ones are not worried about getting a job; they're worried about getting the *right* job. The interviewer's task, therefore, is to determine if this *is* the right teacher and then to represent the job in the best terms possible.

Setting the Scene

The reproducibles in Figures 5–1, **Sample Memo**, and 5–2, **Two-Way Streets**, are therefore necessary in the early stages of the interview process. They emphasize the importance of "putting one's best foot forward," which includes both the prospective teacher *and* the interviewers! Each of the reproducibles avoids being prescriptive; no one wants to squelch the spontaneity of informal give-and-take. On the other hand, we must acknowledge in the development of our processes that, next to reading the newspaper, conversation probably is the least effective form of communication.

It's wise, therefore, to shape the process beforehand so that it accomplishes what we expect it to. If we want to identify the best teacher from among several candidates and present ourselves in such a way that he or she wants the job, we had better do some preliminary planning to influence each of these conditions. The reproducibles will help. So will the **Interview Feedback form** in Figure 5–3, which promotes feedback to the department chair regarding the assessment of those involved in the interview process.

Setting Up the Process

The process of hiring the best teachers consists of four basic steps: recruitment and the application process, the initial screening, interviewing, and selection. Most schools use each of these steps to hire personnel. Some schools use them more successfully than others. Again, process is the answer. Keep these suggestions in mind:

Recruitment and the Application Process. Before becoming involved in administration and supervision, I coached for several years and learned early in my career that the most successful college football programs recruited athletes that satisfied predetermined needs. They recruited someone who could play strong safety or weakside tackle. They looked for youngsters who were self-disciplined and equally accomplished in the classroom. They realized that athletic skills alone don't guarantee success on the football field. I saw some of my most gifted athletes shunned by major college programs because the players didn't project educational success or the kinds of values and behaviors that contributed to team goals.

The experience with college coaches helped when, a few years later, I found myself recruiting and hiring teachers. I learned that intelligence and a solid academic record in college certainly were desirable in a candidate, but that they weren't the only criteria to use in hiring good teachers. I learned quickly that candidates must also possess stability, resourcefulness, energy, social and professional skills, extracurricular experiences, immediate and future goals which were consistent with our needs, realistic job expectations, and the proper 'fit' with the rest of the staff.

Internal Recruitment.   Most generally, I learned that recruitment of personnel can occur inside or outside the building. If conducted inside, three advantages result:

1. The school/department has an adequate amount of time to judge the qualifications of the candidate.
2. Teachers realize that their competence is rewarded, and they tend to commit themselves to the school/department on a long-term basis.
3. The teacher-aide promoted to teacher, the teacher given Advanced Placement classes, or the teacher promoted to assistant department chair are familiar with the culture of the department and can be groomed for positions over a period of time.

If conducted outside the building, it's likely that someone decided that the department needs "new blood," that organizational in-breeding has established a formidable status quo that requires some shaking up. Transferring people from one department to another, therefore, may help the morale of people within the building, but it probably won't promote a challenge to traditional ways of doing things. Preliminary planning regarding recruitment needs should consider the need for change within the department and seek people who can promote it.

Recruitment also requires a knowledge of successful procedures. Internal recruitment can be handled any one of several ways. The posting of jobs is probably the most obvious. Figure 5–4, *Job Posting*, provides a format that includes a job title, salary range, job description, needed qualifications, and application procedures. This procedure is perhaps most popular in the schools.

External Recruitment.   External recruitment is handled in a number of different ways. The two most popular involve recruiting from reputable universities, usually those in your geographical area, and accepting and filing unsolicited applications. Most universities provide placement offices for their graduates. Each generally asks graduates interested in teaching to develop a file containing biographical information, a transcript, and at least three letters of recommendation. Many department chairs notify placement offices of vacancies, request credentials, then screen applicants to determine those to be interviewed.

Although this process helps identify interested applicants, it may not highlight the truly outstanding person for the job. Many good applicants have good grades; most have excellent letters of recommendation. Few job seekers solicit letters of recommendation from friends or acquaintances who criticize them. In addition, all applicants develop impressive cover letters. What is needed is a process that distinguishes the potentially great teacher from the also-ran.

An important part of that process is the development of the specific criteria that will be used to evaluate each candidate. We already have indicated that each candidate must possess certain personal characteristics. He or she may also require specific educational and professional preparation. Figure 5–5, *Staff Input Regarding Departmental Vacancy*, provides a form you may want to circulate among your staff to secure their preliminary input regarding the instructional and/or professional requirements of the position. Figure 5–6, *Sample Memo Regarding Criteria for Candidates*, represents a sample checklist of their criteria. Circulate it among the people who will be doing the actual interviewing and evaluation of each candidate.

Another part of the process is a visit to the campus. Figure 5–7 provides a sample letter to a university placement office; Figure 5–8, *Teaching Vacancy*, provides a reproducible of the major elements to be contained in the posting that accompanies the letter. Trust the placement office to arrange a schedule of interviews with interested applicants during your visit. Following your visit, you'll realize several added benefits.

If you take the time to visit a class or two or to meet with the dean of the college of education, you will have gained a better understanding of the quality of their program. You will have established a working relationship with the college of education and the placement office, and you will have impressed them with the quality of *your* school and department. They are likely to remember you and your visit the next time a student seeks advice from them about schools that represent desirable employment opportunities in the area.

Finally, a file of unsolicited applications sometimes reveals a real diamond in the rough. Many graduates routinely mail applications to reputable school districts. Some of them are exceptionally well-qualified and may not have access to any of your later, more specific requests for applications. It's always a good idea to look through the file for potential standouts whenever you seek to fill a teaching position.

The Initial Screening

Department chairs certainly can't invite every applicant for an interview, nor can they ask others in the department to search through the pool of applicants for those most qualified to be interviewed. The initial screening is the department chair's job, and usually it involves two important considerations, the applicant's biographical information and reference checks on his or her previous employment.

Biographical Information.   Colleges and universities have been saying for a long time that the best way to predict success for college applicants is to look closely at what they have done in high school. The student's past history is the single best predictor of his or her future achievement. The same is true of any professional. While some of us might not like it, our behavior is consistent over time, and we are unlikely to change the good or the bad habits that we have developed.

Biographical information will reveal most of these behaviors. Any preliminary screening, therefore, must look carefully at the substance as well as the appearance of the application, the letter of application, the applicant's résumé, perhaps a writing sample, and undergraduate and graduate credentials. This information will reveal much about the applicant's intelligence, level of achievement, personal and professional goals, awards and accomplishments, and work record. Use the Checklist provided in Figure 5–9 to conduct your evaluation. It will help you touch all the bases.

Reference Checks

In most instances, the information will be sufficient to select the applicants to be interviewed. Sometimes, however, the information in the letter or the applicant's résumé may provoke questions. A high-achieving, apparently accomplished applicant, for example, may have changed jobs several times within a relatively short time. In such cases, it may be wise to call one or two of the applicant's former employers to determine a few specifics that may have been omitted from letters of recommendation.

The Privacy Act of 1974 now permits applicants to read letters of recommendation that have been written about them. Letters that formerly may have identified potential problems now couch them in suggestive phrases or make no reference to them at all. Candidates who survive the preliminary screening, therefore, but have sketchy background information may warrant a phone call to previous employers before an interview is offered. Persons who write positive but imprecise recommendations sometimes fill in the spaces when given the opportunity to speak off the record.

That's why reference checks are often so important. Even a phone call to the previous department chair and principal about an applicant may not illuminate an obscure background issue. Both people may still be celebrating the teacher's departure. Sometimes their recommendations are written more to bury a teacher at home than to praise him somewhere else. Some administrators are not above rewriting local history to bid a less than fond farewell to a talented but problematic teacher. The more talented, the easier the recommendation is to write; the more problematic, the more inclined the administrator is to write it.

Some reference checks, therefore, should be directed to other persons with whom the teacher has worked: fellow committee members, departmental team members, team teaching colleagues, fellow coaches, students, parents, or anyone who depended on the teacher for the completion of shared responsibilities. You may be more likely to get straight answers to important questions from these people. Admittedly, such persons are difficult to contact, so make phone calls or visits only when this kind of information is essential.

The Interview Process

If conducted thoughtfully, the interview can provide some of the most revealing information about candidates. It can also create some of the messiest legal snags a department chair will ever have to unravel. And any fisherman realizes that the best way to deal with snags is to avoid them. So this section considers both the legality and the effectiveness of the interview process. Let's start with the process itself.

Opening the Interview. Most psychologists will tell you that one of the best ways to establish rapport with another person is to match voice tone and posture and to paraphrase comments to show that you are listening. Certainly, that doesn't mean that you have to appear anxious for the occasional person who is overwhelmed by the whole experience. It does mean that you should welcome each candidate with a relaxed and friendly handshake, a smile, and a warm greeting (however, not the good-old-boy slap on the back and knuckle-buster that intimidates even the most stout-hearted).

Following the initial greeting, it's wise to set the tone of the meeting by making brief reference to something in the candidate's background: his college or previous job, a mutual acquaintance, his specific field of study, his extracurricular experiences, anything that promotes a nonthreatening conversation and shows him that you have reviewed his materials. Follow this conversation with a brief explanation of the job and a description of the school, and you're ready to get into the heart of the interview.

Conducting the Interview. Interviewing is like teaching. The key to a successful interview is to get the candidate involved. Good interviewers ask well-coordinated questions and listen carefully to the answers. Like good teachers, they elicit responses, then probe answers, asking candidates to elaborate and evaluate, to make connections, and to express feelings and concerns. Interviewers are well-advised, therefore, to devote most of their involvement in the interview process to listening and evaluating and to talk only when the candidate asks questions of them or needs information about a specific element of the job or school.

All persons involved in the process, therefore, should give preliminary thought to the kinds of questions they must ask during the interview. Sometimes a handout such as *Interviewing (Sample Questions)* in Figure 5–10 provides either the actual questions or samples of the kinds of questions that need to be asked to identify the best candidate. Notice that most of the questions start with one of the five "Ws:" what, when, where, why, and who. Toss in a few "how" questions, and the interview is likely to reveal valuable information about the candidate.

Closing the Interview. Generally, interviewers follow a prescribed routine. They may, in fact, structure the interview so that all candidates are asked fundamentally the same questions. Such a process is more defensible in court than an unstructured format. Usually the last question to be asked of the candidate is something like: "Well, we've asked a great deal of you; what questions do you have for us?" At this point, the better candidates will ask very pointed questions about the nature of the job, the culture of the department and school, and the more subtle expectations of the school and community.

When such questions are answered, the interview can be concluded, probably with some indication that you will be in contact with the candidate within the next several days. How candidates are notified of hiring decisions is a matter of personal preference. Some interviewers notify immediately after the interview; most, especially if an interview committee is involved, indicate that they will call or write within a specified period of time. Fairness dictates that such decisions be communicated as soon as possible.

When a decision to reject is communicated, it is advisable to avoid going into detail about the reasons for the decision. The more specific the reasons, the more likely these will lead to hard feelings. The best comment is one that praises the candidate's qualifications and preparation but indicates that they are not consistent with your job requirements.

Evaluating the Candidates. When evaluating the candidates after each has been interviewed, keep in mind that interviews usually are poor predictors of performance on the job. This is true for several reasons:

- Glib candidates often have a history of selling themselves exceptionally well during interviews; they tend to have problems over the long haul, when behavior speaks louder than words.

- The best-qualified person may not be offered the job because of his or her position in the interviewing schedule. Someone with lesser qualifications may have followed one or two particularly poor candidates and, by comparison, may have appeared superior. Interviewers must take such possibilities into consideration when evaluating the entire pool of applicants.

- Interviewers must also guard against other tendencies. They may assume, for example, that a candidate who is spontaneous and witty is also intelligent and competent. Personal charisma, although sometimes valuable, is often misinterpreted as skill. I've known several school administrators who landed jobs because of their charisma but who couldn't lead their way out of a paper bag. Charisma is a widespread but insufficient substitute for professional expertise.

- Interviewers also make the occasional mistake of projecting one poor trait into a blanket assessment of the candidate. The poor dresser or the initially shy person may be an exceptionally talented teacher. The interviewing process must not allow one negative characteristic to cause the rejection of an otherwise very talented candidate.

- Similarly, interviewers must be aware of their biases. "Fat people are lazy;" "Ghetto-born people have poor values;" "Southerners are slow;" and "Exfootball players are too aggressive" are just a few of the biases that may influence interviewers. Department chairs have to carefully review feedback from interview committees to check for biases or for indications of one negative or positive characteristic influencing committee recommendations.

- Other factors affect the evaluation process. Inexperienced interviewers tend to make decisions about applicants during the first several minutes of the interview. The information gathered subsequently is used to reinforce their initial assessment. Figure 5–11, *Interviewing (Evaluating the Candidates)*, helps overcome this tendency, given the inability of most schools to train their interviewers.

Guaranteeing the Process

In addition to the information provided in Figure 5–11, department chairs can avoid problems with the evaluation of candidates by heeding the following advice:

- Be sure to structure the interview format. Determine in advance the content areas that need to be covered, any specific questions, the persons who will do the interviewing, the criteria they will use to evaluate each candidate, and the processes they must follow to preview the interviews and to provide feedback to the department chair. Many of the reproducibles that are provided in this section are helpful.

- Whenever possible, use interview committees, including colleague, student, and even parental groups. The student groups can meet with candidates before or after school or during lunch periods. Their questions sometimes elicit the most revealing responses from candidates. Each group provides a different perspective, unique insights into and *for* each candidate, with a different set of expectations. Their feedback is helpful not only to the department chair but to the candidates, who will learn more about the attitudes, values, and expectations of the people with whom they may be working.

- Use the interview as one part of the selection process. Subjective assessments are important, but when complemented with the objectivity of transcripts, biographical information, letters of reference, and reference checks such as phone calls and meetings with previous employers, the picture of the applicant becomes clearer.

- Maintain written records. Well-documented records of each interview enable a later comparison of candidates. First impressions fade, and conversations with one candidate spill over into discussions with another. Good records help interviewers distinguish among candidates during the evaluation process. In addition, they provide documented information if legal action results from the rejection of a candidate.

Some of the literature indicates that testing is becoming more prevalent in school districts, particularly in the hiring of principals and other administrative personnel. Aptitude tests, personality tests, interest inventories, and achievement tests are the primary tests administered. Because they are used rarely in the hiring of classroom teachers and other nonadministrative personnel, they will not be given serious treatment in this section.

It is important to recognize, however, that schools may start using test results to help make hiring decisions, given the apparent success of the practice in many businesses. In addition, human resource experts are in general agreement that testing is the single most reliable way to make hiring decisions. Department chairs should consider testing as a potential element in the hiring process, especially as more information about it becomes available. Be careful, however, to assure that the tests have validity, that is, that they test exactly what is needed for the job, otherwise you run the risk of discrimination.

Avoiding Legal Pitfalls

Equal Employment Opportunity clearly deserves all the attention it is receiving across the country, but it has introduced a range of problems for anyone involved in hiring. That we are not allowed to discriminate because of a candidate's race, religion, national origin, age, or sex keeps employers steered in the right direction. Problems arise when interviewers get off course by asking questions that can lead to discrimination. Usually inadvertent, such questions and their answers can provoke significant legal problems.

The best way to avoid them is to be sure interviewers are familiar with the DOs and DON'Ts of appropriate questioning. Federal law, the Age Discrimination in Employment Act (ADEA), prohibits asking the age of an applicant. All teachers have varying degrees of energy and commitment, regardless of their age. It should not be a reason to reject a candidate. Other areas of race and gender are as obvious.

It's important, then, to provide each interviewer with a reproducible similar to the one in Figure 5–12. It provides a concise reference for anyone who wants to scan a legal roadmap before visiting with one or more candidates. You might also want to provide copies of the *Technical Assistance Manual*. The EEOC provides free copies that explain what you can and can't ask at an interview regarding disabilities.

Generally, persons on an interviewing committee have no vested interests in issues regarding disabilities or the age, gender, or race of the candidates. They may have biases that suggest potential problems, but normally any problems they create result from innocent requests for information: "Oh really? Just how old are you?" "How do *you* feel about a career versus marriage and kids?" or "Interesting; just what does your husband *do?*"

These are questions that can result in discrimination suits. That's why it's advisable to have interviewers review acceptable questions, such as those in Figure 5–12, **Interviewing (Questions of Legality)**, and to subscribe to one or more personnel journals that provide periodic updates of changes in interpretations of equal employment laws.

Keeping Written Records

A quick reminder about records. We know already that they enable the comparison and contrast of candidates. Mental comparisons at the time of the actual interview is unavoidable—and unreliable. Better judgments result from a more objective comparison of the notes and observations that have been recorded after each interview. They also stand up to investigations of the EEOC or state civil rights agencies. That's why Figure 5–12 is so important.

Finally, keep in mind that legislation regarding discrimination is changing all the time. This section was not designed to provide a definitive format for avoiding legal pitfalls. It will help considerably, but it also would be wise to seek legal counsel periodically and to maintain contact with important governmental agencies such as the EEOC. They will be able to provide current information for you and the members of your department.

Hiring the Best Candidate

Hiring the best teachers involves asking good questions and then probing for detailed information. Such information will uncover the qualities you want in a good teacher: honesty, commitment, a willingness to learn, insight, self-awareness, the ability to make connections, and curiosity. It's not easy to identify these characteristics with confidence in one interview, even in a series of interviews. That's why it's as important to *listen* as to question carefully.

Candidates reveal themselves as much by what they don't say as by what they do say. The candidate, for example, who provides only superficial answers to relatively complex questions may not have the depth of understanding required of a superior teacher. Similarly, the candidate who asks few questions may not have the curiosity of a life-long learner or the ability to analyze a situation carefully enough to formulate good questions.

The reproducible in Figure 5–13, *Interviewing (Another Look at Evaluation)*, provides a framework within which interviewers can assess the responses they receive, or don't receive. It provides another way to question candidates and ultimately to evaluate them. When combined with the more specific information considered in Figures 5–5 and 5–6, this reproducible promotes decision making and provides something substantive when hiring decisions are questioned by others.

They will help a great deal. While using them, however, interviewers must remember to ask the widest range of questions possible. Interviews are nothing more than benign social gatherings when interviewers fail to unmask candidates through use of insightful questions. Most candidates do an impressive job revealing only what employers want to see. Good interviewers, then, must catch glimpses of the people behind the mask by giving them opportunities to discuss a time when:

- They helped someone else.
- They tried to overcome a challenge.
- They worked hard at something but failed.
- They had association with a person they most—and least—admire.
- They made a mistake and learned from it.

Such discussions must involve elaboration and probe questions that provide an in-depth look at what the candidate learned from each experience. In effect, is this a person who takes responsibility for a failure and learns from it? Is this someone who gives credit where it is due? Is this a person who reflects the qualities we seek in a teacher who will work comfortably and insightfully with groups of kids and who is unafraid of making a fool of him- or herself?

Let's Wrap It Up

We've mentioned already that hiring is one of the most important responsibilities of the department chair. The reasons remain obvious. The process-oriented department chair gets people involved in departmental activities. The more talented the people, the richer the substance of the activities. Again, trust is the key—in others and in yourself, in your ability to lead without drawing attention to yourself and to plan and organize so that others make most of the decisions.

The reproducibles in this section will help. A few may be unnecessary if you decide against interviewing committees or if you can't use them because of union contract, but they help promote the process that is necessary to find and eventually hire good teachers. It probably would be wise to put all or most of the reproducibles in a booklet to give each person who will be interviewing candidates. The information will be helpful to them, and it will affirm your commitment to their involvement in important departmental activities.

Such an orientation capitalizes on the strengths of the people in your department, and it provides the circumstances they need to express their talents. Remember, department chairs promote motivation by providing the circumstances within which people meet their needs. Talented and dedicated teachers come to work each day with a clear desire to succeed. Our job is to help them—by providing opportunities and encouragement. Such is the essence of motivation, the focus of the next section.

Figure 5–1

SAMPLE MEMO

To: Interviewing Committee

Fr.: Greg Royer

Re: Teacher candidates

Our preliminary screening of the credentials of applicants for the position of Freshman English teacher has resulted in the following five names:

Tom Browner
Jim Wilson
Elaine Jenwell
David Mirsch
Glynis Johnson

We have decided on the following schedule for conducting interviews and introducing the applicants to the school:

Monday, April 2

Tom Browner: 8–9:30—Me; 9:30–11:00—Committee; 11–Noon—Principal
Glynis Johnson: 1–2:30—Me; 2:30–3:00—Committee; 3–4:00—Principal
David Mirsch: 8–9:30—Principal; 9:30–11—Me; 11–Noon—Committee

Tuesday, April 3

Elaine Jenwell: (same times as Browner above)
Jim Wilson: (same as Johnson above)

Characteristics:

Please be reminded that during a recent departmental meeting we decided that the person selected for this position would need a strong background in composition, preferably with some published material of his or her own, and coursework and/or experience in Greek mythology and American literature.

Please refer to the other sources I have provided or will provide regarding strategies for identifying the best person for the job. Also be sure to use the feedback form to give me your reactions to each of the candidates. We will discuss them all when the interviews are completed.

Again, thanks for your help with this very important task.

Figure 5–2

TWO-WAY STREETS

The people you will be interviewing come to us prepared to "put on a show," and to *see* one. They will be putting their best foot forward; so should we. A good salesperson once said: "Presentation is half the sell." I don't know who said it, but (s)he understood what it takes to interest people in a product. At the moment, we find ourselves interested in two products, the candidates we are about to interview and ourselves. We are interested in buying the candidate and selling ourselves.

With that thought, please keep the following aspects of our school program in mind when interviewing candidates. Review the School Profile and consider your range of experiences with us, then jot down under each heading a couple of facts and/or observations that might attract qualified people. Because each of you on the committee is likely to come up with different characteristics, your combined effort should result in a variety of very appealing observations for the candidates:

The Relationships and Qualifications of Our Staff:

Our Department's Program:

The Uniqueness of the School:

The Characteristics of Our Student Body:

Our Relationships with the Community:

Figure 5–3

INTERVIEW FEEDBACK

Candidate's Name: _____

Committee Members:

_____

_____

_____

_____

_____

The following are the impressions of the committee regarding the above-named candidate. This feedback includes reference to our perceptions of the candidate's stability, resourcefulness, energy, social and professional skills, extracurricular experiences, goals, job expectations, and "fit" with the rest of the department:

We plan to review each of these feedback documents before making our final recommendations.

Figure 5–4

JOB POSTING

The following vacancy is available within the building. Persons interested in the position are asked to read the information listed below and apply accordingly.

Job Title: _____

Job Description:

Necessary Qualifications:

Salary Range:

Application Procedures:

Persons requiring additional information are asked to contact _____.

Figure 5–5

STAFF INPUT REGARDING
DEPARTMENTAL VACANCY

    As you know, we have a vacancy for next year. In order to hire the best candidate, the department needs your help. If you have ideas regarding the specific instructional, professional, and/or personal requirements needed for the position, please take a few moments to share them in the spaces below. Obviously, we want the best person for the job, and we need your help to hire him or her. Give me this form sometime within the next week or two.

    As usual, thanks for your help.

Instructional Requirements:

Professional Requirements:

Personal Requirements:

Figure 5–6

SAMPLE MEMO

To: The Interviewing Committee
     Science Department

Fr: Vince Malek

Re: Criteria for Candidates

A recent survey of department members and others involved in the hiring process identified several characteristics that are needed by the person who will fill the current vacancy in the science department. While these characteristics are neither exhaustive nor determinative, they provide insights into our department's priorities for the position. They are provided in checklist form for ready reference. You might use the list before and after an interview to help with the evaluation of each candidate. I hope it helps. See me if you have any questions.

Is this Candidate:

_____   Student-oriented or subject-oriented? The department acknowledges the need for a subject specialist but emphasizes the need for a teacher who is student-centered.

_____   Familiar with and/or willing to engage in collegial activity within the department and school?

_____   Energetic enough to deal with four science classes and be available to students after school each day?

_____   The kind of person who will fit into a departmental culture that includes not only planning committees after school but informal weekend get-togethers?

_____   Qualified to teach a load that consists primarily of biology classes?

_____   Willing to be involved and to initiate activities that engage teachers and students in activities that promote environmental awareness?

_____   Open to supervisory processes that involve peer- and self-evaluation?

_____   An independent thinker with an outgoing personality? This one was mentioned by the department recurrently. It may sound as if we're looking for "Superteacher," but we believe in aiming high!

Thanks!

Figure 5–7

SAMPLE LETTER
(University Placement Office)

Placement Office
Midwest University
Anywhere, USA 00000

Dear Placement Office:

Clearfield High School in Township High School District 115 is seeking a qualified English teacher for the upcoming school year. We prefer someone with practical experience in journalism but will be pleased to meet with anyone with a strong background in composition and American literature. Would you be so kind as to post the accompanying explanation of the position and to arrange for interviews? We are interested in meeting with qualified applicants sometime in early March, maybe sooner, so anything you can do to arrange an interview schedule would be appreciated.

We have always been pleased by the quality of your graduates and are anxious to work with you to find someone to fill our teaching vacancy. Please use the accompanying job posting and contact me at your convenience regarding the particulars of an interview schedule. I'll get back to you right away to finalize it.

Thanks for your time. I look forward to hearing from you and meeting you.

Sincerely yours,

John Spearman
English Department Chair

Figure 5–8

TEACHING VACANCY

Job Description:

English teacher
to work primarily with junior
English and journalism
classes

School and District:

Clearfield H. S.
TWPHS District 115
1992 Wauconda Rd.
Clearfield, IL 60000

Job Requirements:

English major with background
in journalism and/or composition
and American literature

Additional Preferences:

Candidates who are
qualified to coach one or
more sports or who can
sponsor one or more
cocurricular activities
will be given preference.

Salary Range:

Base salary starts at $28,000
for teachers with BAs and $33,000
for MAs. Actual salary is dependent
on years experience, credit hours earned
beyond the minimum degree, and
additional responsibilities assumed.

Description:

Clearfield High School is located in the North Shore area of suburban Chicago. It is approximately 30 years old and has a student population of 1100. Each year, 5 to 15 students earn status as National Merit Finalists, the school earns an average ACT score of 24, and approximately 93% of the graduates enroll in four-year colleges. The school enjoys a student:teacher ratio of 15:1, and the average salary is $39,000. The average age of a faculty member is 42, and the average tenure in the high school is 15 years.

The school prides itself on a national reputation of educational excellence and welcomes energetic and student-centered teachers with solid academic preparation. Applicants interested in the above position are encouraged to send a letter of interest, copies of all college transcripts (unofficial copies accepted for preliminary screening), a résumé with at least three current letters of recommendation, and other materials as selected by the candidate to provide evidence of strength in teaching. Send all materials to the above address in care of the principal.

Figure 5–9

CHECKLIST
(Preliminary Screening)

Review the following characteristics periodically to assure a complete look at each candidate's credentials and background during the preliminary screening.

_____ Is the appearance of the application acceptable?

_____ Is the letter of application informative and interesting?

_____ Does the writing sample, if required, reveal a clear command of the language?

_____ Is the résumé complete? Is it up-to-date?

_____ Do the transcripts reveal a well-rounded and accomplished student?

_____ Is the previous work record satisfactory? Does it reveal frequent job changes?

_____ Are there any glaring omissions in the work record?

_____ Does the applicant have sufficient experience?

_____ Does the applicant have the specific academic and personal requirements for this particular job?

If I Reject, Am I Rejecting for the Right Reasons?

_____ Does the applicant really need the experience I am expecting of him or her for this job?

_____ Am I rejecting because of the applicant's poor qualifications, or does the application have insufficient information? Should I call?

Figure 5–10

INTERVIEWING
(Sample Questions)

The kinds of questions we ask each candidate ultimately reveal the kind of information we need to make a hiring decision. Several different elements within the candidate's background must be explored. The following are some sample questions you might either think about or use before each interview.

Job-Focused Questions:

What was your biggest achievement in your last job?
What failures did you experience in your previous job?
How did you learn from them?
Of everything you did on your last job, what did you like best? Least?
For what kinds of things did your former department chair compliment you? Criticize you?
How have you adjusted your teaching style within the past _____ years?
What current topic in the literature do you find most promising? Why?

Personality-Type Questions:

Motivation

Why did you decide on education as a career?
What is your long-term career goal?
What do you seek in this job that you can't find now?

Relationships

What is it you like about your former department chair's methods of supervision? Dislike?
What kinds of committees do you enjoy being involved in?
How do you feel about the movement toward collegiality in education?

Adaptability

What do you do differently now that you didn't do five years ago?
What are some of the biggest problems you faced in the last _____ years?
If you had to keep your current job, how would you change it?
How do you plan to improve your performance within the next few years?

Strength of Character

What has been your biggest professional disappointment?
How did it change you?
Whom do you routinely seek out when you're having problems?

Figure 5–11

INTERVIEWING
(Evaluating the Candidates)

The following are some questions you might ask yourself during the evaluation of each candidate. Pure objectivity probably is impossible during the evaluation process; but these questions can help:

1. Do I favor this candidate because his or her background is similar to my own?

2. Is appearance an overriding factor for or against this candidate?

3. Does this candidate have one outstanding characteristics that somehow has convinced me that everything else about him or her is outstanding?

4. For example, is this person so bright that I'm overlooking other faults?

5. On the other hand, does this candidate have one negative characteristic that has swayed my opinion in other areas as well?

6. In essence, am I looking at the total person when I make my evaluation?

7. Have I missed anything about any one of the candidates that I should know? Do I have to make some phone calls to secure additional information to be fair to all of them?

Figure 5–12

INTERVIEWING
(Questions of Legality)

Each of us must be careful to avoid asking questions that discriminate against applicants. Each question must in some way pertain to the job. Aside from the legal problems involved, we want to make each candidate as comfortable as possible during the interview process. Review the following sample questions as needed before meeting with the candidates.

Do Ask:	**Don't Ask:**
1. Are there any job duties you cannot perform because of any mental, physical, or medical disabilities?	Are you disabled, or have you ever had the following diseases?
2. Have you ever used a different name in your current job?	What's your maiden name?
3.	What are the ages of your children? Are you married? What is your nationality?
4. What languages do you speak fluently?	What is your native language?
5. Of what professional organizations are you a member?	What societies or lodges do you belong to?
6.	What religion are you?
7.	Where does your spouse work?
8.	Should we call you Mrs. or Ms.?
9. Have you ever been convicted of a crime?	Have you ever been arrested?
10.	How old are you?

There are probably a whole lot more. Again, the basic principle to keep in mind is to ask only those questions that relate to the job. Arbitrary questions that may exclude candidates for reasons other than job performance are illegal and should be avoided.

Figure 5–13

INTERVIEWING
(Another Look at Evaluation)

Candidates reveal as much about themselves by what they don't say as what they do say. Be sure, therefore, to probe their answers and to ask them to elaborate on certain points. And keep the following pointers in mind when you evaluate each of them.

We Want:

People who are aware of their strengths and limitations.

People who admit to being involved in a project that failed.

People who are able to see the big picture, who identify the subtle characteristics of a situation.

People who ask a lot of questions, who want to know more and more about the world around them.

People who accept alternative ways of doing things.

People who describe a situation and relate the specifics of how they learned to respond differently.

We Don't Want:

People who have a tough time saying anything about their own weaknesses.

People who find excuses for periodic failures.

People who see situations only superficially.

People who ask few questions, who are accepting of almost everything they are told.

People who prescribe few ways of doing things. They tend to be too rigid.

People who view their situations as being controlled by someone else.

In essence, we're looking for honesty and candor, a solid sense of self, awareness, and a willingness to grow. Be sure to ask the kinds of questions that reveal these characteristics. Review the other materials as needed.

ᴇʀ **Mᴏᴛɪᴠᴀᴛɪᴏɴ**

otivation. Teachers energize ap-
ll programs; parents reform
burned-out teachers. To the
hey are the very real conse-
ntribute to such successes,
others suddenly take an ac-
res prominently in the process.
gives it life?

erstand their role in the process, and
ying effective motivation. They recog-
people *need* to be competent, responsi-
notivators understand that most of us
ce, they trust people, and they seek

ple inherently *want* to succeed; they
as well as the expectations of others.
ust. Whatever it is, the department
nships with the members of his or
without it. Trust is a two-way street. If we
it, and what we give is the simple acceptance that people
involved, and competent in what they do.

re, is a needs-based system; it inheres within the individ-
n comes from within, not from without. They reason that
s; we simply influence the conditions of the work environ-
eds or to capitalize on the needs people bring to work each
may be a bit extreme because it fails to recognize the differ-
ntrinsic and extrinsic motivation, but it does highlight the con-
al focus.

147

So let's define motivation as any internal stimulus to action that is affected by external circumstances and conditions. As such, it is closely related to morale. Morale in schools is the highest, for example, when individuals are able to contribute simultaneously to the goals of the organization and to the satisfaction of their own needs. Even the nonpurists among us, therefore, recognize that motivation isn't necessarily something we do *to* our colleagues. More appropriately, it is something they do *for* themselves, with our help.

This is a very important distinction for all school personnel, administrators and teachers, as well as department chairs. It acknowledges a fundamental difference between intrinsic and extrinsic motivation. Let's take a closer look at both.

INTRINSIC MOTIVATION

Intrinsic motivation, a need operating within the individual, is the quickest way to any desired behavior. That's why coaches live in the best of all possible motivational worlds. Athletes come to them with the need to be successful, with an accompanying willingness to listen and learn and to be challenged to succeed. I discovered over the years that it's a whole lot easier teaching a young quarterback to spot pass than to diagram sentences. Both can be accomplished and both require creative approaches, but "spot passing" satisfies a young athlete's basic needs faster than does diagraming sentences.

Other students may enjoy diagramming sentences more than "spot passing." The point is, I can work with another person most effectively when I focus on the satisfaction of his or her needs. Even coaches fail to acknowledge this fact when they emphasize their need to win over the needs of their players to enjoy the game. The result is often the failure of both to realize their needs. And coaches who confuse periodic inspiration with motivation run into real problems. They fail to recognize that what *they* need, even when accompanied by periodic attempts at inspiration, is considerably less important than what their players need. Let's look at it this way.

To be a motivator, be like a farmer. Plant a seed and work hard to cultivate it. Nourish it; provide the best environment possible; remove obstacles to its growth; watch over it. But, above all, remember that the inclination to grow is in the *seed*, not the farmer. Therein lies the fundamental characteristic of intrinsic motivation. If the seed possesses no inclination to take root and grow, no amount of exhortation or inspiration from the farmer will make it become a plant.

So it is with teachers. Exhortations, pep talks, even threats may provoke movement, but they may not do much to promote motivation. If the extrinsic motivator is a push, I may move, but I won't continue to move until someone pushes me again, or until I realize that the movement I experienced was in some way satisfying. So it is with extrinsic motivation. It is helpful, but, unlike intrinsic motivation, it may not be the quickest way to desired behaviors.

EXTRINSIC MOTIVATION

Extrinsic motivation may even provoke behaviors that are contrary to the goals of the motivator. Keep in mind that intrinsic motivators can be satisfied only by the behavior in question. If young athletes, for example, are motivated to learn spot passing techniques, only the improved use of spot passing techniques will satisfy the need. If they are encouraged *extrinsically* to diagram sentences, they may behave in ways that relate only incidentally to the diagramming of sentences. They may cheat on homework assignments, copy others on tests, promise to do work at some undefined time in the future, or even cut class.

Then again, they may diagram sentences! Extrinsic motivation, therefore, may at times be very effective. Sometimes it is the only way to provoke a need in someone which leads to a desired behavior. Reinforcement theory teaches us that reward and punishment can be effective extrinsic motivators because they provoke behaviors which ultimately become self-reinforcing. The key to effective extrinsic motivation, then, is to transform the extrinsic motivator into an intrinsic need.

"Extrinsic motivation" may not be an oxymoron. It can lead to desirable behavior if it promotes or satisfies the internal needs of others. Problems arise when the needs of the persons to be motivated are inconsistent with the motivator's needs or when the needs of the "others" are disregarded. When the needs of these others are not accommodated, no amount of "motivation" or inspiration will influence their behavior.

This can lead to specific problems, the most obvious of which is the valuing of personal charisma over leadership behavior that is based on solid principles of motivation and organizational theory. I learned long ago to beware of the person with more personality than brains. He or she can be as harmful as he or she is engaging—not petty or mean-spirited, just inconsistent and unaware. Charismatic people without knowledge play "Follow the Leader." The only problem is, the leader doesn't know where he or she is going!

As such, this person doesn't last long as a leader. She may hold a *position* of leadership, but if one day she looks around and sees no one following, has she been *leading?* I don't think so. Similarly, if the person fails to acknowledge the principles of intrinsic motivation, trying to "motivate" people until blue in the face, but failing to influence their behavior, has this "leader" been motivating? Again, I don't think so.

The world is full of self-proclaimed motivators who spend most of their time talking in someone else's sleep. These are the very same people who take bows for someone else's performance. They spend too much time focusing on their own needs instead of the needs of the people they seek to influence. Good department chairs decrease their own visibility by promoting processes that focus on the intrinsic needs of their colleagues. They heed the words of Lao-Tzu, who said:

> As for the best leaders, the people do not notice their existence.
> The next best, the people honor and praise.
> The next, the people fear, and the next the people hate.
> When the best leader's work is done, the people say,
> "We did it ourselves!"

The *best* leaders are exceptionally skilled and generally very well-balanced emotionally. They find their satisfactions in the accomplishments of others and, as such, are willing to stand in the wings and smile as their colleagues accept recognition, knowing that such recognition is a spur to greater accomplishment.

Everyone benefits from this kind of motivation, especially the students who gain the benefits of improved instruction.

This section, then, focuses on the satisfaction of needs and on the processes that both create and accommodate those needs. No theorist provides a better framework to provide such a focus than Abraham Maslow.

MASLOW'S HIERARCHY OF NEEDS

Maslow's Hierarchy of Needs is as familiar to most students of education as *Cliff Notes* publications are to English majors. It is considerably more helpful, however, because it has such a wide range of applications. Because it highlights the progression of general needs from physiological to self-actualizing, it is appropriate for parents, teachers, administrators, and department chairs who want to understand motivation within a well-conceived theoretical framework.

See ***Maslow's Hierarchy of Needs*** that follows. The model is presented as a pyramid to emphasize the foundational characteristics of the lower level needs. Because they are most basic to our survival, the physiological and security needs constitute the base of the pyramid. Each of the lower levels is a motivator until its needs are satisfied, at which point they no longer motivate. Successive levels then become motivators until, ultimately, the need to self-actualize predominates.

Obviously, the need to self-actualize is never completely satisfied, nor do lower level needs always remain satisfied. Persons, therefore, experience periodic movement up and down Maslow's hierarchy. As security needs are threatened, for example, they once again become motivators. As children become hungry, the physiological need becomes a motivator. As teachers experience a sense of exclusion from a peer or colleague group, the social needs become motivators. Very simply, our job as department chairs is to assure that each of these lower level needs is satisfied so that persons within the department can experience improved esteem and self-actualization.

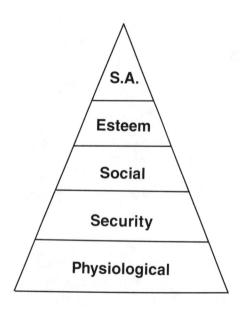

To fully understand self-actualization, one must first understand "potential." As I recall from my undergraduate experiences in metaphysics, complete potential is *nothing*. The youth with outstanding academic potential does not become an outstanding student until he or she actualizes it. The father who tells his son that he could have been a great football player if he had played the game must also acknowledge that he *wasn't* a great football player. Similarly, mediocre teachers with outstanding potential will never be outstanding teachers until they actualize their potential.

Our jobs as department chairs and supervisors are to help them with that task. Maslow's model can help us. It reminds us that teachers are unable to self-actualize when their security, social, or esteem needs are unsatisfied. In essence, they are not motivated to work on self-actualization. Movement along the **Self-Actualization Continuum** illustrated, therefore, is impossible. The key, then, is to guarantee the relative satisfaction of lower level needs.

Nothing	Becoming	Perfection
Complete potential	Partial actualization	Complete actualization

The remainder of this section looks at teacher motivation within the framework of Maslow's theory:

Physiological Needs

Rarely do teachers come to work hungry. We may be underpaid for the magic we sometimes perform with kids, but malnutrition has yet to become an issue—I think! On the other hand, the stomach is not only the quickest way to a man's heart but the surest way to relaxed and informal department meetings, particularly at the end of the day. It doesn't take a feast to loosen everybody up, just a few snacks and soft drinks.

Check with members of the department early in the year to see if they like the idea, then use a memo like the one labelled, **Meeting Schedule for Current School Year**, in Figure 6–1, to list responsibilities. You might even foot the bill for several or all of the meetings. It's common knowledge around the building that you are constantly seeking ways to spend those big bucks the school is paying you. What better way than to satisfy the culinary needs of your colleagues?

Another issue involving physiological needs is much more difficult to resolve. Alcoholism and drug abuse among teachers is alarming hundreds of administrators across the country. Comprehensive statistics are hard to find, but anecdotes and concerns are shared by a wide range of professionals. A recent conversation with a California administrator who is responsible for dealing with substance abuse problems in his district revealed the breadth of *his* concerns.

Of the 400+ teachers in his district's schools, more than *100* of them referred themselves to the district's Employment Assistance Program (EAP) for consultation with a psychologist, many of the problems focusing on substance abuse. When asked to define the importance of the problem, he answered with three words: "It is critical." He then volunteered additional information.

Recent studies by prominent psychologists indicate that a significant number of people who go into education and the support services are the "heroes" of alcoholic families. That is, they are the achievers, the standard-bearers of families in which one or more people are alcoholics. As such, they are codependents and are susceptible not only to chemical abuse themselves but to the behaviors that characterize their codependency.

Such a phenomenon has obvious implications for department chairs and school administrators. Many teachers who are either codependent or chemically dependent are struggling to maintain their professionalism and generally have the ability to be among the best in the school. Our job is to help them whenever possible by referring them to Employee Assistance Programs (EAP) or community agencies when they admit to a problem.

It is important to recognize, however, that our job is *not* to diagnose, confront, or intervene. Most department chairs have not been trained to assist employees with substance abuse problems. Misguided diagnoses or intervention strategies can result in a world of legal problems for the department chair and the school. The department chair's job is to engage in performance appraisal only. If teacher substance abuse affects performance, the department chair should document the performance and deal with it within established procedure.

In the course of a performance appraisal, teachers who acknowledge a substance problem should be referred to the school's EAP or an appropriate community agency. After such referral, the department chair should continue to evaluate performance and avoid any kind of additional intervention. Our desires to help in such cases may be understandable but usually result in circumstances we have not been trained to handle. The best course of action, is to follow established procedure, unless the teacher shows suspicious on-the-job behaviors.

If the teacher's speech is slurred or if he or she seems in any way disoriented, the department chair should document the behavior and report it immediately to the principal. Most schools will have a policy that governs such situations. It is important to emphasize the documentation of *behaviors*. Department chairs must avoid diagnoses or interpretations of these behaviors. A teacher having a stroke may appear intoxicated. Such a misdiagnosis can result in almost anything, ranging from a red face to a substantial lawsuit.

Those few teachers who surrender to, rather than battle their dependency, really do need our help, even to the point where we may have to threaten their security needs to provoke battles with their dependency and the problems it causes for both them and the school. Such circumstances, however, usually result from routine performance appraisal, not from preliminary diagnosis and confrontation. There are times, then, when the security needs of colleagues are the motivators we need to promote improved performance—which leads us to the next level of Maslow's hierarchy.

Security Needs

Like the physiological needs, the security needs of people are powerful motivators. From the billions of dollars spent on massive arms build-ups to the isolationist policies of the 30s, nations have sought security in complementary and sometimes contradictory ways. Individuals are little different. We buy guns, and we install elaborate alarm systems in our homes. When fearful, we fight or flee, feigning aggressiveness or running from it.

Security comes in a variety of forms and is needed for a variety of reasons. The security needs of teachers, for example, exist on a continuum from physical to psychological. On one end of the continuum, teachers in inner city schools take their lives into their hands each day they go to work. The Center for Disease Control reports that 1 in 5 students carries a weapon of some kind and that 1 in 20 carries a gun. They also indicate that nearly 3 million crimes occur on or near U.S. schools every year.

To say that teachers in inner city schools deserve hazardous duty pay may be funny, "but it ain't no joke." The mayor of New York City recently allocated $32 million to place more police in school hallways and install more metal detectors in school entrances. Consider as well that 1 in 10 students is victimized by a bully, 1 in 4 admits to being physically afraid of *someone* in the school, and the leading causes of death among urban adolescents are fights with friends, neighbors, or classmates. It is evident that the security needs of students as well as teachers are threatened.

It's no startling revelation that such schools are populated by teachers who are unable to teach and students who are unable to learn. The social, esteem, and self-actualization needs of teachers and students, the levels most responsible for learning, are never activated as long as security needs remain primary motivators. Department chairs obviously are limited in what they can do to resolve such problems. They are well-advised, however, to keep these few suggestions in mind:

- Reveal yourself as a willing source for teachers who are worried about certain classes or students. Be in such classes often enough for teachers and students to know that you are intolerant of physical threat of any kind.

- Develop a referral process for teachers to document threatening behaviors and to secure administrative and, if necessary, police assistance in dealing with them. Forms to be used in such a process can be found in Section Seven.

- Establish a crisis team within your department that responds immediately to problems, providing appropriate follow-up for all students and teachers.

- If gangs are not a problem within the school, emphasize to teachers and administrators the need for "zero tolerance" of gang activity on or near school property.

- If gangs are a problem in your school, work closely with community officials and agencies to combat the problem.

- Irrespective of gangs, work closely with the community, especially with parental organizations, to develop a cooperative approach to curtail problems of violence or misbehavior on campus.

- Consider the development of a parent advisory council to provide the ideas and the support necessary to deal with such issues.

Psychological Security. The psychological insecurity of teachers is much more subtle and often as difficult to deal with. Such insecurity has a number of causes.

It may relate to instability at home, poor interpersonal relationships outside the school, or a continuing or periodic sense of powerlessness within the school. How department chairs respond to such teacher insecurity depends on its cause(s) and its seriousness.

Basically secure persons may experience insecurity as the circumstances of their lives change. Such circumstances may involve crises such as a death in the family or changes in routine such as a classroom observation. Even with such a relatively benign experience as a classroom observation, teachers experience varying degrees of insecurity. A few may experience none; several will experience a great deal; most will experience some.

The department chair's job is to know the anxiety/insecurity levels of each teacher and to accommodate them as circumstances require. Obviously, we're not mind readers who can spot and relieve every anxious moment in the lives of our colleagues. To the extent that anxiety is baseless fear, sometimes the smartest thing to do is ignore it. But when insecurity results from our behavior or the circumstances of the work environment, we often can and should do something about it. That's what motivation is all about.

Consider your own behavior. I learned a long time ago to look for a mirror whenever I experienced resistance in my colleagues. I asked myself: "What did I do to provoke such a reaction?" When I'm the cause of the problem, I've discovered that it's much easier to resolve. I can change my behavior a whole lot faster than someone else's. It's unfortunate how few organizational "leaders" are willing to look for mirrors when they run into problems.

And if I determine that I am not the problem, it's easier for me to focus on the teacher and to devise ways to threaten his or her security in order to make it become a motivator again. Teachers whose social needs are being satisfied by a cadre of burned-out malcontents need to experience a little insecurity again, if we are to save them. Remember, once the security needs are threatened and become motivators again, the social needs no longer motivate. More of this will be discussed in the section dealing with conflict management.

Rapport.   Speaking of mirrors, consider a behavior as simple as reflecting the attitude of another. Effective motivation requires trust, and one of the quickest ways to create trust with colleagues is to be in rapport with them when they are anxious or insecure. Art Costa and Bob Garmston, two prominent professors of education at Cal State/Sacramento, indicate that a natural correspondence of body gestures and voice tonality helps create rapport.

Department chairs who are well-liked know how to establish quick rapport with their colleagues. They match gestures and tonality to reflect attentiveness. And if the purpose of the meeting is to motivate, they will reflect the primary body-language habits of the other to reinforce important points. Be a chameleon; it's a characteristic of good communicators.

But don't be ridiculous about it. Don't cross your legs when he crosses his legs or rub your eye when she rubs her eye. *That* kind of "rapport" can lead to physical violence. Just be aware of posture, tonality, gesture, language, and breathing and reflect them to create an atmosphere of mutual understanding. If nothing else, it reflects the fact that you are listening.

I remember one of my first days on the job when a veteran teacher sat very deliberately across from me at the table in my office sizing me up. When she first sat down, she leaned on both elbows and perched on the edge of her chair just waiting for my first mistake. I, too, learned forward while we made a little small talk, speaking slowly and deliberately. Eventually, she leaned back in the chair, resting both arms on her lap. I leaned back, crossed my legs, and asked her how life in the department had been during the past few years.

By the end of the meeting, both of us had become more animated: smiling, joking, gesturing, in perfect rapport with each other. We concluded by promising to keep our lines of communication open at all times. We have enjoyed a great relationship every since, even after her retirement a couple of years ago. Since that first day, we have enjoyed a natural rapport that has enabled communication and has promoted growth in both of us.

As a matter of fact, she is the teacher who helped me develop the **_Meeting Feedback_** form in Figure 6–2. It has been invaluable to me over the years. At the conclusion of a postobservation conference, a problem-solving session, a meeting with parents or an administrator, or an end-of-the-year evaluation, I occasionally give the form to the teacher, the parent, or the administrator to request feedback. The process has helped me in two important ways.

First, it has given me another mirror to assess my own performance. Because I use the form with parents and administrators as well as teachers, it provides feedback from a number of different sources. It is also evidence to them that I am constantly seeking to improve my skills. Finally, I have used the results, which usually are positive, to include in my annual report as further evidence of my self-evaluation. Such a procedure may be somewhat political, but that's OK. School organizations as well as the Lord help those who help themselves.

The process has also proven to my colleagues that I am unafraid of constructive evaluation. I always thank them for their help and do my best to accommodate good recommendations. Invariably, they seem less threatened about receiving evaluations when they have the chance to give them to me. Security in teachers usually results from an awareness that we're not in this thing alone.

The Hierarchy.   Sometimes, the hierarchy isolates us, and this isolation is one of the severest detractors of trust. Because the hierarchy also fosters deference between "subordinates" and "superiors," it often fails to promote strong interpersonal relationships, the kind that permit honest communication. Most tragically, the "pecking order" that results in many schools substitutes positional power for expert power and provokes an administrative mad dash to create the *appearance* of leadership.

What, then, do those of us do who really want to improve our schools? First, we recognize that hierarchical relationships are often destructive to open communication and the ultimate autonomy of teachers. Decades ago, writers were shouting for flatter organizations that promoted more interaction among school personnel. They suggested "phenomenarchies," "Ad Hocracies," and a range of alternative organizational structures.

Today, writers are recommending "restructuring," in their own way trying to travel along education's organizational continuum from "most hierarchical" to "most collaborative." Tom Sergiovanni, a prominent author in the field of educational administration, however, reminds us that our schools range not from hierarchical to collaborative but from *most* hierarchical to *least* hierarchical. Teachers find themselves, then, on a continuum ranging not from dependent to autonomous, as much of the current literature would have us believe, but from most dependent to least dependent.

Team Building.   If we hope to change the situation, we must first acknowledge that we did it to ourselves. Divine providence didn't force the hierarchy on us, nor did it create separate departments, self-contained classrooms, and isolated teachers. As a profession, we discovered a long time ago that working alone is easier and safer than working with colleagues, particularly in highly evaluative organizations. Chris Argyris, one of the major transitional theorists to write about educational administration in the 50s and 60s, even went so far as to indicate that the organizational opportunity to be apathetic can lead to strong loyalty within the school.

It was a shocking commentary on schools and seemed to defy solutions. Department chairs who seek solutions, therefore, must accept Marcel Proust's insight that "the real art of discovery consists not in finding new lands, but in seeing with new eyes." We must refocus on the fact that teachers really do want to interact but only when they are secure enough to do so. Maslow is right. Teachers will be motivated to seek a sense of team membership when their security needs have been satisfied, and they will be satisfied when we eliminate many of the threats that accompany traditional hierarchical relationships.

Social Needs

Department chairs must model a sense of interdependence to promote team building. Families become dysfunctional when members are unable to interact. Parents must model such behaviors. To see with Marcel Proust's "new eyes," department chairs must reflect and promote reflection among their colleagues. They must sustain a vision on the department's normative values. They must encourage change to be proactive rather than reactive.

Team building is impossible without consensus building. That's why Figure 6–3, **This Year's Priorities**, is so helpful. Distribute it early in the school year before teachers develop their goals. In addition to promoting in-service themes, it focuses on the department's "vision" and provides opportunities for the department chair to develop planning activities that promote interaction among members of the department. Once they commit to such activities, they are open to the development of behaviors that make teams successful.

Without the necessary skills and behaviors that promote interaction, team building is impossible. Teachers must have the skills to work with each other; they must know how to collaborate. "Collegiality," for example, will exist only in the literature if schools don't provide opportunities for teachers to learn observing and conferencing skills and effective planning activities.

Consider any change in education. Someone becomes dissatisfied with the status quo and discovers or creates a set of desirable principles that lead to the development of a new program. Implementers of the program forget to influence the behaviors of the persons who will bring the program to life. The program fails.

More specifically, consider collegiality as a desirable principle leading to a program of peer supervision within your school. Your teachers are encouraged to participate in the program before they are taught how to observe each other and how to share the results of their observations. Your program fails. Motivation alone is insufficient without knowledge.

Department chairs must acknowledge the equation: *Principles* lead to *Programs* that are expressed in *Behaviors*. Without the last part of the equation, team-building activities within the department will fail. Such activities don't require a great deal of time or money, just the willingness to provide in-service training experiences for your staff, the kinds of experiences that ultimately bring needed programs to life. Review Section Four for a discussion of the processes that promote such interaction.

New Teacher Orientation. New teachers experience a similar problem. They, too, must adjust their behaviors to the tasks at hand. Each school has its own culture, or "how we do business around here," and new teachers must learn to function within that culture. To the degree that they don't, for whatever reason, they compromise their future success in the school.

In recognition of the social needs of new teachers, department chairs must be sure to give each of them a packet containing the following information:

- Explanations of policies involving district and state or federal requirements such as academic honesty, child abuse, and the confidentiality of records.
- Attendance and tardiness policies for students and absence policies for teachers.
- The daily schedule and school calendar with an explanation of their use.
- The use of the class record book and explanations of disciplinary procedures.
- Procedures for building evacuation.
- Procedures for field trips, grade reduction penalties, notices and grade reports to parents, permanent passes, and semester exams.
- Explanations of Student Services.
- Procedures for building supervision, including study halls and cafeteria.
- An explanation of the supervisory and teacher evaluation processes.
- Procedures to join the teacher organization.
- Procedures for securing typing and duplicating services.
- A map of the building.
- A listing of functions and tasks within the building/department and the names of the persons responsible for each one.

Obviously, I could list more. New teachers must know about professional advancement requirements, procedures regarding insurance claims, the use of bulletin boards and display cases, any performance awards, and procedures for making student scheduling changes. Fortunately, most of this information will be provided by the district or building administration, at least it should be. If it isn't, someone, probably you, will have to assume the responsibility.

Most importantly, new teachers must acknowledge the subtleties of school and department culture, in essence understand their prevailing beliefs. They must be introduced, for example, to expectations regarding collegiality, student discipline, professional growth, interactions with the community, and involvement with students outside as well as inside the classroom.

They must understand the accepted rituals of the department and school: relationships with the secretarial staff, behavior at staff meetings, informal relationships outside the school, expectations imposed upon the "new guy on the block," even ways to address the superintendent and principal. Each school has its own expectations in each of these areas. Failure to operate within this framework of behavior can cause new teachers unanticipated problems.

A *New Teacher Handbook* is just one way to accommodate such needs. New teachers also benefit from periodic meetings with you and/or veteran members of the department who can explain such expectations informally and supportively. These should not be presented as mandates but as suggestions, helping hands, brief but substantive words to the wise. How you share the information is as important as what you share. Use a reproducible such as the **Orientation Schedule** in Figure 6–4 to notify the new teacher of the meeting schedule.

More could be said of social needs, but my point has been made. Once the security needs of teachers have been satisfied, their social needs become motivators. All of us desire a sense of belonging. Because we want it, we are all inclined to accept the hand that reaches out to us. For those few who don't accept it, our job is to discover which of their security needs is yet to be satisfied and do what we can to meet them.

Esteem Needs

Once the security and social needs have been satisfied, the esteem needs become motivators. Having gained a sense of belonging, we desire a solid sense of self, a comfortable acceptance of who we are. Such self-knowledge is most complete when the rewards we receive for work well done are found within ourselves. Good department chairs, however, must also do what they can to guarantee recognition for the efforts of colleagues.

We must also recognize the fine line that separates the recognition we give and the autonomy they require within themselves. Generic praise fosters dependency and generally reaffirms your position in the school's hierarchy. Think about it. It acknowledges that you are in a position to give someone a pat on the back and that you can make that person dependent on you for the next pat on the back.

Specific praise, however, acknowledges exactly what the person did that merits recognition and, as such, makes a stronger contribution to his or her sense of self-esteem. Generic praise is a "good ol' boy" slap on the back; specific recognition is a friendly handshake. Whereas the one is sometimes cold, the other is invariably warm. Be sure, therefore, to use the following suggestions but to be specific in your references.

- *Monthly newsletters.* You can write them or delegate the task to someone in the department who has a romance with the language, but keep them short and distribute them at departmental meetings or in mailboxes. Be sure to include specific references to the activities and accomplishments of department members. You might also consider forwarding the newsletter to appropriate parental groups such as Parent Advisory Councils, Parent/Teacher Organizations, and Booster Clubs.

- *The student newspaper.* Inform the newspaper sponsor of the goings-on in the department and the achievements and activities of department members. See **Monthly Highlights** in Figure 6–5. Notice that the form also refers to monthly reports and a district newsletter. You might also share the memo with the principal and anyone who might put together a district newsletter.

- *Memos to the administration.* Send thank-you notes to individual members for special contributions to the department and forward copies to the building principal. Figure 6–6, **A Big Thank You!**, provides an excellent reproducible.

- *Press releases.* Send periodic press releases to local newspapers to request feature stories where appropriate and to otherwise notify them of the accomplishments of individual teachers. See the **Press Release** form in Figure 6–7 for a reproducible.

- *Workshops and conferences.* Provide funds and/or free time for members of the department to attend workshops, conferences, and conventions. Such experiences are enriching and revitalizing for the teachers, and they affirm your confidence in them.

- *Requests for input and help.* The best way to show respect for colleagues is to ask for their help, but do so in moderation. We don't want to ride our best horses to death. On the other hand, we don't want to forget that if we're careful not to push them to the point of exhaustion, the horses enjoy the ride as much as we do.

- *Performance or merit increases.* Psychologist Frederick Herzberg indicates that salary is a lower-level motivator. Well, you and I know that it does motivate, especially when performance increases are accompanied by specific reference to the reasons for the recognition. To Herzberg, recognition is a higher-level motivator. Performances increases, if handled appropriately, motivate teachers as well as anything else we do. If your district doesn't have any kind of merit pay, find a way to work with the administration to devise a program. If it does have a program, be sure to incorporate a form like **Performance Award** in Figure 6–8 to include the reasons for the merit increase. Remember, generic praise fosters dependency; specific praise leads to autonomy. Figure 6–9 provides an example of how the form is used.

- *General professional growth.* Madeline Hunter, who gave education, among other things, her widely used 7-step lesson design, reminds us constantly that corrective feedback is a motivator. The emphasis is on the word "feedback," especially the kind that leads to teacher self-evaluation. At the risk of overemphasizing an obvious point, ongoing administrative evaluation is not a motivator, unless the administration wants to threaten the security needs of the teacher. At times, as already indicated, this may be appropriate, especially for the unwilling and unable teacher; normally, however, a program of professional growth such as the one outlined in Section Two of this book will best satisfy the esteem needs of your staff.

To conclude, consider the words of Confucius: "He who wishes to secure the good of others has already secured his own." This is an important message for all of us. By assisting with the self-esteem of others, we enhance our own. Organizationally, it's also important to recognize that we do much to reinforce our working relationships with our colleagues.

Self-Actualization Needs

This is the top of Maslow's pyramid. Only when all our other needs have been satisfied are we ready to seek self-actualization. And what is self-actualization? As indicated earlier in this section, it is "putting our potential to work." It is pushing ourselves toward perfection, realizing its unattainability but its desirability as a goal. All of us require help to actualize our potential, especially teachers, who must constantly grow in so many different areas: emotionally, socially, and intellectually.

Maslow indicated that self-actualized people find themselves in constant association with what he described as the *metavalues:* truth, beauty, justice. In fact, he indicated that, for the rest of us, the continued denial of these metavalues is pathogenic; that is, it causes sickness. Constantly surrounded by ugliness, we become depressed, even physically ill. Constantly denied truth, we become paranoid. Plato indicated that the best education is for a child to play among lovely things.

Persons interested in becoming department chairs, therefore, undertake a large responsibility. They must satisfy not only the many routine tasks that the administration expects of them but also the self-actualizing needs of their teaching colleagues. In Maslow's terms, our job is to promote for our colleagues daily associations with beauty and truth. It's that simple. To paraphrase Plato, the best motivation is for a teacher to work among lovely things.

Let's Wrap It Up

The initial definition of motivation in this section emphasized that it is an internal drive state influenced by external circumstances and conditions. Such a definition is consistent with current emphases on "Control Theory," which explains that we are always motivated from within, and that what happens outside us is rarely the cause of anything we do. The purpose of this section, however, was not to discard earlier motivational theory nor to provoke semantic scuffles.

Whatever theory of motivation you choose, the material in this section will help establish the kinds of relationships you want with your staff and encourage their investment in the success of departmental programs. The section has emphasized much of what is consistent with current learning research, namely, to invite success for teachers by helping them believe in themselves and to encourage them to work together in cooperative rather than competitive situations. If we believe these principles will work for students, they can do the same for teachers.

And perhaps the best way to perceive our role in this process is to conclude with the words of Albert Camus:

> Don't walk in front of me;
> I may not follow.
> Don't walk behind me;
> I may not lead.
> Just walk beside me
> And be my friend.

Figure 6–1

MEETING SCHEDULE FOR
CURRENT SCHOOL YEAR

The following is the meeting schedule for the current school year. As usual, we will meet from 2:45 until about 4:00 on Mondays. As in the past, should you have a pressing engagement that requires you to leave at 4:00 (if the meeting runs a little late), please feel free to leave but be sure to check with me on the following day to pick up any information you may need. I also have included the name of the person who will be responsible for providing the "treats" for the meeting. If you have any problems with any of this, be sure to see me ASAP. The in-service schedule will follow.

Meeting Dates:

Sept. 6—Tom
     13—Glynis
     27—Ralph

Oct. 4—Pat
    18—Mike

Nov. 8—Dorothy
    22—Marybeth

Dec. 13—John

Jan. 11—Alice
    25—Tom

Feb. 8—Glynis
    22—Ralph

March 1—Pat
    15—Mike

April 5—Dorothy
    19—Marybeth

May 10—John
    24—Alice

Figure 6–2

MEETING FEEDBACK

Please take a moment or two to answer each of the following questions for me. I need your help to assure productive and purposeful meetings. Just circle the appropriate answer and provide comments where necessary. Thanks, in advance.

1. Did I explain the purpose of the meeting clearly early in the conference or seek to identify the purpose with you?

Yes _____   No _____

Comments:

2. Did I maintain a focus on the purpose(s), even as other issues may have been discussed?

Yes _____   No _____

Comments:

3. Did I strive to maintain a relaxed, informal exchange of ideas?

Yes _____   No _____

Comments:

4. At the conclusion of the meeting, did I summarize its focus as well as the expectations of "next steps?"

Yes _____   No _____

Comments:

Please provide any additional, specific suggestions that may be helpful to me for future meetings:

Again, thanks for your help!

Figure 6–3

THIS YEAR'S PRIORITIES

Please read each of the following learning experiences for students and add others where appropriate, then read the directions at the bottom of the sheet. In advance, thanks for your help. Your input will help identify a few of our priorities for the current school year.

Our Department Should Help Our Students:

1. Identify the reasons and the rationale for their responsibilities to other people.
2. Learn how values, attitudes, facts, and logic affect decision making.
3. Understand the values of risk taking and deal with uncertainty.
4. Accept other people as allies instead of obstacles.
5. Develop an understanding and an appreciation of cooperation.
6. Enjoy the intrinsic pleasures of accomplishment.
7. Learn to accept limitations and strengths.
8. Under the moral and social worth of their work.
9. Develop and maintain a positive self-image.
10. Learn how to interact with others.
11. Put democratic principles into practice.
12. Engage in experiences that lead to lifestyle and vocational choices.
13. Others—Please list.

At the bottom of this sheet, please identify in priority order three of the above goals that require our attention this year. On the back of the sheet, write a brief paragraph that describes your reasons for selecting your number one priority. I'll get back to you with a summary of the department's priorities. Thanks.

Figure 6–4

ORIENTATION SCHEDULE

Teacher's Name: _____

Please plan to attend the following activities at the designated times. These meetings are designed to introduce you to the people and programs at Deerfield High School. If you should have a conflict with one or more of these meetings, please discuss alternatives with your department chair.

Thursday, Sept. 12, 3:30 P.M. in Room J108

> **Presenter:** Bill Barnett, Assistant Principal
>
> **Focus:** Internal and External Communication
>
>> Referral forms, notices to parents, departmental liaisons, faculty and department meetings, relationships with student services, et al.

Wednesday, Oct. 20, 3:30 P.M. in Room F105

> **Presenter:** Fred Harvey, Director of Financial Affairs
>
> **Focus:** Fringe Benefit program, District committees, extracurricular program

Thursday, Nov. 11, 3:30 P.M. in Room J108

> **Presenter:** Pat Moorhead, Guidance department chair
>
> **Focus:** Informal discussion of DHS "school culture"

Thursday, Dec. 16, 3:30 P.M. in Administration Building conference room

> **Presenter:** Phil Jackson, Assistant Superintendent
>
> **Focus:** District program of teacher supervision and evaluation

Tuesday, May 25, 3:30 P.M. in Room J108

> **Presenter:** John Scornavacco, Principal
>
> **Focus:** End of the year wrap-up

Figure 6–5

MONTHLY HIGHLIGHTS

Please accept this monthly update of the goings-on and accomplishments of our department. Feel free to use the information for upcoming publications, monthly reports, or district newsletters. If I can provide additional information, be sure to give me a call.

Departmental Activities:

Teacher Accomplishments:

Student Accomplishments:

Figure 6–6

A BIG THANK YOU!

Just a quick note to thank you for what you did recently for the department:

cc: Principal

Figure 6–7

PRESS RELEASE

(Put title here: teacher's name, name of organization)

Copies to: (Names of local papers)

For Immediate Release

(Your name, address, and phone number here)

Figure 6–8

PERFORMANCE AWARD

Name of Teacher: _____

Amount of Award: _____

At a recent Board of Education meeting, the administrative recommendation that you receive the above Performance Award was approved. This amount will be added into your next year's contract. The award is given to recognize your special contribution to the students of this district. The specific reasons are described below. The amount is not guaranteed for the future but is renewable upon recommendation.

Again, please accept our personal appreciation for your continuing and outstanding service to the students of this district.

_____
Department chair

_____
Principal

Figure 6–9

PERFORMANCE AWARD
(Completed Sample)

Name of Teacher: _____Tim Brown_____

Amount of Award: _____$1200_____

At a recent Board of Education meeting, the administrative recommendation that you receive the above Performance Award was approved. This amount will be added into your next year's contract. The award is given to recognize your special contribution to the students of this district. The specific reasons are described below. The amount is not guaranteed for the future but is renewable upon recommendation.

Aside from the several presentations you have made at national conventions regarding the needs of LD students and the three articles you published this year, your chairing of the committee to assess the changing needs of our parent and student populations has had a dramatic effect on the job descriptions of counselors and special education personnel. Your committee's report revealed several very important insights, particularly in relation to the college application process and the changing value systems of our students. We were intrigued, for example, by the committee's observation that so many seniors seem to be applying to prestigious schools more for the status involved than for any real reason to ultimately attend those schools. Such an observation does provoke thought about the scores of recommendations written by counselors and teachers early in each school year. It also causes a lot of thought about the entire college selection process for students and parents.

We look forward to hearing more from you and your committee about these issues. At this point in time, however, the committee work is much appreciated by us, and we'd like to recognize your efforts.

Thanks for all you've done.

Again, please accept our personal appreciation for your continuing and outstanding service to the students of this district.

_____
Department chair

_____
Principal

MEETING THE CHANGING NEEDS OF STUDENTS

Growing up on Chicago's south side in the fifties, I watched several friends drop out of high school during their junior or senior years. Only football and a nagging intellectual curiosity prevented me from joining them. I also had role models like Jim Anderson on "Father Knows Best" to set standards for me. You see, most 50s homes not only watched the Andersons, they shared common characteristics with them. Life in these homes may have involved more than sitcom fantasy and the wisdom of idealized fatherhood, but most of their families were intact and the steel mills and other blue-collar jobs were in abundance for the several who decided to trade in report cards for paychecks.

The steel mills are gone; the blue-collar jobs have dwindled to a precious few; and the stereotypical American family has suffered the slings and arrows of outrageous fortune. The foresight of the Andersons may not have surrendered to the myopia of the Simpsons, but the building blocks of the family institution, like so many of our urban buildings, is discovering cracks in its foundation.

The Father-Knows-Best prototype describes only 25% of today's households, down from 40% twenty years ago. Today, 1 in every 4 or 5 children lives in a single-parent home, and more than 60% of mothers with kids under 14 are working. Two-thirds of black children are born out of wedlock. Nine million preschoolers spend most of the day with someone other than a parent, and our society may have as many as 10 million latchkey youngsters. And when these children eventually qualify for the labor force, they will discover, as we did in an earlier section of this book, that only 10% of the jobs in our society are blue-collar.

Given the demands of our economy and the lifestyle and personal preferences of many Americans, even a contemporary Margaret Anderson might trade in her food processor for a word processor. Her decision would be consistent with contemporary values and the career choices of millions of women. With neither parent at home, however, family roles become obscured and children experience less supervision.

Students have been affected in other ways by their families. A full 20% of American children now live in poverty. Twenty-two percent live in single-parent homes, nearly 3% with no parent at all. The poverty rate of single-mother families is 50%. One in three Americans is a stepparent or a stepchild. In the 1930s, 70% of us lived in agricultural areas. Interdependence among family members was high, most having one or more grandparents as role models in the family unit. Values were consistent from one generation to the next, and work responsibilities were spread throughout the family.

In the evening, families read or talked. The value-shaping entertainment of television and other technologies hadn't influenced the lifestyle habits and sexual mores of teenagers. Today, more than 60% of 16- to 18-year olds have had sex, and "handgun homicide" is the second leading cause of death for boys aged 15 to 19. The nation's schools experience more than half a million shakedowns, robberies, and attacks each month. It's not surprising that in the 1980s the number of private high schools in the nation grew almost 30%, while the number of public schools declined.

Fortunately, however, we don't have to restrict ourselves to pictures of gloom and doom. Ninety percent of all high school students do not use drugs frequently; 94% do not drink alcohol every day; 97% have never struck a teacher; and 85% of teenaged girls never get pregnant. But all of them are subject almost daily to the temptations that involve drugs, alcohol, violence, and sex. Our job, therefore, is to continue to assure attractive alternatives to such temptations and to affirm the kinds of normative values that most schools emphasize for their students.

WHAT ARE THE NEEDS?

The ego and social needs of human beings as identified by sociologist Henry A. Murray decades ago are still relevant today. All students require a sense of achievement, order, and understanding to develop ego strength. Their social development still requires the needs to defer to someone, to affiliate, to impress others, to gain a sense of autonomy, and to console others. These needs haven't changed, and our understanding of them is important if we hope to devise ways for schools to help satisfy them.

The problem is, our jobs are complicated by a range of social issues that were unheard of thirty years ago. Approximately 2,000 youths are listed as suicides each year; 500,000 kids are diagnosed as anorexics, and 10 to 15% of them will die. One in every nine kids will be in court by the age of 18 and thousands will die each year of child abuse. Finally, consider the tragedy of almost 600,000 child prostitutes in the United States.

Most recently, a national resource committee for the Carnegie Corporation identified several factors leading to the high drop-out rate among minority groups. Heading the list were differentiated tracking, lack of identification with teachers and counselors, poor attitudes and low expectations from teachers, and lack of support systems. While reviewing the committee's report, I was struck by the similarity of these factors with several that were identified for me as a doctoral student more than 20 years ago.

One of my professors at the time suggested that schools can help students realize their ego and social needs by reducing competition, adjusting standards, eliminating punitive control, increasing affective as well as cognitive learning, developing support structures, and creating special classes. Comparing these factors with those identified by the Carnegie Corporation reveals that education has yet to accommodate the most significant of student needs.

This section, therefore, will use these six factors I gleaned so many years ago from an education class as the framework to discuss what you and I can do to help meet the changing needs of kids. They were appropriate then, have been identified recently as still appropriate, and may help us think systematically about the issues affecting our students.

Reducing Competition

That this issue is still appropriate today is a cause of some concern. Certainly, you and I will never eliminate the reality of competition in our classrooms. From football after school to class rank during the day, we promote competition as much as we praise cooperation. The key for you and me is to accept some competition as inevitable but to advance cooperation wherever possible.

We do this for several reasons. First, and without making any attempt to document what must be obvious, our society is full of uncooperative and inconsiderate people who emphasize "me-first" in almost everything they do. Certainly they're not a majority, but if you want to find a few, try your local freeway. Second, statistics prove that students who volunteer their time and/or engage in extracurricular programs are more successful in later life than their uninvolved classmates. Third, business and industry are looking for graduates who know how to think and who can work cooperatively in groups to solve problems.

Consensus Building.   Fortunately, the opportunities for cooperative experiences in the school and community are endless. All of them give students the chance to help their classmates and to reach out to others in the community. A first consideration involves cooperation in the classroom. If we hope to develop more of it among students, we must first assure it among teachers. As indicated in an earlier section, one of the best ways to assure it is to engage the staff in consensus-building activities.

Figure 7–1, *Achieving Consensus,* involves a checklist of characteristics identified by a friend several years ago. The characteristics go beyond cognitive classroom experiences for students and provide affective elements that promote increased awareness of the needs of self and others. Several allude to cooperation and consideration; one addresses it specifically. Most of them promote school experiences that involve students in some kind of cooperative interaction with their classmates. Most are as appropriate for math and fine arts classes as for English and social studies.

This kind of consensus building complements end-of-the-year needs assessments and offers the department a sense of direction. Most importantly, once completed, it fosters a common purpose and prompts teachers to seek solutions that promote the desired characteristics. An obvious solution involves "cooperative learning" as developed by Johnson and Johnson and others. If used thoughtfully, it reduces competition and engages students in cooperative educational experiences.*

Other techniques and strategies are available to do the same thing. What is needed first, however, is teacher awareness of the advantages of cooperative experiences for students and a consensus within the department to provide them. Forms such as Figure 7–1 will help. Once such a consensus is achieved, the department chair will be in a position to provide or receive suggestions for ways to promote cooperation and group interaction among students. Such suggestions can come in the form of in-service activities or meeting agendas. The form, *Ideas for Further Study* in Figure 7–2, provides a useful reproducible to secure such suggestions.

The American classroom, according to much of the literature, is in need of change. From the introduction of "cooperative learning" to the elimination of ability grouping, writers and researchers are encouraging a variety of changes—and let's admit it, organizational adjustments in classrooms have to start somewhere. They might as well start with you and me, if you agree that cooperation among students is more important than competition between them.

The purpose of this section, however, is not to outline plans to implement cooperative learning or eliminate ability grouping. Section One suggests ways to do that. Our intention is to specify the need, to provide a format for studying it within your department, and to identify one or two other ideas for reducing student competition.

Tutorial programs can be one way of accomplishing this goal. These programs will be discussed in more detail in this section under "Developing Support Systems." The Early Bird Tutoring Assistance program is especially designed for student volunteers. Other resources can come from parents, other adults, or other members of the student body as volunteers or paid workers.

Students can assist students in other ways as well. Figure 7–3, *Peer Guides*, invites students to volunteer their time to help transfers adjust to a new school environment. These students don't have to be whiz kids in math, science, or English. They simply have to want to help new students feel more comfortable in unfamiliar surroundings. Again, such a program may ultimately function on an all-school basis, but you might as well be the one to start it.

Adjusting Standards

Culture, whether of an entire society or an individual school, serves two primary functions. At times, these functions may be contradictory. One, culture provides the processes for accommodating or generating new information and understandings. Such processes enable the culture to change, to survive. Two, it provides traditions and ritualized behaviors that promote predictability for people within the culture. Such predictability promotes comfort and reduces the anxiety that problems and change provoke. Therein lies a problem for education.

*For an enlightened treatment of cooperative learning, I suggest you read: Johnson, David W. and Roger T. *Circles of Learning: Cooperation in the Classroom,* Interaction Books, Edina, MN, 1990.

The very traditions and rituals that comfort us may also interfere with our ability to change.

Consider the classroom. The assumption that "homogeneous classrooms" contain students that learn at the same rate and in the same way is a comforting aspect of the school's culture. It provides the predictability teachers need to teach their subject areas. It offers a rational organizational structure that enables them to teach large groups of students. The problem is, teachers teach kids, not a subject area.

We already have discussed that systems are, by definition, resistant to change. Some of the resistance results from fear of change, a nonrational element that operates in any school. It perpetuates assumptions like the homogeneous classroom and the belief that all kids learn the same way. What, then, of that old Chinese proverb: "I hear and I forget; I see and I remember; I do and I understand?" If it's so old, why has it taken so long to influence our classrooms?

The answer to this question is also found in system theory. Aside from hiring old Chinese teachers, perhaps we need to get into the system's environment and determine its expectations of us. Specifically, if we want to adjust standards for our students, we need to give the students and their parents the chance to look at these standards and identify issues requiring our attention. Figure 7–4, *Looking Back*, provides a process for securing such input from parents and kids.

It can be extremely effective. I know of one school, for example, that used it and discovered a remarkable insight about freshman final exams. Parents and a subsequent investigation of semester report cards indicated that a sizeable number of freshmen were earning As and Bs during the semester but were receiving Cs and Ds on their semester exams. The poor showing on the exams was dropping their semester grades and highlighting the continuing perception of teachers that freshmen simply didn't know how to study for finals.

A closer look, however, by the school's English department revealed that the school was disregarding a fundamental characteristic of freshmen. They discovered that most freshmen were not ready developmentally to handle the high level abstraction that was required for successful completion of the exams. Most of the teaching during the semester had accommodated all the modalities of the students, but the final exams had emphasized only their visual and abstraction skills. As one teacher indicated: "We forgot that just two months before these kids entered our front door they were eighth graders. Most are just making the transition from concrete to abstract thinking."

A result of their study was the elimination of final exams for freshmen. Instead, teachers assigned final projects that synthesized what the students had learned during the semester and provided chances for them to work with the material again. Tests during the sophomore year covered progressively larger amounts of material, so that the students eventually were able to handle the demands of a semester exam.

The process, a clear adjustment of standards, resulted in appropriate assessments of student achievement, a sense of professionalism for the teachers, and an awareness of parents that their input was valued by the school. It was an awareness that promoted a mutually enjoyable partnership between the school and community and, not too surprisingly, resulted in more parent volunteers and an increased willingness to pass referenda!

Special Accommodation.   Less dramatically, the adjustment of standards is reflected in the department's willingness to meet the needs of kids, who, for a variety of reasons, require special accommodations. The ***Pass-Fail form*** in Figure 7–5 provides a pass-fail option for students who want to keep a class but don't want to worry about the grade. Such an option is appropriate for the student who likes a course but finds it very difficult and doesn't want the grade to affect his or her class rank.

Figure 7–6, ***Extended Time***, provides a sample form for students who require extended time on tests. Such students may be involved in special education or may have been identified by the family doctor as requiring untimed tests. This particular form is from a math department and is another example of how growing numbers of schools are adjusting their standards to meet the individual needs of students.

Eliminating Punitive Control Models

Punitive control is reactive. Discipline in schools must be proactive. The school that is able to anticipate student misbehavior and "cut it off at the pass" is a school with a nurturing learning environment. It is a school that understands the nature of self-discipline and seeks to promote it in students. Consider once more our discussion of adjusting standards. The expectations we impose on students provide the framework within which they find their successes.

Unrealistically High Standards.   If standards are too high, students become frustrated. The next step is to act out their frustrations and to misbehave. When the only standard of success is superior achievement, we send the wrong message. Consider the message sent by the International Olympic Committee when they allowed professional basketball and tennis players to compete in the Olympics. Sport for its own sake gave way to the desire to win.

The Gang Problem.   When significant accomplishment becomes the only standard for success, lesser performers fall short necessarily, and many of them inevitably seek a sense of belonging in subcultures that reward alienation. In the case of schools, gangs result. Unmotivated students result. School discipline involves much more than adult responses to misbehavior. Certainly students must realize the consequences of their misbehavior, but, more importantly, they must learn the values of self-discipline within an environment that promotes their self-esteem. Remember that punishment is the external response when self-discipline breaks down. The key to effective discipline in schools, therefore, involves opportunities for students to learn to discipline themselves.

This is not pie-in-the-sky unreality. It can be done, even in schools battling inner-city disregard. Consider the extreme example of gangs. What are some of the factors in schools that feed their growth? If we accept the assumption that kids join gangs because they don't feel respected anywhere else, then it's critical for schools to respect their students. It's that simple.

Young people don't respect the institutions that don't respect them. Schools spend more money on vandalism than they do on textbooks. Much of this vandalism is gang-related. In addition to assessing their climate, curriculum, and teaching methods, schools must find ways to explore and discuss values and to make kids feel welcomed every time they come to school.

Recognizing the Symptoms.   In schools where gangs are a potential problem, teachers must be proactive. They can't wait to *re* act to them. Anyone who has had experience with gang activities in schools realizes that once established, gangs are virtually impossible to remove. It's important to share information such as the ***Profile of a Student Who Is Susceptible to Gang Membership*** in Figure 7–7 with teachers, counselors, and, if possible, parents. This particular form was developed by a psychologist for a suburban school district. Similar forms should be developed for inner-city or rural communities.

Such information helps alert adults to the susceptibility of some students to gangs. When accompanied by pictures and explanations of gang symbols and colors, it increases the proactivity of the school. Proactivity, however, involves much more than a sharing of information, and it extends well beyond the obvious problem of gangs.

The most obvious problems are the easiest to diagnose. Some may be subtle, but when a dog is snapping at your heels, you know you're in trouble. The *solution* may not be as obvious, but the problem is hard to avoid. The gang issue falls into this category. Other problems involving student misbehavior in most schools, however, are much more subtle and usually require the input of several different specialists to diagnose and resolve.

Teachers, administrators, deans of students, counselors, special educators, social workers, and department chairs all have specialized and important perspectives on student behavior. Each has a body of knowledge and a different perspective to contribute to the analysis of student behavior and to the resolution of any problems. It's important that the school coordinates these perspectives to help diagnose problems and find the best solutions.

Referrals.   Some schools have developed teams of special services personnel that meet two or three times during the week to discuss individual students and, occasionally, to anticipate or respond to systemic problems. Such teams coalesce the expertise of guidance, administration, social work, and special education. They also provide support to the team members when solutions are hard to find or implement. It is a process that involves the best of collegial interaction.

The department chair's responsibility in the process is critical. He or she is the first level of intervention whenever a referral is made within the building. Consider, for example, the referrals in Figures 7–8, ***Unauthorized Absence Contact Record;*** 7–9, ***Behavior Referral,*** and 7–10, ***Learning Referral.***

- The first, a referral recording a student unauthorized absence, provides notification of the absence and instructs the teacher, counselor, and dean of their responsibilities at certain stages of the process.

- The second, a behavioral referral, identifies the nature of the misbehavior, seeks a description of it, asks about prior intervention attempts, and defines the school's response and any additional referrals.

- The third, a learning referral form, as illustrated in Figure 7–10, is used by teachers to refer students to counselors and other special services personnel when they suspect behavior problems or learning interferences. The form is not for *mis*behavior specifically, but for any behavior that causes concern for the teacher, such as apparent student disorientation, sudden depression, or a significant change in study habits and achievement.

I recall the time I received such a referral from a teacher. She was concerned about the student's inability or unwillingness to "tune in" to class activities. She documented behaviors such as sleeping on the desk, gazing out of the window, and scribbling on tests and quizzes. The documentation of such specific behaviors, by the way, is very important for special services personnel to diagnose the student's problem.

I responded to the referral by sending for the student to talk with him. When he discovered that I had no intention to "discipline" him, he opened up and made a comment I'll never forget: "I spend most of my time in school *someplace else!*" Our job was to find out why. After a screening and a full case study evaluation, we discovered a learning disability, subtle but easily documented. With the proper support program, he began to tune back into classroom activities and ultimately found his way to college.

Documenting Referrals.   All these referrals should first go to the department chair who, in turn, meets with students as I did, forwards them to appropriate support personnel, or meets with such personnel to discuss the student's situation. The department chair is in a key position to document the incidence of misbehavior, the teachers with whom it most frequently occurs, the attendance patterns of students in particular classes, the incidence of specific learning interferences, and the kinds of interventions attempted before the actual referral.

This kind of information is revealing for the department chair. Most obviously, it provides an opportunity to help solve student problems and to be seen by the department staff as a helpmate and source of support. It also describes in considerable detail the kinds of problems that are occurring in the department, and with whom. A simple summary of the different kinds of information sometimes provides remarkable insights.

I worked with a group of department chairs one year who confessed that "Their use of such referrals resulted in their departments referring *themselves.*" In essence, the referrals that the teachers were writing were identifying student problems that to some extent were being caused by the teachers themselves, the curriculum, the expectations of the school, or the control models being used in the classrooms or the dean's office!

Gathering Referral Data.   Without the department chair organizing a "central clearinghouse" to summarize and coordinate such information, the data generated by the referrals would have been lost as a supervisory and planning tool. In addition, when such information is combined with teachers' grades, it provides a revealing picture of both student and teacher activity. The Teacher Referral Tally in Figure 7–11 provides a reproducible for gathering information about individual teachers. The **Referrals form** in Figure 7–12 provides a summary sheet for developing a comparative analysis among members of the department.

Obviously, the forms themselves involve confidential information and should be used only by you. Even the teachers should not see them because of the misinterpretation that may result. The information they provide, however, is revealing and may be used during end-of-the-year conferences or even dismissal proceedings, certainly during departmental planning activities.

Each of these forms can be very helpful during departmental planning activities and for supervisory activity with the staff. More importantly, they promote needed interaction among school professionals. Routine processes must be developed to accommodate this interaction. They operate in the best interests of students *and* teachers.

Discipline.   Such forms provide a "picture" of the activities of students and staff and help identify problems in the department. They ultimately encourage the prevention of such problems by identifying areas of actual or potential conflict. Department chairs can help coordination even more by providing a form such as the one titled ***Establishing Limits*** in Figure 7–13 that encourages teachers to work with their students to develop reasonable rules for classroom behavior. The form is consistent with years of research that have emphasized everything from judicious discipline to assertive discipline.

The basic premise is to provide opportunities for students to have a voice in the development of rules of behavior. Having done so, students are more likely to follow them, at least to understand any punishment for violating them. Once completed, the form can be distributed to each student, and the teacher can refer to it when misbehavior occurs. During the development of the rules, teachers can emphasize their high expectations of students, indicating among other things that:

- The focus of classroom activities should almost always be on learning.
- Character is an outgrowth of self-control.
- Ours is a first-class department with first-class students.
- We're in this *together*.

Clearly, some kids are going to test the limits. Preventive discipline may work with most students, but it's lost on others. For these few, punitive control is appropriate. It is sometimes the only thing they understand. It must always, however, involve the child's parents, not necessarily just in meetings. Phone calls or letters from the teacher, you, or another administrator are equally effective. In fact, a phone call home is sometimes the ounce of prevention that is worth the school's pound of cure.

Increasing Affective Learning Experiences

Sometimes the meetings that result with parents regarding student misbehavior are the best way to increase affective experiences for students! And they have far-reaching consequences for the right kinds of affective experiences in the classroom. The dictionary indicates that "affective" means "of or relating to feelings or emotions." Educators generally contrast affective with cognitive experiences in the classroom, cognitive relating to the intellectual or nonemotional elements in a relationship.

I am convinced that teachers have made great strides in this area. Emphases on question-and-answer techniques in the classroom and cooperative learning have provoked classroom interaction among students and teachers. Harvey Silver, an educational consultant from New Jersey and a frequent speaker at conventions and workshops, has influenced thousands of teachers to accept answers from students as "gifts," to value them as we would a remembrance on Christmas or a birthday.

Valuing Student Opinions.   Accordingly, when students feel that their opinions are valued, they "feel good" in the classroom. They relate to the teacher more comfortably and are more inclined to take risks because they know they won't get hurt when they do. The affective elements of education, then, simply involve making students feel good when they come to school—confident in themselves and in their relationships with teachers.

The concept that "teachers teach and students learn" is often confused with the outdated notion that "teachers talk and students listen." Such a notion doesn't leave much room for affective experiences in the classroom. Department chairs must use in-service activities and supervisory and evaluative experiences with the staff to underscore the importance of current research and to share the "gifts" that theorists like Silver are offering us. A brief review of earlier sections in this book will help.

Showing a Caring Attitude.   A terrific example of communicating a caring attitude is illustrated in *Commendation,* the form in Figure 7–14. Teachers should be encouraged to mail these by the score! They make parents and students happy by providing specific praise for accomplishments in the class. The form also leaves room for additional specific praise and should be used by the entire staff. Generally, when the affective needs of students are satisfied, so are the affective needs of teachers.

You can do your share, too. Travel back in time a few years and recall your feelings in college when you banged your head on the bureaucracy. You and I both know that nothing is more frustrating and more likely to provoke a *negative* affect than bureaucratic disregard. If we promote processes that encourage teachers to relate to their students affectively, we must do the same. *Cutting through the Red Tape,* the form in Figure 7–15, gives students the chance to identify organizational obstacles, bureaucratic or otherwise, in your department.

Believe me, the kids will use it. They will identify problems that genuinely warrant your attention, and when you respond to their concerns, they, too, will see you as a helpmate in school. Increasing the affective experiences of students, therefore, isn't restricted only to the classroom.

Developing Support Systems

To some extent, the entire school shares the responsibility of increasing affective experiences. However, individual department chairs can develop programs that are unique to their subject areas. They can provide resource centers, tutorial help, assistance with study skills, advice regarding registration, arbitration with conflicts between students and teachers, advice regarding subject requirements for college admissions, and a range of other services.

Tutorial help from classmates and adult volunteers can often turn the academic tide for a student who is struggling with a subject. A program called Early Bird Tutoring Assistance engages a group of students on an "early-bird" basis, 30 to 45 minutes before the start of the regular school day, to help classmates understand coursework and/or complete important assignments. Take a look at the ***Departmental Tutoring form*** in Figure 7–16.

This form is easily reproduced and distributed to students within your department. Many students will volunteer their time. Some will do it out of a sense of concern for their classmates. The less altruistic among them may do it to pad their resumes for college applications. Whatever their motivations, the result is a group of talented students that can provide tutoring to lesser-talented classmates.

If teachers in the department are encouraged to refer students to the program by using the ***Early Bird Tutoring Assistance form*** in Figure 7–17, the program can become a potent force for kids, become a prototype for teachers throughout the school, and will be an example the community approves of and appreciates. Under the leadership of Jan Jordan and Dick Moore, two English teachers at Deerfield High School in Illinois, such a program is highly successful, to the point of being copied by schools across the country.

The reproducible, ***The Ins and Outs of Tutoring***, in Figure 7–18 provides specific information for tutors. It discusses an overview of the tutoring process, specific responsibilities of the tutor, suggestions on how to start tutoring students, and a word about positive tutoring relationships. Depending on the amount of time available to you, you might also provide one or two preliminary training sessions for tutors.

The sessions and the materials in Figure 7–18 help tutors do their jobs well and underscore the importance of their responsibilities. Other tutorial services can be provided formally in a tutorial center or informally by upperclass students who are willing to visit the student's home to provide help. To find tutors, use the forms in Figure 7–19, ***Student Tutors***, for students and Figure 7–20, ***Adult Tutors***, for parents.

Obviously, the student form can be circulated throughout the school. The parent form and its information should be included in community newspapers, PTO bulletins, and the school newspaper. The form itself might also be shared with parent groups such as advisory councils, Booster Clubs, and PTO or PTA committees. Mail it directly to parents who have volunteered in the past. The effort it takes to circulate the form is well worth the contributions made by the upperclass students and parents who volunteer their time to work with students who need help.

Finally, the ***Student and Adult Tutors*** form in Figure 7–21 lists those tutors who are available to assist with completion of assignments and preparation for tests and quizzes. You may be able to get them to donate their time; more likely, they may request a slight fee. The form indicates *donated* time; change it accordingly to reflect an hourly rate if a fee is involved. And recognize that this list of tutors is designed to complement, not replace, the Early Bird Tutoring Assistance program. Some students may want to take advantage of both.

Study Skills. Helping students with their study skills can be accommodated in a couple ways. Department chairs can include such help in resource center activities; they can encourage teachers to provide after-school assistance to students on selected days; or they can include forms such as the *Study Skills* form in Figure 7–22 in teacher handbooks or somewhere in the department office.

I once stacked some shelves on a wall close to the door in the teachers' office and posted a sign immediately underneath entitled Professional Growth Materials. Then I put xeroxed copies of materials like those in Figure 7–22 for teacher use. I was pleased to see how often the staff referred to them during observation conferences and general discussions. They are indeed helpful, particularly when they provide specific examples that teachers can use in their classes immediately.

Help from Guidance. Sometimes the characteristics of the support system are unique to the department. The forms in Figures 7–23, *Request for Social Work Services*, and 7–24, *Peer Helping Referral*, are most appropriate for guidance departments. Academic departments may not find them useful, but guidance and special education departments will benefit from them greatly, particularly from the additional dimensions they provide for helping kids.

The form in Figure 7–24 will be helpful if you should decide to develop such a peer program. We discovered it to be very helpful for students who fear speech class activities or who are having problems with their peer groups. Significant emotional or adjustmental problems obviously require the services of professionals, but a good peer helping program often provides the intervention a student needs to resolve a minor personal problem.

Problems between Student and Teacher. Regarding the resolution of problems, department chairs often find themselves wedged between students and teachers who, for whatever reason, decide to do battle. Usually minor squabbles, they nonetheless have far-reaching implications for the relationships you may enjoy with the teacher or the student. It is critical, therefore, that you have the right information before you try to resolve the problem. The reproducible, *Confidential Statement*, in Figure 7–25 will provide such information. It will serve other purposes as well.

- It documents the incident in the event parents or other school authorities become involved.

- It forces the student to objectify the situation by recording exactly what he or she thinks happened. My experience has been that once I ask students to fill out this form, they rethink the incident and discover that they contributed to the problem or that it wasn't as serious as they thought originally.

- Along with other such incidents, it provides accumulated evidence of continuing conflicts between students and a particular teacher.

Mention to the student, however, that if he or she chooses anonymity, you may be unwilling to confront the teacher. You can indicate that you will keep the form on hand and use it, without the student's name, if additional situations such as this one arise. One incident involving an anonymous student, however, unless the circumstances are significant, is not probable cause to confront a teacher.

If the student indicates that it's all right to use his or her name, then you must make a decision based upon the circumstances of the situation and/or the teacher's past history whether or not a meeting is appropriate. If you choose to have a meeting, identify a time that is mutually convenient for both the student and the teacher and meet with both beforehand to share the "ground rules:"

- No confrontation in the meeting.
- No other parties to attend unless discussed and agreed upon beforehand.
- Stick to the facts.

With the proper preparation for such a meeting, the experience can be helpful for both the student and the teacher. My experience has been that once such a meeting is held, the student and the teacher invariably have a better relationship for the rest of the year—considerably stronger than it had been.

Absenteeism as a Red Flag. I have learned almost as much as I have taught during my 30 years in public education. I learned long ago, for example, that high school students are as slick as used car salespeople at camouflaging the truth. Some of them can hide personal problems better than these salespeople can hide faulty transmissions. But the system, if used properly, doesn't let them do it for long.

Even the most careful student sooner or later waves a red flag. The flag probably comes in the form of one or more of three characteristics: behavior, grades, or absenteeism. Because the reproducibles already provided in this section accommodate behavior, grades, and unauthorized absences, we need only one more to alert teachers and counselors to excessive *authorized* absenteeism.

These kinds of absences often escape our attention and sometimes signal some of the biggest problems. Have your attendance office alert you each time a student accumulates 20 or more absences in one semester, then use the ***Absence Record form*** in Figure 7–26 to notify the teacher in your department, the student's counselor, and the dean, if your school has one. Notice that the form not only alerts other professionals to the situation but requests a response from them.

As such, it requests documented follow-up to a potentially serious problem. You, too, might call the student's home to request information from the parents and, if needed, offer your help to them. Sometimes even parents don't realize the number of absences a child may accumulate, and sometimes don't care. You'll want to know that, too. Many schools don't have a policy in this area. If yours doesn't, develop one for your department, using the process as provided on the form. I have seen this process provide a tremendous service to some students and their families.

You'll also want to know when students can't afford to pay for textbooks, fees for certain classes, costs for field trips, or the expenses that may occur routinely during the school year. A form may cause some embarrassment for students, so it's wise simply to mention in announcements or letters home the opportunity to petition for financial help with book costs, lunch prices, or fees for such things as field trips or lab costs.

Special Classes

This area of student need has been accommodated for the most part by special education in most schools. Special education has done such a nice job, in fact, and has probed so insightfully into the learning process that it may have outdistanced many classroom teachers regarding the diagnosis and remediation of learning problems. It also can provide unique insights into the development of curriculum. That's why the two sample memos in Figure 7–27 can be so helpful.

Current trends in special education are encouraging mainstreamed classes for many learning- and behaviorally-challenged students. The movement seems to be redefining special education teachers as partners, consultants if you will, in regular classrooms. Some departments are working closely with special education to promote team teaching with mainstreamed teachers in order to work collaboratively with certain students. They are also inviting special education personnel to join them on curriculum committees.

My experience has been that such partnerships work extremely well. Administration may have to make the time for certain special education teachers to provide such services, but they'll discover improved student achievement in these classrooms, a reduction in behavioral referrals, professional growth in mainstreamed teachers, and curriculum that responds to the developmental and learning needs of kids.

Department chairs must see such assistance as a way to complement their efforts with teachers and curriculum. In the true spirit of everything that is sacred about recent concepts of management, the synergy that results from collaboration between special education and regular classrooms can be of tremendous value to the school's planning activities and, ultimately, to the students themselves. You are emphasizing a strength, not a weakness, when you seek the help of someone who can contribute to a good idea.

In the absence of team teaching and committee partnerships, schools can still coordinate the relationship between special education and other departments by devising ways to share information and recommendations about certain students. The ***Confidential Information*** form in Figure 7–28 provides a reproducible for special education teachers or case managers to forward information to mainstream teachers regarding the characteristics and needs of certain learning- or behaviorally-challenged students. Figure 7–29 provides an example of what the form might look like for a particular student. Mainstream teachers really appreciate this information, and it does much to solidify their relationship with special education.

Maintaining Contact with the Home

The only time people really fail is when they make mistakes—and don't learn from the experience. You and I can't allow that to happen to our students. That's why we use forms similar to the ***Notice to Parent*** in Figure 7–30 to notify parents of their child's unsatisfactory progress regarding course objectives. Such forms can be mailed at any time, with or without an accompanying phone call. In the case of significant problems, however, teachers should always be encouraged to call the home to alert parents to the specifics of the problem, even to request a meeting to discuss the child's behavior and academic progress.

Should the problems eventuate in a course failure, students can still learn from the experience, if it is handled by the school sensitively. That's why I recommend the use of a form such as the **Notice of Failure** in Figure 7–31 to provide information to the counselor or advisor who might be in contact with the family. Either the teacher or the counselor should make a phone call to the family to discuss the implications of the failure for continuation in the course, future courses, or possible enrollment in summer school. This particular form is used by a math department for freshmen and sophomores. Obviously, you can use it as a model to develop other such forms.

These forms, and the others in this section, emphasize to everyone associated with the school that we are, in fact, student-centered, that we are teaching children, not just a curriculum, and that we *expect* our students to succeed. In fact, we will do whatever we can to assure that success.

The principle to emphasize with your staff, therefore, is to maintain *Parent Contact*. Teachers should be encouraged to contact parents whenever a student persistently misbehaves or fails to live up to course expectations. On that basis, they should have easy access to phones and recognize that continuing communication with the home is one of the standards of their professional performance. Nothing establishes positive relationships with the community or works for the well-being of students better than ongoing dialogue with parents. In fact, parent/school partnerships are the current focus on many of the nation's schools.

What Else Does the Future Hold?

The number of students who come to school each day hungry, chemically dependent, abused, poor, violent, or alienated has risen dramatically within the past several years, and it doesn't seem to be diminishing. Certainly, schools cannot be expected to treat chemical dependency or cure chronic depression, but we must acknowledge such realities and discover ways to work with our communities and political institutions to deal with these issues. And we must consider such interferences when we promote learning.

Schools must encourage political and social commitment among students in spite of their cultural dissimilarity. Like their counterparts in higher education, schools must not simply preserve and impart knowledge, they must create it—in exciting and relevant ways. New technologies and new social issues require new processes. We must seek more than answers to questions; we must formulate new questions. Department chairs play a major role in this responsibility.

Let's Wrap It Up

This section provides you with a lot of material. Certainly, you won't use it all, but what you do use will open the door to an increased awareness of the changing needs of students. Hopefully, the volume of material will help you with your responsibilities. It will also underscore the fact that student needs are not satisfied by prepackaged solutions or quick fixes. The forms in this section are simply elements in the *processes* that coordinate the collaborative and continuing efforts of professionals. Only by working together with their colleagues will department chairs create the organizational synergy needed to respond to the significant social, environmental, and political issues that transform the lives of students on a daily basis and that challenge the vitality and adaptability of schools across the country.

Figure 7–1

ACHIEVING CONSENSUS

To the Department:

Please respond to the following checklist. It consists of several characteristics that readdress the fundamental purposes of education. Identify the five or six most important purposes that require our mutual attention. Identify the most important with a 1, the remaining four or five in descending order. Your help is appreciated.

We Must Help Our Students:

_____ Develop social skills.

_____ Value the processes of education (learning how to learn).

_____ Analyze experiences and relationships that have brought them the greatest happiness.

_____ Identify strategies for relating to society's institutions.

_____ Explore experiences that lead to lifestyle and vocational choices.

_____ Explore their personal strengths and weaknesses.

_____ Understand the increasing interdependence among segments of society.

_____ Experience and study democratic principles in action.

_____ Develop a positive self-concept.

_____ Explore people, relationships, interests, goals, et al. in relation to their basic values.

_____ Discuss the what and why of their responsibilities to other people.

_____ Explore and understand the difference between needs and wants.

_____ Learn positive ways to assert their influence on society.

_____ Explore family roles and determine the appropriateness of their own role.

_____ Practice decision making as it relates to values, attitudes, and logic.

_____ View other people in a cooperative, not a competitive way.

_____ Develop a willingness to take risks in the face of uncertainty.

_____ Practice good physical health.

_____ Appreciate beauty.

_____ Learn to appreciate the moral and social value of hard work.

_____ Experience the satisfaction of a job well done.

_____ Other. (Please specify.)

We probably will require help from other people in the building to see these characteristics emphasized throughout the school. Most importantly, however, we will have achieved consensus among ourselves and will have a stronger sense of how we hope to satisfy the changing needs of our students. This information will also be important to us during future planning activities.

Figure 7–2

IDEAS
For Further Study

Thanks for your help with the consensus-building form. It provided some great ideas. Now that we have developed a general sense of direction in our recent department meeting, we're in need of some specifics to move us along. Please use this form to suggest in-service topics or agenda items for upcoming meetings that relate to our top-priority items. I'll get back to you once I collate the results. Thanks!

1.

2.

3.

4.

5.

6.

7.

8.

9.

10.

Figure 7–3

PEER GUIDES

Students interested in volunteering their time during the school day to help transfer students make new friends and find their way around the building are invited to fill out this form and drop it off in Room ____. Each year our high school receives ten or more transfer students, all of whom appreciate the help they get from our department's Peer Guides. We hope you will help out. In advance, thanks for your help, and we'll be in touch.

Your Name: _____

Year in School: _____

I have been in the program before.   Yes _____   No _____

Please list your free periods or study halls this year:

_____

_____

_____

_____

Please list other extracurricular activities:

Again, thanks for your help. Programs such as this one wouldn't be possible without students like you.

Figure 7–4

LOOKING BACK

Input from students and parents is very important if our department is to continue to meet the educational needs of our student body. We are always seeking to improve the standards we use to assess student achievement. As you know, we use a combination of homework, papers, projects, quizzes, tests, and final exams to determine student progress toward the completion of course objectives and requirements. As each of these relates *to your child* in his or her recently completed course, please identify any issues that you would like to bring to our attention. First, indicate the name of the course, and please *don't* include the name of the teacher. Then return this form to the department office.

Course Name: _____

1. *Homework*

2. *Papers*

3. *Quizzes*

4. *Projects*

5. *Tests*

6. *Final Exams*

Thanks a lot for your help!

Figure 7–5

PASS/FAIL POLICY

Students:

The purposes of taking a class of Pass/Fail are

1. To encourage the exploration of new areas of study.
2. To encourage the taking of more difficult courses.
3. To relieve excessive academic pressure.

Please be advised that you may want to consult with the admissions office of the college(s) to which you are applying as to how they interpret a pass/fail on an applicant's transcript.

Please be sure to read excerpts from the Pass/Fail policy as listed below. If you have any questions, please see me before September 25. The deadline for submitting your request for Pass/Fail is September 25.

Excerpts from Pass/Fail Policy

1. A student may elect any course (full or partial credit) offered in the school for a Pass/Fail grade under this policy EXCEPT THOSE REQUIRED FOR GRADUATION.

2. All students must have at least 37 of the 41 credits required for graduation in courses graded regularly. Only four may be taken on a Pass/Fail basis. This includes students who elect to graduate in fewer than eight semesters.

3. Any students taking five or six courses may elect any one of them on a Pass/Fail basis (except those exempted in item 1). A student taking seven courses may elect any two of them on a Pass/Fail basis. Once a student has earned 37 regularly graded credits, he or she may elect to take two courses on a Pass/Fail basis if he or she is enrolled in six courses, or one course on a Pass/Fail basis if enrolled in five or fewer courses, again excepting those exempted in item 1.

4. To obtain a "Pass" in a course, the student must obtain a grade of "D" or better, in accordance with standards of that course. The student must meet the same attendance requirements as students graded regularly.

5. A student may *not* take a sequential or prerequisite course on a Pass/Fail basis. Except with the permission of the department chairperson, only the last semester in an intended sequence may be taken Pass/Fail.

6. Students and their families are responsible for decisions made to carry a course on a Pass/Fail basis. Counselors will work with students and their parents on this matter.

7. A senior student on Pass/Fail may elect not to take the final exam during their final semester if they have an average of at least 80% at the time of the exam.

Figure 7–5, continued

Designation of a Subject to be Taken on a Pass/Fail Basis

1st Semester 1993–94

Student: _____ Year in School: _____

Counselor Signature: _____ First Period Teacher: _____

I request that I be permitted to take the following on a Pass/Fail basis:

Subject: _____ Teacher Signature: _____
                                              (for purpose of teacher notification)

Accept the conditions as set forth below:

1. To obtain a "Pass" in a course, I must obtain a grade of "D" or better, in accordance with standards of that course. I must meet the same attendance requirements as students regularly graded.
2. Credit toward graduation will be granted for a "Pass" grade, but courses taken Pass/Fail are not used in calculating class rank.
3. Courses required for graduation cannot be taken on a Pass/Fail basis.
4. This decision is for one semester and must be renewed each semester.

_____ _____
Student Signature   Parent Signature

This form must be completed and turned in to the Guidance Office no later than Friday, September 25, 1993.

Figure 7–6

EXTENDED TIME EXAM

Student: _____

Teacher: _____

Math Tests

Check List

Please check the following conditions that apply to the administration of this extended time exam.

1. Date of Exam _____

2. Periods _____

3. Students may use:

    _____ calculator

    _____ notes

    _____ books

    _____ work to be turned in with exam (please specify)

    _____ other

Time Started: _____

Time Completed: _____

Test Administrator: _____

Figure 7–7

A PROFILE OF A STUDENT WHO IS SUSCEPTIBLE
TO GANG MEMBERSHIP

Generally speaking, teenagers who are most susceptible to gang influences and possible membership are male, and immature. They may be intelligent but are usually lacking in cognitive development. They probably are fourteen to sixteen years of age and are products of single-parent or dysfunctional families. In middle or upper-class communities, such dysfunction may be caused partially by "fast-track" parents who are unavailable to their children, abusive or neglectful parents, or, in some cases, parents of reconstituted families. There are myriad causes of family dysfunction. The result, is a quality of parenting that fails to meet the developmental needs of the children.

Other significant factors that contribute to the susceptibility of some teenagers to gang influences are delinquency, arrest, or early contact with the police. Such students also tend to evidence chronic adjustment problems throughout their schooling such as truancy, acting out, or other aggressive and sometimes hostile behaviors. They tend to avoid school activities and maintain records of poor academic achievement, which may result in leaving school prematurely.

Unlike teens in low income areas, where friends or family members are in gangs or where they come in frequent contact with gang members, some teens in middle or upper-income communities are susceptible because of their underdeveloped social skills, their low resistance to peer influences, or their economically or socially deprived backgrounds. They tend, however, to be "streetwise" and to seek social control through any means available.

Teens who use drugs or live with a chemically dependent parent are also susceptible to gang influences. This latter characteristic, while one of the most obvious, is also one of the most disturbing because of the strong relationship between gangs and drug use/distribution. Addicted teens, particularly if they evidence additional characteristics of gang susceptibility, are prime candidates for gang involvement.

Obviously, no one characteristic is determinative; several of them may not suggest gang involvement. Any teen, however, who possesses a combination of these characteristics warrants watching and possible referral to the appropriate person(s) if gang involvement seems probable.

Figure 7–8

UNAUTHORIZED ABSENCE CONTACT RECORD

Student Name	Year	Counselor

Course	Instructor	Period

Unauthorized Absence # (✓)	Initiator	Action
( ) 1	Teacher	Call parent
( ) 2	Teacher	Call parent, implement consequence
( ) 3	Counselor	Contact student and parent
( ) 4	Dean	Contact parent, require Saturday detention
( ) 5	Dean	Conference to re-evaluate student status
( )	_____	_____

Date of Unauthorized Absence _____

Person Contacted _____

Contact Summary:

Action taken:

I am aware that if I am absent without authorization from class again I will receive the following consequence. A grade reduction may also be applied.

_____ Teacher consequence

_____ Conference

_____ Saturday detention

_____ Other: _____

Student signature	Date

Initiator signature	Date

Figure 7–9

BEHAVIOR REFERRAL

Log In _____
Log Out _____

Student's Name		Year	Sub/Area	Per/Time
Counselor	Date of Incident	Teacher		Date of Referral

Level I involves minor misbehavior on the part of the student and is usually handled by the teacher and sometime requires the intervention of the counselor. The purpose of this referral is to document Level I misconduct or report *Levels II, III or IV misconduct.*

Level I

CAP ☐ Cafeteria Disturbances
DRB ☐ Disturbances
EAA ☐ Excessive Absences
OBS ☐ Inappropriate Language
ICH ☐ No I.D.
☐ Other _____

Level II

FSD ☐ Absent from Detention
ACD ☐ Cheating/Lying
DIS ☐ Disrespect
PAR ☐ Driving/Parking Violations
GAM ☐ Gambling Card Playing
FOR ☐ Invalid Passes/Notes/Excuses
OCW ☐ Off Campus/Loitering
FGT ☐ Pushing/Shoving/Running
UNA ☐ U-Absence Study
☐ Other _____

Level III

FSD ☐ Absent Detention
SUB ☐ Drugs/Alcohol
FGT ☐ Fighting
DEC ☐ Gross Insubordination
DRB ☐ Inappropriate Behavior
OBS ☐ Profanity to Staff
UNA ☐ Repeated Absences
VAN ☐ Vandalism
SMO ☐ Tobacco Usage
☐ Other _____

Level IV

AST ☐ Assault/Battery
DTB ☐ Bomb Threats/Fire Alarm
DRB ☐ Disruptive Behavior
SUB ☐ Drugs/Alcohol
DTB ☐ Extortion
DTB ☐ Possession Weapons
TFT ☐ Theft
VAN ☐ Vandalism
☐ Other _____

- -

Description of Behavior (frequency, duration, intensity)

Figure 7–9, continued

Interventions Prior to Referral

DTP ☐ Discussion With Student
TTP ☐ Parent Contact
PCD ☐ Warning/Reprimand
DET ☐ Detention(s)
     ☐ Other

Referral Disposition:

    ☐ Documentation Only
    ☐ Further Intervention Requested (Describe)

_____

Signature

- -

Counselor/Dean Actions

DOC ☐ Documentation
ESS ☐ Essay/Assignment
DCP ☐ Conference with Students
CCT ☐ Conference with Teacher
APP ☐ Conference with Parent
RST ☐ Restriction from _____
DET ☐ Detention(s) _____
RIS ☐ Saturday Detention
ATP ☐ In-School Suspension
SUS ☐ Out-of-School Suspension
CON ☐ Special Education Consultation
     ☐ _____

Referral to:

RSW ☐ Social Worker
SCR ☐ Screening Committee
RSE ☐ Special Education
TMR ☐ Team
     ☐ _____

_____   _____

Signature   **Date**

White-Teacher's Copy   **Yellow-Dean's Copy**   **Green-Counselor Copy**

Figure 7–10

LEARNING REFERRAL

Logged In _____

Logged Out _____

Student: _____   **Counselor:** _____

Initiated By: _____   **Year in School:** _____

Class: _____ **Period:** _____   **Date of Referral:** _____

1. *Reason for Referral:* (Describe those behaviors, attitudes, habits, levels of achievement or production, and so forth about which you have concerns.)

2. *Assessment:* (Please comment on student skills, ability, appropriateness of placement, learning style, and so forth.)

3. *Interventions:* (What steps have you or others taken to intervene on behalf of this student, specific to the reason for referral?)

Disposition: **Comments:**

_____ A. Counselor Contact with Student

_____ B. Counselor Contact with Parent

_____ C. Referral to:

    _____ 1. Social Worker

    _____ 2. Screening Committee

    _____ 3. Special Education

    _____ 4. Other _____

_____ D. Consultation With:

_____

_____

_____ E. Other Interventions:

_____

_____

Signature: _____

Figure 7–11

TEACHER REFERRAL TALLY

Name of Teacher: _____

Learning Referrals

Date   *Reason for Referral*   *Previous Intervention*   *Disposition*

Attendance Referrals

Date   *Student's Name*   *Number of UA*   *Teacher Action*   *Disposition*

Behavioral Referrals

Date   *Description of Behavior*   *Prior Interventions*   *Disposition*

Figure 7–12

REFERRALS
(Departmental Summary)

Teachers	Students with UAs	Highest Number	Behavioral Referrals		Learning Referrals	
			Reason	Disposition	Reason	Disposition

Figure 7–13

ESTABLISHING LIMITS

Use this form during the first week of school to discuss with your students attendance and proper behavior in class. The expectations you establish with them should complement the all-school rules and regulations but should represent the starting point for appropriate behavior in class. This form and the process it involves should provide you and your students the chance to deal with student behavior proactively, in essence to cut off misbehavior "at the pass." In addition, as you already know, most of the research out there is telling us that students tend to follow rules and regs more willingly if they have had a hand in their development.

Please give me a copy of the form when you've completed it. I may need to make reference to it with one or more of your students as the year unfolds! Please give them copies, too! Thanks.

Attendance:

Mention the school policy first:

First unauthorized absence _____

Second UA _____

Third UA _____

Fourth UA _____

Subsequent UAs _____

What constitutes a tardy? _____

What happens if tardiness is persistent? _____

What is a reasonable expectation for the make-up of tests, quizzes, and homework

assignments when students cut classes? _____

Behavior:

Why is appropriate behavior important in the classroom? _____

What behaviors cannot be tolerated? _____

For each of these behaviors, what is a reasonable response from the teacher?

Behavior: _____   Response: _____

Behavior: _____   Response: _____

Behavior: _____   Response: _____

Behavior: _____   Response: _____

More as needed:

Figure 7–14

COMMENDATION

Student (Last Name first)

Subject

Advisory Teacher

Counselor

Date

Soph.　　Jr.　　Sr.
Grade to Date: _____

1. Participates in class effectively and enthusiastically.
   _____

2. Is prepared for class consistently.
   _____

3. Consistently tries to do his/her best.
   _____

4. Earned a(n) _____ on the most recent test/quiz.
   _____

5. Is an enjoyable presence in the class.
   _____

6. Exhibits outstanding leadership in class.
   _____

7. Exhibits an excellent understanding of this subject.
   _____

8. Recent work shows considerable improvement and increased effort.
   _____

9. Is to be congratulated for a job well done.
   _____

10. Helps create a positive environment for other students.
    _____

Comments

Teacher

Yellow-Parent/Pink-Counselor/White-Fr. Adv. Teacher/Blue-Classroom Teacher

Figure 7–15

CUTTING THROUGH THE RED TAPE

Sometimes the "system" prevents us from helping each other. My job is to do what I can to help the students and the teachers in this department be as successful as possible. To do that effectively, I may need your help at times identifying obstacles that sometimes get in the way. If you have had a problem getting to see me, making a schedule change, or finding the right place to get an answer to a question, use this form to bring the issue to my attention. Be sure to describe the circumstances of the situation and not to use names. This process is not to be used to "get someone" but to make it easier for students to get answers to their questions.

Thanks for your help. I promise to review your comments and get back to you right away.

What Are the Specifics of the Problem?

What Time of the Day Is Most Convenient for You to Talk?
(Please list your study halls, free period, or lunch period)

Figure 7–16

DEPARTMENTAL TUTORING

Students interested in volunteering their time and knowledge to be departmental tutors are invited to fill out this form and submit it to me by _____.
Please recognize that Early Bird tutors in our department must be at school 45 minutes before the start of the regular school day to work with the students who have been assigned to them. Tutors may be involved on a daily basis; it is a large commitment of their time. If you are willing to make such a commitment, please fill out this form and return it by the time specified at the top.

Name: _____

Year in School: _____

Subject Area Specialty: _____

Average Grades in Specialty While in H.S. _____

Have you been involved in any honors or advanced placement courses in your area of specialty? Specifically, what were they?

_____

_____

Thanks for your willingness to be involved in our tutoring program. Our school needs more students like you. We will be in touch soon regarding the need for an interview or our decision. Again, thanks.

Figure 7–17

EARLY BIRD TUTORING ASSISTANCE

Early Bird Tutoring Assistance Referral Form

(Persons referring students for EBTA tutoring are reminded that this form needs to be *completed on both sides entirely* and *signed by the tutee* before being submitted to EBTA for processing.)

Student: _____   *Course and Level:* _____

Counselor: _____   *Classroom Instructor:* _____

Tutee's Academic Grade: _____   Referred by: _____

Tutee's Year at DHS: _____   Today's Date: _____

Tutee's Parent/Guardian Name: _____

Home Address: _____   Town: _____ Zip: _____

Tutee's Telephones: Home: _____   Personal Phone: _____

Date of Parent Contact by Classroom Teacher/Counselor: _____

Parent Comments: _____

_____

_____

_____

_____

Reason(s) for Referral to Early Bird Tutoring Assistance

(There are differing reasons for referring students to EBTA for one-on-one tutoring sessions. Please mark as many of the following items as may be necessary.)

This student has not met (is not meeting) the academic expectations of this class in the following ways. . . .

_____ Being Prepared for Class   _____ Questionable Study Skills

_____ Completing Homework on Time   _____ Working Independently

_____ Completing Make-Up Work   _____ Preparing for Quizzes, Tests

_____ Comprehending What's Read   _____ Memorizing Terms, Vocabulary

_____ Being Accountable for Assigned   _____ Perseverance in Completing
        Work   Assigned Work

_____ Following Directions for   _____ Accurately Completing Steps in
        Written Assignments   Problem-Solving Processes

Figure 7–17, continued

(It is *very helpful* when the person initiating this form can provide the tutor with some specific direction(s) about where and how to begin with an individual tutee. Not all tutees come to tutoring sessions prepared, so having some idea about how to proceed does make a positive difference. Please use the following space to provide the tutor with any specifics you care to mention that will help make the tutoring sessions productive.)

_____

_____

_____

_____

_____

_____

To the Tutee

When this referral form is received by EBTA you will be called at home with specific information about your tutor and the mornings you will meet for tutoring sessions. In order for tutoring to work for *your personal benefit,* you need to be aware that *you are responsible* for attending the morning (7:30 AM through until 8:05 AM) tutoring sessions *regularly* and *on time.* Your tutor is *volunteering* to help you be more successful, after all. Your signature below tells us that you agree with what you have read in this paragraph and are willing to attend *regularly* and *on time.* Consistent *unexcused* absences from EBTA tutoring *could* result in your being dropped from the program.

Tutee's Signature: _____

Today's Date: _____

(Please call _____ or see _____ with any questions that may arise concerning the EBTA referral process. We want to do the best we can for *all* the tutors and tutees involved in Early Bird Tutoring Assistance.)

Figure 7–18

THE INS AND OUTS OF TUTORING

You have just assumed a very important responsibility. The student(s) who work with you will depend on you for knowledge of the subject area, the ability to share that knowledge, and a genuine willingness to help them do a better job in the class. The following are some time-tested suggestions that might help you in each of these areas:

Overview

You have become a departmental tutor because you have experienced some success in one or more subject areas, and you have just undertaken the responsibility to meet with someone who is struggling to achieve his or her own level of success. Recognize that much of your success resulted not only from your basic intelligence, but your ability to become academically independent. You will want to help your students do much the same thing, so don't *Enable* him or her by doing the work for him. Ask lots of questions and suggest ways for him to complete assignments, projects, or make-up work. Generally, a good question is "How can I help from where you're at now?" or "What do you plan to do about it?"

Just keep in mind that your ultimate responsibility is to become dispensable. Every student with whom you work should eventually be able to function very successfully without you. That's the biggest part of your job.

Responsibilities of the Tutor

First of all, these are not orders. They are responsibilities that you have undertaken by volunteering your time to help your schoolmates. If you have a problem with any one of them, see me.

Be on time. This one is really important!

Seek a replacement if you are unable to meet on certain days.

Be honest with your student. If you don't have an answer, say so—then check with us.

Communicate. Talk to me if you're having a problem.

Getting Started

1. Before your student arrives, ask me for the referral forms from the teacher and/or counselor. Be sure you read them to have a sense of the student's needs before starting work.

2. When the student arrives, introduce yourself and make a little small talk before actually getting to work.

3. Have the student tell you in his or her own words what the problem is. This is very important if he or she is to address it realistically.

4. Show the student the referral form to make sure both the teacher and the student are in agreement about the nature of the problem.

Figure 7–18, continued

5. Look at such things as the student's notebook and assignment book. He or she may need your help to get organized.

6. Conclude each session on a positive note and summarize what has been accomplished. Then talk about what each of you plans to do for the next session. Discuss materials that must be brought and assignments that must be completed.

The Nature of the Relationship

A positive relationship is very important if you are to help your student. Keep these suggestions in mind when developing one:

1. Don't be worried about an initial negative attitude from your student. He or she may be a little embarrassed or resistant to the whole idea. That will change as you get to know each other.

2. Exhibit a caring attitude. It does show in what you say and do.

3. Develop trust in your relationship. Will he or she be able to share confidences with you and feel free to talk?

4. Follow through on any promises made. Your student must have confidence in you.

5. Show that you understand his or her situation. Place yourself in your student's shoes and be empathetic.

6. Be sure to communicate clearly. If your student is having difficulty understanding you, don't blame him or her first. Ask yourself, "Am I expressing myself clearly? Is there a better way for me to say this?" Be an active listener.

Always keep in mind that it takes a long time to build a trusting relationship and a very short time to destroy one. Good Luck!

Figure 7–19

STUDENT TUTORS

The department is in need of volunteers who are willing to help their fellow students with their academic achievement. If you are accepted into the program, you will be needed sometime before the start of the regular school day to work with students who have been referred by a teacher for tutorial help. Students who have volunteered in the past have found the experience to be very rewarding. It is particularly valuable for those of you who are interested in education as a career.

If you would like to be involved in our tutoring program, please provide the following information and deposit the form in the department office. We will be in touch soon. Thanks for your help.

Student's Name: _____

Year in School: _____

Area(s) of this subject you are particularly well-qualified to tutor:

_____

_____

_____

_____

Again, thanks for your help!

Figure 7–20

ADULT TUTORS

It's time for our annual attempt to tap into the talents of our parent community. It's not enough that you give us such wonderful kids to work with; we also want *you!* Every year we enjoy the association with several parent volunteers who help our school in a variety of ways, from working in resource centers to tutoring students in specific subject areas.

We are seeking your help in the area of tutoring. If you are available at any time of the week to come to school for at least an hour, hopefully more, to work with students on the completion of projects or preparation for tests and quizzes, we would appreciate your help. If interested, please provide the following information and return the form to my office at your earliest convenience. In advance, thanks *a lot* for your help.

Parent Name: _____

Home Phone Number: _____

Areas of Specialty in this Subject Area:

_____

_____

_____

_____

Preferred Days and Times of Involvement:

_____

_____

Again, thanks for your help!

Figure 7–21

STUDENT AND ADULT TUTORS

The following are the names of student and adult tutors who have volunteered their time to be available to students who need help from someone to prepare for tests and quizzes and complete homework assignments and class projects. Recognize that these people have not volunteered their time to do the work for the student but to *help* him or her to better understand the material. You might share this list with your teacher or counselor to identify a tutor most appropriate for you. In addition, keep these points in mind:

1. During your first meeting with the tutor, discuss with him or her an appropriate meeting schedule, one that will accommodate your short-term as well as long-term needs for the course.

2. Make certain that the tutor is going to have the availability of time you require. Some students have time commitments of their own that could interfere.

3. Have the tutor meet with your teacher to identify any special needs that he or she should address with you.

4. Have the tutor maintain periodic contact with your teacher to accommodate special needs as they may arise.

Student Tutors	Subject Specialties	Phone No.

Figure 7–22

STUDY SKILLS

Student study skills are *not* unrelated to teacher behaviors.

1. **Kids can *learn* to think creatively!**
   Encourage them to:
   - Describe their feelings and apply what they have learned to some aspect of their lives.

     "How would you feel if. . . ?"

     "What are your feelings about. . . ?"

     "Of what importance is _____ to you in your life?"
   - Relate objects/thoughts as they come to mind.

     "What words come to mind when I say. . . ?"

     "What do you think of when you listen to. . . ?"

     "What do you think of when you see. . . ?"
   - Identify and describe.

     "Describe the facts of. . . ."

     "What did you observe specifically?"
   - Explore and predict alternatives concerning cause and effect.

     "How many different ways can you. . . ?"

     "What would happen if. . . ?"
   - Summarize what has been observed, heard, or experienced briefly.

     "Draw a picture which summarizes. . . ."

     "The point of view of the lecture was. . . ."

     "What title would you give this story?"

2. **Kids need clarity and specificity.**
   They must:
   - Receive concepts and directions logically/clearly.
   - Work with appropriate materials.
   - Understand objectives and expectations.

     "Today we will be looking at. . . ."

     "Yesterday we looked at. . . . How do you suppose ___ relates to ___?"

     "Last year you learned_____. Now it's time to. . . ."

     "If you are going to be able to _____, you must be able to_____."

3. **Kids must see the structure in the material to be learned.**
   They must:
   - *Not* have to guess the purpose of the lesson.
   - See that instruction moves smoothly from concept/skill to concept/skill.
   - Experience a definite beginning, middle, and end to the instructional session.
   - Be exposed to the natural structure that inheres in all bodies of knowledge.

     "Now that we understand _____, let's look at _____."

     "OK, let's wrap it up. To review, ..."

     "Now that we've seen the big picture, let's look at the specifics. First, ..."

Figure 7–23

REQUEST FOR SOCIAL WORK SERVICES

To: _____ **Date** _____

From: _____ **Counselor** _____

Re: _____ **Case Manager** _____
        Student

Year: _____ **Phone** _____

Services Requested: *Availability*

_____ Diagnostic Interviews   *Period*   *Assignment*

_____ On-going Casework Services   _____   _____

_____ Consultation   _____   _____

_____ Social History/Update,   _____   _____
         if necessary

Supporting Information:

Parent Informed? _____ Yes _____ No

   If no, who will inform? _____

Student Informed? _____ Yes _____ No

   If no, who will inform? _____

Assigned Social Worker _____ Date _____

Disposition _____ Date _____

Figure 7–24

CONFIDENTIAL
PEER HELPING REFERRAL FORM

Note: Persons referring students to the Peer Helping Program must discuss the referral with the student prior to submitting this form to the student's counselor.

This recommendation for peer helping services will remain confidential. PLEASE return this form to the Peer Helping mailbox in I-107.

Student: _____   **Referred by:** _____

Counselor: _____   **Today's Date:** _____

Year _____: _____   **Free Periods:** _____
(Study Hall, Lunch, Resource)

Home Phone #: _____

Reason(s) for Referral:

Note: Please be reminded that the Peer Helping Program is designed to be an early intervention for students who are exhibiting low levels of difficulty in the following areas: (please check all appropriate categories)

_____ academic pressure/stress   _____ family problems

_____ student/teacher conflict   _____ harassment/bullying by other students

_____ problems with friends   _____ adjusting to the class and/or school

_____ boyfriend/girlfriend relationships

_____ other (please describe) _____

_____

For Peer Helping Use Only:

Date referral received: _____

Step 1: Counselor's Recommendation: _____

_____

Step 2: Peer Helper Assigned: _____ Date: _____

Step 3: Number of Contacts: _____

Step 4: Summary of Outcome:

Figure 7–25

CONFIDENTIAL STATEMENT
(for Teacher/Student Problems)

This form is provided for students who have experienced a "situation" with a teacher and want to talk about it with someone. Because I am the likely "someone," I will need some information if I am to be helpful. Please provide the information below and leave the form with me or my secretary. I will be sure to contact you as soon as possible.

Your Name: _____ **Today's Date:** _____

Date and Time of the Incident: _____

Class, Period, and Teacher's Name: _____

_____

In Your Own Words, Please Describe What Happened:

It's OK to use my name: _____

I'd prefer that my name not be used: _____
                    (Please check one.)

Figure 7–26

ABSENCE RECORD

This is to inform you that the following student has accumulated 20 or more authorized and unauthorized absences for the current semester. Please call the student's home to identify the reasons for such an attendance pattern, indicate the student's achievements to date, including grades and completion of assigned work, and forward the information to the student's counselor. If I can be of assistance in any way, let me know.

Teacher's Name: _____ **Student's Name:** _____

Class: _____ *Period:* _____ *Absences:* _____

Grade to Date: _____ *Incomplete Work:* _____

_____

_____

Reasons for Absences:

Phone call made: (Date) _____

Referred to Counselor (Date) _____

Interventions Made by Counselor:

Counselor signature: _____ **Please return to:** _____

Figure 7–27

MEMOS

Date:

To: Special Education Department

Fr:

Re: Teacher Assistance

One of our teachers is having problems dealing with a particular class and has asked for assistance from a teacher in special education. I have worked with him for the past three months, visiting the class and discussing possible strategies with him in postobservation conferences. The unique perspective provided by special education should help complement my efforts. So I guess both he and I are hopeful that one of those special few you have in your department can spend a few periods team teaching with him. The experience should help resolve some of the problems in the class and will help him with his professional growth. We might even call it in-service.

I'll be in touch soon to discuss possibilities. Thanks.

Or

Date:

To: Special Education Department

Fr:

Re: Curriculum Revision

Our department's curriculum committee is about to get off the ground with a much-needed audit of our course offerings. Because we anticipate some significant changes—course revision, elimination, and addition—we want to involve as many perspectives as possible. Is someone from your department available to meet with the committee on an adhoc basis? The involvement may not be required for every meeting, just for a select few, to be determined in conjunction with the committee chair.

I'll be in touch soon to discuss possibilities. Thanks.

Figure 7–28

CONFIDENTIAL INFORMATION
(for Special Ed Mainstreamed Students)

Date:

To:

Fr: Special Education

Re: Student: _____

    The above-named student is enrolled this semester in your class. I thought you might find the following information helpful to assist you with the development of instructional strategies and materials.

1.

2.

3.

4.

5.

6.

7.

    If you should have any questions about the above information, please feel free to give me a call. If I am not available, I will be sure to get back to you.

_____
(Case Manager)

Figure 7–29

CONFIDENTIAL INFORMATION
(Completed Sample)

Date: March 3, 1995

To: Fred Thomas, Bruce Hightower, Carrie Hanson, Peggy Koehler, and Bud Sexmith

Fr: Special Education

Re: Student: _____Fred Wilson_____

The above-named student is enrolled this semester in your class. I thought you might find the following information helpful to assist you with the development of instructional strategies and materials.

1. Seat him near the front of the class. He is distracted by other students easily.

2. Fred is a young man who benefits considerably from extended time on tests.

3. Outline your expectations of his behavior very clearly, and stick to your guns. Fred has been known to test limits!

4. You may at times have to explain material for him more than once.

5. His parents appreciate contacts as needed. They are very helpful. A quick call will work miracles! Mom can be reached at home.

6.

7.

If you should have any questions about the above information, please feel free to give me a call. If I am not available, I will be sure to get back to you.

_____Margaret O'Reilly_____
(Case Manager)

Figure 7–30

NOTICE TO PARENT

Unsatisfactory _____
Failing   _____
Incomplete   _____

Student   (Last Name first)

Counselor

Subject

Date

Advisory Teacher

Soph.   Jr.   Sr.

Quarter Absences to Date _____

Grade to Date _____

Suggestions for Improvement

Comments

1. Increase quality of daily preparation for class.   _____

2. Improve study habits.   _____

3. Reduce absenteeism and/or tardiness.   _____

4. Stay on task in class.   _____

5. Improve behavior in class.   _____

6. Prepare carefully for tests and quizzes.   _____

7. Bring appropriate materials to class.   _____

8. Participate in all class activities.   _____

9. Seek additional help.   _____

10. Improve preparation on major assignments/projects.   _____

11. Complete assignments listed at right.   _____

Teacher
Telephone: _____ **Ext.** _____

White-Parent/Yellow-Counselor/Blue-Fr. Adv. Teacher/Pink-Classroom Teacher

© 1993 by Michael D. Koehler

Figure 7–31

NOTICE OF FAILURE

Mathematics Department

Notice of Course Failure
First Semester

Counselor: _____

2nd Quarter Grade _____

Exam Grade _____

_____ has failed _____

Department Recommendation:

This student

_____ must continue to Essential Math 2.

_____ may continue to Essential Math 4.

_____ may continue to Algebra 2, III.

_____ is recommended to transfer to Algebra 2, III.

_____ may continue to Geometry 2, III.

_____ is recommended to transfer to Adv. Algebra.

_____ may continue to the second semester of the course.

_____ should drop this course.

Comments:

Classroom Teacher _____

These forms are to be given to _____ as soon as possible,

but no later than _____ .

PLANNING FOR SUCCESS

Several years ago, when I still had administrative stars in my eyes and was convinced that the surest way to resolve a problem was to convene a committee, I found myself chairing a task force to study the implementation of variable modular scheduling. It was a popular topic at the time, operational in some schools, studied in others. Ours was one of the others. The committee was a high priority for the school year and was composed of a few teachers, a couple department chairs, and the building principal. It provided one of my lasting professional memories.

Early in our very first meeting, I asked the principal why we were convened to study this issue. His answer? "Mike, why do you always ask *why?* It's a great idea that will resolve a lot of our scheduling problems." If not convinced, at least intimidated by his argument, I shut up and, along with the other members of the committee, embarked on a year-long study of variable modular scheduling.

Several school visits and a 170-page resource book later, we found ourselves planning how to present the information to the faculty for their reaction. Someone recommended that we distribute the resource books prior to a faculty meeting and that the principal lead a discussion of our ideas at the meeting. Said the principal: "If I suggest the idea to the faculty, there's no way it gets off the ground. Mike, you lead the discussion." A principal's argument can be very convincing to a young teacher, so I acquiesced again and found myself standing in front of a faculty of 150 teachers to extol the merits of variable modular scheduling.

The meeting went well enough, but when the faculty returned the forms we provided them for a reaction, an overwhelming majority indicated that it wasn't a topic they cared to pursue. Their reaction was a death knell for a concept that we had been struggling for a year to bring to life. The last of those resource books has long since been cleaned out of the school vault. Some of the members of that committee have retired; the rest find themselves in the same school, following the same schedule that dictated our committee meetings some twenty years ago. And I'm still asking why.

Ours was not the only school that experienced such problems. Let's admit it, educators fall in line somewhere behind our nation's budget makers when it comes to planning. The *New World Dictionary* defines a plan as "A scheme or program for making, doing, or arranging something." My experience has taught me that an *educational* plan is "a standard that can be used later to document unrealized intentions." You see, very little changes in education. In part, the problem results from what I call education's "Bandwagon Syndrome."

Educational trends come and go, and then usually come again. They march along education's parade route in a succession of bandwagons attracting excited onlookers. The most excitable among us find one, jump aboard, and anticipate the thrill of sudden discovery. Some of us actually believe we're going somewhere, but when the ride seems headed nowhere, we finally jump off and are left only with the prospect of finding our way back to things as they were.

As indicated elsewhere in this book, such trends usually are well-researched and conceptually sound, so sound, in fact, that some educators use them as immediate solutions to persistent problems. We educators are pretty good at identifying solutions; we get a lot of help. Some of the trends have even made dents in our systems, but none has provoked their elaborate reconstruction. Maybe that's because we're not very good at identifying problems. Prepackaged solutions, no matter how exciting they seem, just don't work for poorly defined problems.

This section looks at an effective planning process, from the identification of problems to the selection of appropriate solutions. It looks at the budget as a planning tool and discusses the importance of recordkeeping, particularly for the monitoring of solutions. It provides a set of principles that you will use to guide your administrative behavior as well as your planning activities.

IDENTIFYING THE PROBLEM

A colleague used to scoff at my need to take the time to identify problems by saying: "When you find yourself up to your armpits in alligators, what do you have to study? You ought to *know* you have a problem!" My response? "Maybe if you had studied the situation earlier, you wouldn't find yourself up to your armpits in alligators!" Planning is proactive; surprise is reactive.

You and I must eliminate surprises if education as a social institution is to survive. It's up to you and me to guarantee it. The best way to assure survival is to anticipate the unexpected by guaranteeing planning processes that make alligator omelets instead of alligators. If I have to wrestle an alligator, I want to do it when it's still in the egg.

The first step, therefore, is to identify our problems when they're still small and manageable. Easier said than done? Maybe, but if department chairs commit their departments to routine planning processes, they will uncover problems that, with immediate attention, can be resolved much easier than if they are allowed to grow. And the best place to start is with a definition of the problem.

To get a handle on just how good teachers are at identifying a problem, ask a colleague to give you a definition of the term. Compare the answer to this one: "A problem is a measurable or observable discrepancy between 'what is' and 'what should be.'" It's the tightest definition I've seen. Figure 8–1, *What is a Problem?*, presents it visually. Use the figure in meetings to explain the concept.

The point is, most teachers are solution-oriented. They are so quick to implement prepackaged solutions that they usually overlook the essential requirements of a problem. Consider these typical responses from teachers asked to identify needs/problems:

- We need more in-service training programs.
- We need longer periods to accommodate the English curriculum.
- We need another dean to handle the increase in discipline problems.
- We need new textbooks.

Although the implementation of some of these ideas might make life somewhat easier in schools, they don't do much to identify problems. They are all *solutions*. More in-service training programs may introduce us to new ideas; longer class periods may provide time for additional activities; another dean might hand out more detentions; and new textbooks might provide a different look at the subject matter.

But what problems do they resolve? Consider just the need for another dean. What if the school took the time to study the problem and decided: "Within the past three years, Jackson High School has experienced a 32% increase in class cutting and a 45% increase in tardiness to class?" This kind of statistic, especially when combined with analyses of other aspects of student behavior, provides a problem statement that offers a sense of direction for the school.

Obviously, the school needs to reduce the incidence of class cutting and tardiness. Another dean might help address the problem; more likely, however, an adequate solution will involve much more. It will provoke answers to such questions as "Why are students cutting more classes?" "What factors have contributed to the increase in tardiness to class?" "What must we do as a department or school to assure improved attendance?"

Once the department or school answers these questions, it might decide to phone the home at the first class cut, invite the parents to school for a meeting if the student cuts again, or develop an *in-school* suspension area for persistent violators. These are less expensive solutions and more responsive to the actual problem. The school that hires a new dean allows an unidentified problem to persist and doesn't do much to promote improved learning for students.

Focusing on Values

The identification of problems is complicated further by the failure of some departments to seriously consider "what is" or to sustain a focus on "what should be." Identifying "what should be" is relatively easy. The school's philosophy and objectives proclaim it for everyone to see and hear. The department chair's job is to assure that teachers see and hear it often enough to focus on the *school's* values more than their own.

Consider the relatively common example of teachers who refuse to accept late assignments from students, even if only a day late. They usually reason that students should learn to complete their tasks on time, that they will develop self-discipline as a result of the classroom policy. They forget, however, that the more important value in their departments is to teach the students the subject matter.

The teacher who focuses on the subject matter accepts the students' assignments, even if they are late, makes appropriate corrections so that they learn from their work, *then* grades them down, and may even fail them for being late. Such a combination of personal and normative values enables the students to learn the materials *as well as* the importance of being punctual. Teachers who sometimes confuse their personal values with the normative values of the school need the help of a good department chair to focus on "what should be." In fact, this may be one of the top two or three responsibilities of the department chair, to sustain a focus on the normative values of the school and department.

The Mission Statement

You know as well as I do that statements of philosophy gather dust between visits from accreditation associations. Each 7 years or so, they are resurrected from relative obscurity, assigned to a committee, reworded somewhat, and included in the accreditation results.

They deserve much more. Mission statements such as the one in Figure 8–2 provide a sense of direction for schools and establish a tone that promotes excellence. This particular philosophy has been the guiding light for the Deerfield/ Highland Park School District in Illinois for more than 20 years. It has undergone periodic revision, but its missions are framed and posted all over the schools and are used by department chairs as standards for planning and evaluation activities. You might even develop one for your department, frame it and post it in your department office prominently, and provide forms for teachers, students, and parents to identify issues that may deviate from the departmental missions. The form, *"Issues to Look At,"* in Figure 8–3 has worked well for me. I didn't receive copies every day; in fact, I received them only a few times a year. But when I did, they signaled an important aspect of "what is" and provided needed information for the future identification of problems.

Problems within the System

As indicated, identifying "what should be" is not difficult. Schools are very good at establishing standards, "visions" for the future. Their difficulties involve translating such standards into teacher and student behaviors and keeping the "visions" in focus. Nothing is more destructive of a vision than the day-to-day routine and the recurring problems it provides. No matter how small these problems are, their immediacy consumes time.

It's important for department chairs to sustain a focus on the school's missions and to encourage teachers, students, and parents to respond to needs assessments and other forms and processes that result in problem identification. Several have been provided in earlier sections and can do much to get a handle on "what is." Department chairs should also consider reviewing the recommendations made in the reports of classroom observations. If several teachers received similar recommendations, the department chair has a fairly clear indication of "what is" regarding classroom instruction and can use it to identify a potential problem and to suggest one or more themes for in-service activities the following year.

The chair who fails to address such issues on a department-wide basis disregards one of the exhortations of W. Edwards Deming, the patriarch of what is currently known as Total Quality Management. Deming advises managers to accept the fact that 80 to 90% of problems in organizations are systemic. That is, they are related not to individuals but to elements within the system. Department chairs, then, are well-advised to look beyond the resistance or incapacity of some teachers to find problems *in the system* that may be promoting that resistance or incapacity.

In essence, when something goes wrong in the department, the good administrator looks for the nearest mirror to ask, "What did I do to contribute to this issue?" or "What is it about the department that has caused this situation?" The department chair who accepts Deming's observations will use the answers to these questions as further indications of "what is" and as guides to the discovery of the real problems. The department chair who fails to seek the larger problems within the system may be inclined to blame others for problems that occur.

A Story about Systemic Problems.   I am asked sometimes to lead in-service programs for high schools. I recall walking into one school about an hour before such a presentation and meeting the superintendent of schools in the principal's office. We small-talked for a couple minutes and finally he said, "So you're the guy who's going to lead today's in-service."

"Yes," I said, "I'm the guy."

Winking at the principal, he shot back, "Well, good luck with this group. You're going to need it." And then he walked out the door.

He was right. By and large, the audience was surly and unresponsive. After about half an hour of planned presentation, I stopped and asked them simply to talk about their school. Many of them remained surly, but most of them were anything but unresponsive. The floodgates opened, and stories of managerial control, poor communication, threatening evaluations, a recent salary strike, and teacher dismissals poured out.

Perceived by the superintendent and principal as resistant and oppositional, this was a faculty that was afraid. These were not teachers who were creating problems for the system; this was a system that was creating problems for the teachers. Someone in the school had to look for that mirror, introspect a little, and accept Deming's insistence that 90% of the problems in organizations are systemic.

Focus on "What" for Problem Identification

Searching for problems is hard work. It's a whole lot easier to blame someone else than study an issue and risk self-analysis. We forget, however, that it's easier to climb the ladder yourself than to try to push someone else to the top. Always look at yourself first, then the system, then the people within the system. My experience has taught me that if I devise ways to look at things in that order, most of the time I'll find the problem in me or in the system.

Also keep in mind that the identification of problems involves the word "what."

- "What" is the current situation?
- "What" factors are interfering with the realization of our goals?
- "What" is it about this program that's getting in the way?
- "What" expectations in this department are causing those behaviors?

A focus on the "what" of a situation leads to the identification of problems. A premature consideration of "how" leads to solutions. Reconsider our earlier example: "We need another dean to handle the increase in discipline problems." Which of the two questions does this statement address, "what" or "how?" "What" is it about this situation that is causing us a problem? Or "How" will we resolve the problem? When we judge issues within the light of these two questions, we can see that another dean answers the question "how." It resolves an unidentified problem.

We do this too often in education. Department chairs must safeguard against this tendency among their teachers. That's why the form in Figure 8–3 makes such specific reference to particulars. Even when an occasional teacher uses the form to identify a "how," you must correct the process by probing the issue further with the teacher to find the *problem*.

Let's use an example throughout the remainder of this section to illustrate these points. Figure 8–4 provides the form, ***Issues to Look At,*** submitted by a senior English teacher. It does a nice job identifying the "what" of the situation and serves as a good starting point for some worthwhile planning.

WHERE DO WE WANT TO BE? _____

The information in Figure 8–4 does indeed identify a problem. Enrollment in senior English shows a steady decline and ultimately may require the dismissal of a teacher. Because the information provided by the teacher doesn't suggest any solutions, it focuses on the specifics of the problem and provides a clear sense of direction for the department.

This direction would not have been as clear had the teacher indicated that the department: "Needs to develop a newsletter to send to parents to explain the importance of senior English for college-bound seniors" or "Needs to develop a handout for junior English teachers to distribute to their students at registration time encouraging them to register for senior English." Each of these is a solution which may or may not resolve the problem.

Until we know the characteristics of a problem, we are unable to identify the most appropriate solution or combination of solutions. As important, if we identify a problem correctly, our objectives are easier to develop. In fact, we might find them in the problem statement. The objective we might develop with the teacher who submitted the form in Figure 8–4 might be to increase the enrollment in senior English by 49 students, in essence to get enrollment back to where it was five years ago.

This depends, of course, on other factors that may relate to the situation. The department may have introduced an etymology or a creative writing course that is taking students away from the senior English classes. If that is the case, the "problem" is understood more easily and doesn't warrant a great deal of attention, unless the department wants to increase enrollment anyway.

If no new courses have been introduced and both you and the department can think of no other acceptable variables that might have an impact on enrollment, then you have to start searching for unacceptable variables. The ***Search for Solutions*** in Figure 8–5 will provide the framework. It asks the seven questions that must be answered for any planning activity. Depending on the nature of the problem, some of the questions will be less important than others.

The problem with student enrollment in senior English, for example, may not require exhaustive answers to most questions, but you will want to develop an objective and seek alternative solutions to realize it. Because of their complexity, other problems, such as modifying the curriculum, developing a supervision format, or improving reading achievement may require a comprehensive look at *each* of the questions, which involves the entire department.

For our senior English problem, the objective can be found in the problem statement. The problem, as identified by the teacher, indicated a 17% decline in student enrollment within the past five years. After a preliminary look at all the variables involved in the situation, you may agree that it is a problem and that the objective should be "Within the next two years, the English department will increase enrollment in senior English by a minimum of 5% per year." This will be our target for action and the standard we will use to determine the success of eventual solutions.

How Do We Get There?

Now is the time to look at solutions. "How" do we accomplish the "what" of our initial planning? An obvious first step is to brainstorm a variety of alternative solutions. This should be done without restriction or judgment. You and I both know that some of the best solutions sound the most ridiculous when first mentioned. With a slight overhaul, these often get the job done. What is needed, then, is a process to identify the alternatives and to select one or combine several to resolve the problem.

Figure 8–6, ***Let's Brainstorm***, provides an excellent way to brainstorm alternatives. It gives departmental planners the opportunity to think about and identify alternative solutions without the possible distraction of colleagues laughing up their sleeves. In addition, because the form can be completed at home, planners can give dimension to an idea before colleagues have the chance to prejudge it.

Figure 8–7, ***Solution Analysis***, provides a follow-up reproducible that looks at each solution and aims at consensus. It explores the operational requirements of each solution, any negative consequences that may result from implementation, and the solutions' contributions to the realization of the planning objective. After using the form to analyze each suggested solution, the planning group (it may be a "group" of two) should indicate a rating for the solution in relation to the others that have been suggested. Following the ratings of all the suggested solutions, one or a combination of several can be selected by the group.

Consider the following examples for the senior English enrollment problem:

- Because senior English is not required for graduation, reassign the current teachers to the required courses and give senior English classes to the more popular but equally qualified teachers in the department.
- Modify the curriculum to make it more exciting and relevant while maintaining its quality.
- Circulate statistics and statements from university officials regarding senior English as an admissions requirement and as necessary preparation for college work.
- Change senior English from a full-year course to a series of one-quarter courses which focus on differing but related learning experiences.
- Eliminate ability grouping across the senior English curriculum and incorporate cooperative learning experiences for all students.
- Petition the Board of Education to make the course a requirement for graduation.

A group of teachers who have a vested interest in the course if likely to brainstorm more solutions, perhaps several better than those mentioned here. Let's assume, however, that the planning group has developed its list, used the forms provided in this section to select the best solution(s), and has decided that curriculum change and the statements from university officials will provoke the fewest negative side effects and promote increased student enrollment.

Monitoring Solutions

The next steps, then, involve implementing solutions and monitoring their progress. The success of solutions is relatively easy to monitor when planning has involved measurable or observable objectives. The senior English objective was to increase enrollment by 5% within each of the next two years. If such increases aren't realized, the solutions aren't working. At this point, notice what happens.

The "what should be" of our solution(s) was a 5% increase in student enrollment. The "what is" of our current situation is another decrease, this time of only 1%. To that extent, we can assume that some elements within our solution(s) may be working, but we still have a problem. It's time, then, for another planning activity.

Effective planning, then, is cyclical. It starts with the proper identification of a problem and concludes with the monitoring of solutions, which may identify another problem. On the other hand, monitoring may affirm the success of solutions, at which point we seek other problems to resolve. The reproducible **Progress Update** in Figure 8–8 provides an excellent monitoring process. It focuses on the measurable or observable evidence of completion, the persons responsible for implementation, and the current status of the original problem. As such, the information can be used by the department chair in monthly and annual reports. It also can be used as part of the evaluation of individual staff members at the end of the year.

Don't Take the Easy Way Out. Compromise? That's trying to stay warm with a coat that's too small. It doesn't quite do the job, but it's better than nothing. And educators are wearing small coats. They are fine coats, of good fabric and well-constructed, but no longer stylish. Outsiders occasionally laugh at our appearance in them; some even criticize us for our apparent unwillingness to change them.

But we wear them anyway because they are all we have. Compromise has become a professional way of life for us. Reconsider the parade of trends that come and go. Some have shifted the building blocks of what we do, but none has provoked an elaborate reconstruction of our jobs and workplaces. Several have provoked compromises, the kind that result not in the school's primary program but in the development of ancillary programs that provide needed but generally insufficient change.

Changes rarely occur within the primary programs in most schools. Curricula, methods of instruction, organizational arrangements, decision-making processes, and delivery of services to students are fundamentally unchanged in schools within the past few decades. Consider, as just one example, the study skills that students need to succeed in different curricula.

Study skills in geography are different from those in algebra. Studying an American literature anthology is different from conducting a biology lab experiment. Study skills are so critical to learning that the subject recently received broad examination in the literature. Did it provoke widespread change in most schools? Did it encourage a majority of teachers to include time in their classrooms to give students the skills they need to master their subjects?

Perhaps in some; certainly not in all, not even in most. Several conscientious teachers read the information and did what they could to work more closely with their students to improve their study skills. Most disregarded the information and proceeded with business as usual. A few immersed themselves in the information, recognized it as an important solution to an obvious need, introduced needed changes in their classrooms, and even developed ancillary programs for their schools.

Their administrators applauded them because the programs were relevant, consistent with the literature, and proclaimed to the community loudly that their schools were on the cutting edge of change. They pumped a few dollars into the programs, gave one or more teachers released time to coordinate them, and invited students to seek them out when they needed help with their study skills. Some schools even encouraged teachers to refer students for specific help.

Having done so, the school pats itself on the back and stakes its claim to the forefront of American education. And no one in the school recognizes that the new program is little more than an expression of an unresolved problem in the school's primary program. The students who really need help with their study skills rarely refer themselves, and the teachers who should be teaching study skills in their classrooms now feel they don't have to—because of the program.

At this point, the study skills program has become a *part of the problem.* So it is with many, maybe most, ancillary programs in schools. Their existence responds to a need but doesn't resolve it, except in the minds of the teachers and administrators, who are convinced that student study skills have been accommodated. Such self-deception regarding ancillary programs simply reaffirms George Bernard Shaw's assertion in *Man and Superman* that "change is an illusion."

System theorists may think Shaw's belief extreme, but they acknowledge that systems, *by definition,* are resistant to change. Systems develop steady states that seek only the status quo. It follows, then, that schools find it easier to develop ancillary programs than to change the primary system. Department chairs and administrators must ask themselves a few important questions when involved in program planning:

- Who supports this program?
- Why do they support it?
- What does it do exactly?
- What experiences are provided by this program?
- Do these experiences *extend, modify,* or *replace* elements in the primary program?

This last question is the most critical. The answer to it helps determine if curriculum, instruction, or school organization are being affected. Then planners must ask, "If they are not, should they be?" If the problem exists in the primary program, most of it should be resolved in the primary program. That's perhaps the biggest irritation when identifying problems. Someone invariably expects us to do something about them. Many schools have discovered that the easiest way to do that is with an ancillary program.

It is not the best way. An ancillary program to assist students with their study skills probably doesn't affect the majority of students, certainly not the majority of those who most need help. Similarly, ancillary programs involving collegial supervision for teachers may or may not be functionally integrated within the professional development activities of the entire staff. If they are not, they probably won't influence the instructional strategies of teachers who most need the help. Again, at this point, the ancillary program is less a solution for the problem and more an indication of the problem itself.

An ancillary tutoring program for low-achieving students often gives tacit permission to teachers to leave immediately at the end of the school day. An ancillary study skills program gives tacit approval to teachers to disregard the topic in the classroom, where it is most needed and where it can be presented to every student. An ancillary peer supervision program gives supervisors and administrators tacit encouragement to emphasize evaluation over formative supervision with teachers. A writing resource center for students gives tacit approval to teachers in all subject areas to disregard planned instruction on writing skills. And so it goes.

Each of us must ask ourselves to what extent should there be the development of ancillary programs: student study skills programs, peer supervision programs, writing workshops, tutoring programs, signal problems within the school's primary programs. Then we must ask the tough questions. Should we find more time during the day, possibly after school, for teachers to tutor students? How do we incorporate study skills into classroom instruction? How do we emphasize writing skills across the school's curriculum?

How can supervisors work more closely with collegial groups and individual teachers to assure their formative growth? Without the knowledge and focus of answers to such questions, schools everywhere will expend their efforts only on the periphery of substantive change, and they will allow the critics of education to continue shooting at stationary targets.

THE BUDGET AS A PLANNING DOCUMENT _____

The budget—a mathematical confirmation of our worst fears. No educator ever has enough money. Spending wisely, therefore, is one of the department chair's biggest responsibilities. Wise spending is always goal-related. Money is one of the tools that helps us realize our purposes.

Unlike businesses, that *earn* their budgets, schools operate on *deserved* budgets. They receive tax monies and donations from local communities and use it to maintain allocations that remain fairly constant from year to year. Such "promises" of money hold the potential for abuse. Spenders are sometimes quick to "use up" their allocations before the year ends in order to assure a similar or better allocation next year.

Department chairs avoid such budgetary abuses when they ask teachers to relate budget requests to annual goal statements. Certainly not all budget requests relate to goal statements. Some expenditures on supplies and material are fixed costs that change only if budget-minded visionaries in the department can buy them cheaper. Most others, however, can be related to professional goals.

When requesting budget items from members of your department, therefore, use the budget request memo, *It's Budget Time Again!*, in Figure 8–9. Include a copy of each teacher's goals for the school year and a copy of their budget requests from the previous year. As indicated on the form, not every item must relate to a goal statement, but those that do are more defensible when departmental requests come under administrative review.

Distribute the forms in a department meeting to review the process and explain any changes in that year's budget picture. School budgets are as dependent on the state and local community as any other part of the educational program. The availability of dollars can change as quickly as a teenager's behavior. Department chairs, therefore, must explain changes in the school's financial picture and encourage teachers to operate successfully within them. Because most budget planning in schools occurs in the spring of the year, the process provides excellent additional opportunities for program planning. You might even conduct needs assessments a few weeks prior to budget discussions.

Once the forms in Figure 8–9 have been received, you should review them, meet with individuals or groups of teachers to discuss significant or questionable items, and plan to incorporate appropriate elements into your department's budget document. Because it serves as one of your most significant planning activities for the school year, the completed budget should be discussed in another department meeting before submission for administrative approval.

The goals included in *Program Description and Goals* in Figure 8–10 should be the first items in the document and the first to be discussed in the meeting. This discussion accomplishes at least three things: one, it provides another chance to discuss and reaffirm the importance of the department's goal statements for the coming school year; two, it shows that you have incorporated the intentions of staff members into departmental planning; and, three, it relates the budget to departmental planning, a necessary link when trying to increase budget allocations for your department.

The remainder of the document should include specific departmental requests, some from the teachers, some from you. The reproducible forms in the following figures are very helpful for categorizing specific requests. Most of them are self-explanatory, but the following is a brief description of each:

- *Figure 8–11, Capital Equipment, Additional.* Each request should be specific and probably should be in priority order. Make sure the person who reads the form has a clear understanding of the equipment requested. Any room or building renovations or installation requirements should be listed on the next form. Remember, this form is for equipment in addition to what you already have in the department.

- *Figure 8–12, Capital Equipment, Replacement.* This form is for replacement of capital equipment and for renovation or installation.

- *Figure 8–13, Expendables.* This form is for any instructional supplies, items from central stores, student travel other than field trips, or supplies for teacher rooms. Again, items should be listed specifically. Any confusion caused by nonspecific requests usually results in denial of funds.

- *Figure 8–14, Expendables, Equipment Rental or Repair.* Use this form to identify equipment that needs repair or that needs to be rented. In some instances, purchase of equipment is unnecessary and, if rented, can result in considerable savings to the district.

- *Figure 8–15, Professional Travel.* List all travel requests on this form. This form is to be used for conferences, conventions, workshops, or any other kind of professional travel approved by you.

- *Figure 8–16, Library Expendables.* This form, after approved, should go to the person responsible for the school library. It involves all printed materials and audio-visual supplies and equipment that ultimately will be housed in the library.

- *Figure 8–17, Budget Projected Planning.* Use this form to project expenditures for the next three years. The best planning involves long-range projections. You will not be requesting these items on this form; you will be preparing the way for future requests. This probably will be one of the most important forms in your department's budget document and the one that will require the most collaboration within the department.

Figures 8–10 through 8–17 will constitute your complete budget document. It will include the input of every member of your department and reflect the planning that has taken place throughout much of the year. More important than the document itself is the process you followed to develop it. It *should* convince the administration of your financial needs; it *will* convince the members of your department that you are all working collaboratively to seek the best for them and their students.

THE ART OF GRANTS _____

Unless yours is a particularly generous school system, your departmental budget rarely meets your needs. Like most other department chairs, you'll want to supplement it. Grants are a ready source of revenue, overlooked frequently by most public school teachers. Professors in many universities are hired for their ability to supplement the university coffers with grants from a wide range of sources.

Obviously, the bigger the grant, the longer the proposal. University professors may have the time to organize 100+ pages of grant proposals. You probably don't. I say "probably" because good department chairs make commitment and dedication visible every day by the way they use their time. Some of you, therefore, may be inclined to try your hand at 100+ page proposals. The point is, you don't have to.

An Example. A few years ago, I was working closely with a local junior high school principal trying to find ways to improve the communication between his school and our high school. Cooperative planning is difficult enough in unit school districts; in independent school districts it is virtually impossible. So Al (Al Cohen, principal of Caruso Junior High School in Deerfield, Illinois) and I met several times to find ways to promote increased interaction between his staff and ours.

Our principal strategy was to find teachers in each building who were interested in working on collegial teams to supervise each other's teaching. We reasoned that junior high and secondary teachers would benefit from:

- Watching each other use different strategies to accommodate the varying cognitive levels of their students;
- Alternating their time between the two buildings to see "how the other half lives;"
- Experiencing the different challenges confronting junior and senior high teachers;
- Getting a closer look at each other's curricula;
- Getting to know each other better in order to make future communication easier.

The idea caught on. Each of us found several volunteers who wanted to try the program and enjoyed the support of our respective district administrators. Our next step, then, was to find the money for the substitute teachers that would be needed to release the teachers to visit each other's classrooms. We also wanted to tie in two local consultants to provide in-service activities for the teachers. The total cost for the program was $2500, certainly not beyond the fiscal capability of our two districts but an add-on that *might* not be funded by them.

We decided to apply for a small grant through the Educational Consolidation and Improvement Act, Chapter Two. The 6-page form provided by the Regional Superintendent of Schools took only an hour to complete and, ultimately, resulted in a grant to our two schools to implement the program. The entire process involved only 3 or 4 meetings for Al and me and a 6-page proposal. But it also resulted in a $2500 grant, an enthusiastic response from the involved teachers, and kudos galore for the two of us for developing and financing such an important program for our two districts.

The "What" of Proposal Writing.   Let's look first at the kinds of grants available to you. Federal, state, and local governments provide approximately half the grants given to most schools. The *Federal Register* is the primary source to identify available funds from the federal government. The *Catalogue of Federal Education Grants* is another good source. Perhaps the best source, however, is the information you'll receive by contacting your Regional and State Superintendents' Offices and asking them for information on state and regional grants.

They will provide information about the types of grants available and the processes needed to receive them. Follow their instructions very carefully. Grant writing is an activity absolutely dictated by their rules. Read these rules very carefully, then do justice to the grant proposal.

The "How" of Proposal Writing.   Most proposals require very specific information about:

- a statement of the problem, the target population involved, and the proposed solution;
- the objectives of the proposal;
- the activities that correspond with each objective; and
- the evaluation design.

It's also wise to provide a review of the literature that is pertinent to your proposal and perhaps a copy of the needs assessment that you used to identify the problem. Remember as well that most funding agencies will not fund workshop registration fees, salaries for additional staff, office or secretarial help, extensive consultant fees, or food for meetings. Also keep these few additional suggestions in mind.

Don't try to make a financial killing. Funding agencies usually offer finite amounts anyway, and they are interested primarily in cost effectiveness and your future ability to fund the project yourself. Be sure to explain the correspondence between the objectives of your project and the goals of the funding agency. Refer to these objectives frequently throughout your proposal. Reviewers often like to relate various parts of the proposal to its objectives. Make it as easy as possible for them.

General Guidelines for Proposal Writing

Remember to read the proposal form very carefully. If you overlook one key section, you might compromise an otherwise excellent proposal. Avoid educational lexicon when writing the proposal. State your position clearly and simply. You want the funding agency to understand the purposes of your request, not stand in awe of your vocabulary.

Be sure to justify the personnel who will be involved in the project and to highlight the expertise of the people who will have primary responsibility. Heed all deadlines and make the proposal presentable, bound if possible. Identify the varying populations that will benefit from it. The more, the better. Funding agencies prefer to support proposals that reach out to large numbers of people.

Finally, the proposal will be rejected if it suggests nothing new or is weak conceptually. Wherever possible, validate your program or research plan with empirical evidence and/or expert opinion. Refer to these sources often. They are perhaps the most important part of the proposal's selling points. You can also expect a rejection if the proposal is unfocused or unclear regarding its methodology. Lay everything out chapter and verse.

Once you establish a relationship with your regional and state offices of education and become familiar with the variety of grants available to you, you'll apply for more and more of them. And if you don't succeed with your first couple attempts, keep trying. Accept the first few rejections as learning experiences; and, sooner or later, you'll be supplementing your departmental budget with grants that will underwrite significant activities in your department.

GENERAL PLANNING PROCEDURES

This final section discusses a few "nuts and bolts" activities for your department and provides several reproducibles that will help with their coordination. These reproducibles are provided in no particular order and relate to planning only to the extent that their use avoids rather than resolves problems.

A little forethought can help you to avoid major problems. That's why it's a good idea to maintain an inventory of everything in your department and to share it at the beginning of the year with your staff. The **Room Inventory** form in Figure 8–18 provides a simple format that enables you to maintain a yearly account of the equipment and supplies for which you and your staff are responsible. The form also provides ready information at budget time to document possible equipment needs.

You will also want to provide a calendar for your teachers and the administration that outlines the year's activities. Figure 8–19, **Monthly Calendar,** provides a reproducible that can be used each year to identify:

- the opening and closing days of the school year
- in-service days
- vacations
- planned field trips
- conferences and conventions
- days and times of department meetings
- dates and times of faculty meetings
- due dates for teacher goals
- curriculum submissions
- final exam schedule
- due dates for approval of final exams

- administration dates of other tests such as the PSAT, SAT, and ACT.
- evening and weekend student activities.

In addition, the calendar can be individualized for teachers to indicate the dates and times of:

- classroom visitations
- end-of-the-year evaluation conferences
- periodic meetings to discuss progress toward goals
- informal "sit-downs" to talk about "how things are going"

You will be able to come up with many more pieces of information to include in the calendar. After using it for a short time, you'll discover, as I did, that it virtually eliminates the "Gee, no one told me" syndrome. More importantly, you'll see that teachers come to depend on it and are grateful to receive it. It provides them with the opportunity to plan ahead, too. I developed one each month for the staff; that way, the information it provided didn't somehow "get forgotten."

Teachers also appreciate being notified of the days when school has been cancelled. When heavy snow or a power failure at school provides an unexpected day off, the **Telephone Chain** in Figure 8–20 can make your job a whole lot easier. Early in the year, distribute this form to the staff and tell them to keep it on hand in the event school is cancelled unexpectedly or important information must be communicated within the department immediately.

The **Recommended Placement** form in Figure 8–21 can also make your life easier. If your department has leveling or some other form of ability grouping, you may need this form for parents who disregard your department's recommendations for placement. Your recommendations may not always be right, and sometimes it's hard to disregard a mother's insights about her child, but schools usually put a lot of time, effort, and expertise into recommendations for placement.

Parents who refuse these must understand that a later change of mind may be impossible to accommodate. Class sizes and scheduling restrictions may interfere with a later schedule change, even if the new placement is consistent with the department's earlier recommendations. If your school has ability grouping, you'll find that this form promotes careful planning in parents and often causes them to think twice about rejecting departmental recommendations.

The reproducible in Figure 8–22, **Substitute Teacher Schedule**, is a form that teachers provide for substitute teachers. It involves a schedule, the locations of necessary materials, and any special instructions the teachers care to leave with the substitute. Figures 8–23 and 8–24 provide forms for student field trips. The first involves the actual request for the trip; the second, the names of the students taking it.

The form in Figure 8–24 is purely procedural. Once completed, it should be duplicated and distributed to the rest of the faculty some time before the actual field trip to notify them of the explained absences of the students involved. The form in Figure 8–23 involves the actual request, but it also promotes additional planning on the part of the teacher regarding the purposes of the trip. As such, it may involve some dialogue between the teacher and the department chair.

Let's Wrap It Up

Dialogue between teachers and department chairs is essential to good educational planning. I'm not the first teacher advocate to praise their contributions to improved education. Recently, both the National Education Association (NEA) and the National Association of Secondary School Principals (NASSP) recommended that teachers play an active role in decisions about school budget, the evaluation of administrative personnel, staffing needs and decisions, curriculum, professional growth, and instruction.

In a document entitled *Ventures in Good Schooling,* they indicated that the leadership capabilities of teachers are an untapped resource for school improvement. It is a willing and accessible resource that increases with use. The key for the smart department chair, therefore, is to tap into it as often as possible with processes that engage teachers in departmental decisions routinely. Their involvement will increase their sense of professionalism and solidify their stake in the educational process.

Many teachers jokingly refer to school committees as groups of the unwilling, picked from the unfit, to do the unnecessary. Teachers are anything but unfit, but they *are* sometimes unwilling, primarily because they are the unselfish, who, unarmed informationally, are asked by the ungrateful to face the unknown, to make recommendations that ultimately are unheeded and unrewarded.

The processes to get teachers involved in decision making involve much more than committees. Sometimes committees really do take minutes and lose hours, so get teachers involved, individually or collectively, at every stage of the planning process to use your time and their expertise effectively. They bring an important perspective to the identification of problems, the development of plans, and the selection and implementation of solutions. Involve them as often as you can.

Figure 8–1

WHAT IS A PROBLEM?

"What Should Be"

$\left.\begin{array}{c} \\ \\ \\ \end{array}\right\}$ *This Is the Problem*

"What Is"

Figure 8–2

MISSION STATEMENT

To inspire inquiry, creativity, and achievement;
To foster integrity, compassion, and respect;
To promote commitment, service, and lifelong learning.

Philosophy

We believe in the dignity and worth of each individual. Therefore, we recognize that our school system must address a variety of individual student needs within an educational program that stimulates each person to realize his or her maximum potential.

Implementing this belief requires diversified, current, and comprehensive programming to provide students with the opportunity to develop intellectually, physically, socially, creatively, and emotionally. A school environment that promotes student growth in these areas is important in developing young men and women into respected and respectful citizens who responsibly balance personal freedom with the needs of a democratic society.

Goals

We see this overall process as a cooperative effort between the community and the school district. To implement these philosophical beliefs, we establish the following goals:

- To provide a program of curricular courses and cocurricular activities through which students develop critical and creative thinking, assess their talents and interests, and increase their respect for others and their appreciation of individual differences;
- To structure a program that will enable all students to acquire the education necessary for future endeavors;
- To promote physical and emotional well-being;
- To select and maintain a professional staff that is sensitive to the instructional and personal needs of each student and is dedicated to quality education;
- To design a meaningful sequence of educational experiences that continually promote academic and personal growth by challenging students to reach their full potential;
- To foster active, open communication among all constituencies of the school district and community;
- To maintain physical and technical facilities that enhance effective teaching and learning;
- To create an environment which fosters integrity, requires commitment, provides opportunities for service, and nurtures a love of learning;
- To maintain, through on-going self-evaluation, a school district that performs in a manner consistent with its stated philosophy.

Figure 8–3

ISSUE(S) TO LOOK AT

Teacher's Name: _____

Date: _____

The following are the particulars of a situation that may identify a problem in the department. Please consider this information and get back to me with a time we can meet to discuss it. Thanks.

The particulars that concern me: (Remember to specify the "what" of the situation; we'll discuss the "how" later.)

Figure 8–4

ISSUE(S) TO LOOK AT
(Completed Sample)

Teacher's Name: _____

Date: _____

The following are the particulars of a situation that may identify a problem in the department. Please consider this information and get back to me with a time we can meet to discuss it. Thanks.

The particulars that concern me: (Remember to specify the "what" of the situation; we'll discuss the "how" later.)

I have reviewed registration figures for senior English and have discovered that enrollment has fallen off by 17% within the past five-years. We have experienced an average decrease of 3% per year while the total student population in school has remained the same. One year ago, for example, we enrolled 253 students within a total school population of 1201. This year, within a total school population of 1205, we are enrolling 243 students. Five years ago, we enrolled 292 students. It seems we have a problem somewhere. Let's talk.

Figure 8–5

THE SEARCH FOR SOLUTIONS

Consider these questions or suggestions when seeking solutions to a problem. Try to provide written answers to them before planning meetings.

1. Eventually, what will we want solutions to do? How must they perform?

2. What interferences might or will continue to get in the way?

3. What specifically is the objective we are hoping to accomplish?

4. What alternative solutions will help us realize this objective?

5. What selection criteria must we establish to choose from among the best alternative solutions?

6. What do we get when we apply these criteria to the alternative solutions?

7. What is the single best solution or combination of solution elements?

8. What kind of process do we want to follow to implement the solution and monitor its success?

Figure 8–6

LET'S BRAINSTORM
(Thinking about Solutions)

Use this form during a moment of free time, to think about solutions to the problem we've been discussing in our group. If any or all of your ideas sound silly, *don't worry.* Sometimes the ideas that sound the silliest at first make the best solutions later on. Just let the ideas flow, then bring the completed form to our next meeting. Thanks for taking the time to do this.

Remember, the solutions are designed to realize the following objective:

My Alternative Solutions:

1.

2.

3.

4.

5.

6.

7.

8.

9.

10.

Figure 8–7

SOLUTION ANALYSIS

Suggested Solution: _____

1. What tasks must be completed to make this solution effective?

    Things about which we agree.

    Areas for further work.

2. What resources are needed and/or available to help with this solution?

    Things about which we agree.

    Areas for further work.

Suggested Solution: _____

3. To what extent does this solution contribute to the realization of our objective?

    Things about which we agree.

    Areas for further study.

4. What are some possible negative consequences of this solution?

    Things about which we agree.

    Areas for further study.

On a scale of 1 to 10, 1 being the highest, rate this solution in relation to all the others.

Rating: _____

Figure 8–8

PROGRESS UPDATE
(Monitoring a Solution's Progress)

To:

Fr:

Re: Planning Update

Please fill out the bottom of this form by _____. Thanks for taking the time to do this. Your input will provide important information for the planning activities in the department.

Title of planning activity: _____

Solution targeted for completion by: _____
(Date)

Persons responsible for implementation:

_____

_____

_____

_____

What is some of the measurable or observable evidence of completion:

Current status of solution, as of: _____
(Date)

(Use reverse side as needed.)

Figure 8–9

IT'S BUDGET TIME AGAIN!
(Budget Request Memo)

To:

Fr:

Re: Next Year's Budget Requests

Attached is a copy of your goals for this year and the budget requests you made last year.

1. Please submit your itemized budget requests for next year by _____. Include projected costs for all meetings, memberships, local programs, publications, and projects at school. Please be specific and try as much as possible to relate budget needs to your goals for this year and next year. Obviously, you will be unable to do this in all instances, but do it whenever possible. It will help clarify our needs to others.

2. Please list departmental goals from your perspective or programs that you are working on that will involve a cost next year. These goal statements will be incorporated into the department's budget document. Such statements might include physical renovations/changes (furniture, ventilation, special programs we should be studying, staffing needs, consultative services, and the like.)

3. Separately, please list two or three projected needs (as stated above) that may or may not involve an initial cost next year. I am interested in anticipated equipment or supply needs that will probably face us sometime within the next three years.

Thanks! I'll be in touch or you can get a hold of me if we need to discuss any of this.

Figure 8–10

PROGRAM DESCRIPTION AND GOALS

1. *Program Elements and Population(s) Served*

2. *Objectives for the Coming Year*

3. *Evaluation Process*

4. *General Comments*

Figure 8–11

CAPITAL EQUIPMENT, ADDITIONAL

School _____

Department _____

Forms Completed by _____

Description of Items	Explanation of Need	Unit Cost	Total Cost	Adm. Notes
Capital Equipment—Additional				
	Total Cost			

Figure 8–12

CAPITAL EQUIPMENT,
REPLACEMENT, SPACE RENOVATION

School _____

Department _____

Forms Completed by _____

Description of Items	Explanation of Need	Unit Cost	Total Cost	Adm. Notes
Capital Equipment—Replacement				
Total Cost				

Space Renovation (Include equipment installation)				
Total Cost				

© 1993 by Michael D. Koehler

Figure 8–13

EXPENDABLES

School _____

Department _____

Forms Completed by _____

Quantity	Description of Items	Unit Cost	Total Cost	Adm. Notes
	Instructional Supplies			
	Total Cost			

Figure 8–14

EXPENDABLES
EQUIPMENT RENTAL OR REPAIR

School _____

Department _____

Forms Completed by _____

Description of Items	Suggested Source	Unit Cost	Total Cost	Adm. Notes
Repair of Equipment				
		Total Cost		

Description of Items	Suggested Source	Unit Cost	Total Cost	Adm. Notes
Rental of Equipment				
		Total Cost		

Figure 8–15

PROFESSIONAL TRAVEL

School _____

Department _____

Forms Completed by _____

Teacher's Name	Conference Name and Location	Cost Estimate	Adm. Notes
		Total Cost	

Figure 8–16

LIBRARY EXPENDABLES

School _____

Department _____

Forms Completed by _____

Name of Category	Budget Code	Cost	Adm. Notes
Printed Materials			
Total Cost			

Name of Category	Budget Code	Cost	Adm. Notes
Audio-Visual Supplies			
Total Cost			

Name of Category	Budget Code	Cost	Adm. Notes
Audio-Visual Materials			
Total Cost			

Figure 8–17

BUDGET PROJECT PLANNING

School _____

Department _____

Forms Completed by _____

In the spaces provided below, I have projected my view of the possible major needs for my department in the years listed. The form includes expenditures that may become necessary to continue or develop our program. It is particularly responsive to major equipment replacements. The costs are estimates.

	Projected Cost
School Year _____	
1.	
2.	
3.	
4.	
5.	
School Year _____	
1.	
2.	
3.	
4.	
5.	
School Year _____	
1.	
2.	
3.	
4.	
5.	

Figure 8–18

ROOM INVENTORY

The following is an inventory of the equipment and supplies in each room in the _____ department. Please notify the department chair if any of the following items is removed from the room and not returned.

Room Number: _____

Number of Desks: _____

Equipment and Supplies: (Include such items as overhead projectors, screens, maps, file cabinets, tables, chairs, textbooks, and so forth.)

Figure 8–19

MONTHLY CALENDAR

Please review this calendar periodically for important departmental and school activities. It will provide information regarding the opening and closing days of school, in-service days, vacations, days and times of department and faculty meetings, due dates (teacher goals, self-evaluations, et al.), the final exam schedule, the beginning and ending days for each semester, administration dates for the ACT, SAT, and other tests, evening and weekend student activities of interest, and other important all-school information.

It also provides personally relevant information such as the days and times of your classroom observations, the days and times of pre- and postobservation conferences, end-of-the-year evaluation conferences, periodic meetings for us to discuss your progress toward your yearly goals, informal sitdowns to talk about "how things are going," and other relevant information.

Obviously, if you have any questions regarding the calendar, you can contact me at your convenience. I hope this is helpful with your planning activities.

Month: _____

Teacher: _____

Figure 8–20

TELEPHONE CHAIN

In the unlikely event that school should be closed, it will be necessary to spread the word quickly. Please help me by calling the next person on the list. Remember to take this form home with you!

Your Name and Number
(   )

Figure 8–21

RECOMMENDED PLACEMENT MEMO

Address

Recommended Placement: _____

_____

Dear _____:

As you know, our department has used a combination of your child's test scores, transcript, and former teachers' recommendations to determine the above placement. Our primary concern is that your child experience as much success as possible in our department. We will continue to work with you toward that end regarding your decision to seek a placement other than the one we have recommended.

Feel free to contact me or your child's teacher to assist you both with a successful adjustment to the expectations of the class. Please contact me as well if you decide to reconsider your decision to accept our recommendation. Please recognize, however, that we may be unable to accommodate it once either semester begins. Class limits and scheduling restrictions may prevent a schedule change of any kind.

If you have questions about any of this, please call me at your convenience.

Sincerely yours,

cc: Registrar's Office

Figure 8–22

SUBSTITUTE TEACHER SCHEDULE

Name _____

Substituting for _____ **On** _____

Department _____ **Chairperson** _____ **Office** _____

Period	Class	Room	Time

Information for Substitute Teacher

Location of . . .

1. Attendance Cards: _____

2. Seating Charts: _____

3. Cabinet/file keys: _____

4. Supplies/Equipment typically used: _____

5. Names of colleagues for whom to seek assistance: _____

_____

6. Comments or special instructions: _____

_____

_____

Daily routine information available from the Department Chair

Figure 8–23

REQUEST FOR FIELD TRIP
(Including In-School)

1st Semester   **2nd Semester**

Due to Department Chairperson:

Department _____

Subject _____ Approximate No. of Students _____

Teacher _____

Day and Date _____

Departure Time _____ Return by _____

Destination _____

_____

_____

Purpose of Trip _____

_____

_____

_____   _____

Signature: Department Chairperson   Approval: Assistant Principal

*Reminders:
  Bus request due to _____ 2 wks. prior to trip.

  Roster due to _____ noon Monday of the
  week preceding the trip.

  Schedule 2nd semester trips beween _____
  and _____ .

A copy of the approved Request Form will be returned to the Department Chairperson.

Field trip rosters and bus request forms are available from Department Chair.

Figure 8–24

FIELD TRIP PREARRANGED ROSTER

Sponsor(s) Name(s) _____

Date of Trip _____

Class Periods to be Missed _____

Destination/Purpose _____

[Complete *either* Part 1 *or* Part 2, below]

---

1. To be completed in cases where the entire class or activity organization (or all but a few students) are expected to participate in the trip.

   Course #: _____ *Activity Code #:* _____

   Section #: _____

---

2. When part 1 is not applicable, please list the name and I.D. number of *each student expected to participate* in the trip. You *may* wish to attach a copy of your class roster which clearly indicates those who *are* expected to participate.

I.D.#	NAME	I.D.#	NAME
_____	_____	_____	_____
_____	_____	_____	_____
_____	_____	_____	_____
_____	_____	_____	_____
_____	_____	_____	_____
_____	_____	_____	_____
_____	_____	_____	_____
_____	_____	_____	_____
_____	_____	_____	_____
_____	_____	_____	_____
_____	_____	_____	_____
_____	_____	_____	_____
_____	_____	_____	_____
_____	_____	_____	_____

MANAGING AND AVOIDING CONFLICT

I worked closely one year with a man named Dick who had the potential to be a marvelous English teacher. He was bright, knew English and enjoyed his continued study of it, and related well with kids—in a nonclassroom setting. In his classroom, Dick was so focused and bright that he often intimidated his students and forgot to cover important material because, like so many veteran teachers, he began to assume that much of it was obvious to them.

Dick often found himself in trouble with the administration. Parents were calling counselors at the beginning of every school year trying to get their children switched to another teacher, and they were calling periodically throughout the year complaining of his teaching techniques. Students were racing in and out of counselors' offices with one horror story after another. With each passing day, he became increasingly defensive, to the point of bringing a lawyer to school and tape-recording his evaluative conferences with his department chair and other administrators.

The school responded by assigning an administrator to observe each of Dick's classes, every day, for one week. Having gathered their documentation, they scheduled another meeting with him to discuss it; he again brought a lawyer. And so it went for another three or four years until the school hired a new principal who decided immediately to take a different approach with him. Recognizing that ongoing adversarial relationships rarely result in anything positive, he asked me to work with Dick.

I have been an advocate of a philosophy similar to W. Edwards Deming's long before it became fashionable. I have believed that if a problem exists *in* the system, the first place to look is *at* the system. Deming reminds decision makers that 90% of the problems in schools and other organizations are systemic; I tell administrators and department chairs to look for a mirror as soon as a problem is discovered. What they will discover in that mirror is the likelihood that the system is at fault. The concepts are complementary.

The first thing I did was to look at the system and the strategies that had been used with Dick, and I found myself asking the question: "Why is increased evaluation the administrative response to poor performance?" Think about it. Evaluation really is a form of measurement, and since when does measuring something make it grow? If farmers counted on bumper crops by measuring corn-stalks each day, we'd all be in trouble.

MANAGING CONFLICT

Obviously, then, we needed a different approach with Dick. Recurring evaluations weren't the answer. They may have been helpful, even essential, if the school's sole purpose was to dismiss Dick, but ostensibly that wasn't their purpose, or so they said. Certainly it wasn't the purpose of the new principal, so I began to look at strategies other than evaluation to improve his teaching. I wanted to find a win-win situation, one that satisfied him as well as the school.

Conflict Resolution Strategies

My subsequent experiences with Dick taught me a great deal about avoiding and resolving conflict. The first thing I realized was that as long as neither party is willing to change, the conflict cannot be resolved. No startling revelation. My 30-some years in public education, however, indicate that few people enmeshed in conflict, although they understand this fact, are willing to do anything about it.

When decades of tradition sanction evaluation as the primary response to a perception of poor teacher performance, the school's administration in Dick's case felt justified in their position. And Dick didn't change because he was pushed into a reactive position, in essence a fight for survival. In such a situation, the conflict will persist, unless the circumstances somehow change. In this case, the administration changed, and Dick discovered a window of opportunity.

Suddenly I found myself looking through the same window. I saw several alternatives to help resolve the problem, developed by a few of educational administration's finest minds. Fremont Kast and James Rosenzweig, the authors of *Organization and Management: A Systems Approach,* developed five strategies I might have used:

- *Withdrawal.* Dick could have resigned from his job, or I could have tried to convince the new administrative team to simply back off. Neither of these ideas seemed realistic.

- *Forcing.* I could have exercised my hierarchical authority and tried to force Dick to accept the administration's position, but this strategy had already failed.

- *Smoothing.* I could have tried the ploy that is so often effective in some situations: "Dick, why don't you just go along with them? This is really no big deal anyway; just play the game for a while, and they'll back off. It's really a whole lot easier. . . ." And I could have said to the new principal: "We're making pretty good progress. I'm pretty sure he's going to come around. Maybe if folks just back off for a while. . . ." I reasoned, however, that the vested interests on both sides were too strong for this strategy.

- *Compromise.* I could have found some bits and pieces from both sides and tried to get each to give and take a little. Such a strategy would have made me an intermediary, a carrier of messages, the guy who calms the waters and eliminates the waves that are so threatening to many administrators. This would have been too pragmatic for me and, frankly, not enough of a challenge.

- *Confrontation.* This strategy is the favorite of Kast and Rosenzweig. It involves both parties in a mutual airing of their respective positions. Each is asked to explain and examine reasons behind the conflict and to seek ways to resolve it. This can be an effective strategy, if both parties are willing to devote the time to a reasonable discussion of the issues. This situation had gone beyond that point, however, so I looked elsewhere.

    Mary Parker Follett started writing about management at the turn of the century and identified three conflict resolution strategies that have become the paradigms for much contemporary thought. She said that administration can do three things:

- *Dominate.* Like Kast and Rosenzweig's "Forcing," domination involves the use of hierarchical power, sometimes referred to as the "Or Else" line of reasoning.

- *Compromise.* Follett reasoned that compromise left both parties dissatisfied, suggesting the likelihood of another conflict at some time in the future, so she favored her third strategy:

- *Integrate.* Instead of seeking a compromise, both parties seek a new solution that will be mutually acceptable. The search for an integrated solution to a conflict precludes victory for either side. Both sides win. Usually, it involves a focus on a higher-level goal, encouraging both parties to ultimately abandon their competing positions. This seemed to me the reasonable way to handle Dick's conflict with the administration.

After a couple of meetings, when Dick and I strengthened our mutual trust, we finally arrived at an integrated solution, one that also was likely to satisfy the administration:

"Dick, let's forget what's happened up to now. How do you prefer to use our meetings? What specifically can I do to help?"

"Maybe you can explain exactly what the administration wants. I've heard so many different things."

"Can I make a suggestion? Let's forget those administrative evaluations. Let's focus on what *you* want. What would make you feel better in your classroom?"

"Well, frankly, ..."

Before steering Dick in this direction, I had to consider all the variables involved in this conflict and, during my earlier meetings with Dick, identify some of the facts behind it. Above all, I had to avoid a "win-lose" situation and identify a solution that advanced the interests of both Dick and the administration. The process is very similar to any planning activity.

The Conflict Resolution Process

Normally, this is a process that engages all parties involved in the conflict. This is especially true if the resolution strategy is "Confrontation" or "Compromise." In this case, however, Dick and I were the only key figures in the strategy, so he and I engaged in the following process. There was nothing formal about it. In fact, I'm sure he didn't even know we were doing it.

"What are the reasons for this disagreement?"

Ostensibly, the administration's reasons involved the "feeling tone" in Dick's classroom. Each of the evaluators had indicated that students felt uncomfortable inmost of the classes. As I reviewed their reports, however, I discovered that most of their observations involved value judgments; almost none involved anecdotal and objective evidence of student behavior to document their discomfort. And none suggested future professional growth activities to resolve the "problem."

The reasons, however, were nonetheless valid. The administration felt that they were dealing with an incompetent and perhaps insubordinate teacher, and their perceptions were reinforced every time a parent called to complain about Dick's teaching. They also had a considerable number of student complaints registered with counselors. The counselors, in turn, were wondering why no one would confront the issue with Dick to either resolve it or dismiss him.

After lengthy discussion, I learned from Dick that his primary reason for taking on the administration was fear. He was fighting back, blindly at times, so preoccupied with actual and anticipated battles that he had little energy left to deal with classroom problems. His reasons also seemed valid. Few people in the school had worked with him formatively to analyze and overcome his problems in the classroom.

Having put the reasons on the table, Dick and I then decided to look at the facts, an essential part of the conflict resolution process. This part of the process is more difficult, because it usually involves "hidden agendas" and less obvious motives. The word "facts" doesn't always involve clear documentation. Questions must be asked that go beyond assumptions and opinions, that provide a clear look at the reality of the situation. Fact-finding sessions should be designed to broaden the areas of agreement and to narrow the areas of disagreement.

"What are the facts behind this conflict?"

Fortunately, facts exist outside the world of words. As facts are uncovered, opinions become transparent increasingly. Experience had taught me, for example, that administrators don't like waves, particularly if the ripple effect reaches into the community and affects parental perceptions of the school. The people who make such waves become the focus of administrative attention. This is a fact.

It also became clear to me that the waves created by Dick were only partially a result of his relationships with students. They also resulted from his frantic attempts to get out of the hot water created by the administration. My job was to calm the waters and to find a middle ground that would be acceptable to everyone involved. This is true for the resolution of all conflict, if compromise or integrated problem solving is the most desirable strategy.

"What is acceptable to all the parties involved in this conflict?"

Remember, compromise requires some give and take from both parties. As indicated in the previous section, it involves trying to stay warm with a coat that's too small. It doesn't quite do the job, but it's better than nothing. Sometimes it's the only strategy possible and almost always involves a mediator or, in some instances, a negotiator to actually make the decision. I can't think of one time in my experience, however, when arbitration was needed for a departmental conflict, and mediation often leaves both parties dissatisfied.

My strategy of choice is usually integration. Recognizing that the administration wanted Dick to improve his teaching and to stop making waves, and that Dick wanted to find a way out of the hot water, I decided to seek a new but related solution to the problem. I reasoned that an unpressured focus on Dick's professional growth would accommodate the administration's concerns and might provide the relief Dick needed to feel more comfortable with his classes.

We met for almost a year and a half, alternately observing his classes and discussing the data I collected. The experience became so productive that Dick would call me periodically to request that I gather more data for him. We used several different instruments, and each time I gave him one, he analyzed the information so carefully that he forgot about me standing alongside him. On a couple of occasions, I leaned toward him and asked if he needed anything else. Focusing only on the paper, he would shake his head and mutter thanks. I would leave the room, and a couple of days later he would call wondering if I might observe another of his classes.

After about a year of observing, sometimes meeting to discuss teaching strategies, and often just touching base over a cup of coffee, Dick was suddenly a different person. He no longer wore the neck brace that symbolized the stress from his earlier confrontations with the administration. He was smiling more and actually enjoying the relationships with his students. And, most importantly, his teaching had improved significantly. Counselors were even reporting to me that they were now receiving phone calls from parents *requesting* him as a teacher.

The waters had calmed, and Dick had waded his way to that middle ground that ultimately provided a solution for him and the administration. It was not a compromised solution, and it didn't represent complete resolution of the problem. In fact, any time a conflict is resolved, department chairs and others must be careful to heed this final element in the process.

"Is this conflict likely to have any after-effects?"

Conflicts usually result in hurt feelings, even when resolution strategies advance the causes of both parties. Fortunately, in Dick's case the new administration sent him memos praising his hard work and commending him for the comments they had been hearing from students and parents. Sometimes, however, hurt feelings can persist beyond the apparent resolution of the problem and cause another conflict.

It's wise to continue to monitor the behaviors and feelings of the parties involved in the conflict, even to be aware of the intentions of others who may be relatively new to the situation. Dick, for example, had alienated a couple of other teachers in his department during his conflict with the administration, one of whom was about to become the new department chair. To avoid a recurrence of the problem, the principal and I met with her to discuss the strategies that I had used to get Dick reinvested in his professional growth.

She agreed that they had been successful and promised to consider them or something like them when she started working with Dick. Fortunately, she was able to forget old animosities and develop a very positive relationship with Dick, who continued to grow professionally, eventually to become a completely satisfactory teacher.

The Need for Flexibility

I had made a conscious decision to seek an integrated solution to Dick's conflict with the administration. A different situation with Dick or another kind of conflict in the building may have provoked a different strategy. Some require a unique sensitivity to the particulars of the problem. Consider other kinds of issues you might face: the assassin on your staff, who, for whatever reason, seeks to destroy you within the building; the intransigent who won't agree to *anything;* or the power monger who has seduced the principal and pays little attention to anything you say.

Such conflicts are insidious and require a special brand of insight in order to find and apply the right solution. In Dick's case, the new principal used good old common sense, not an intellectualized logic but an emotional awareness of the right thing to do. American author Josh Billings once said that common sense is instinct, and enough of it is genius. It is the knack of seeing things as they are, and doing things as they ought to be done. Conflict resolution in education requires this kind of common sense—unfortunately, a very uncommon commodity in many schools.

AVOIDING CONFLICT

Perhaps common sense dictates avoiding conflict in the first place. I have discovered that close attention to four general areas avoids potential trouble: communication, consensus building, team membership, and effective planning. Department chairs who attend to each of these areas significantly reduce conflict in their departments.

Communication

Communication is important for several reasons, but in schools it is necessary to promote common understandings, common purposes, and a common vision.

When students inquire into the primary responsibility of a building principal or a department chair, my pat answer is "to sustain a focus on the normative values of the school or department." Obviously, our responsibilities involve much more, but if we maintain such a focus, everything else seems to fall into place.

I sat in a meeting the other day with a young administrator and two parents to discuss homebound instruction for a girl who was recently hospitalized for a kidney infection. Early in the meeting, the administrator explained to the parents how difficult it was to find teachers who were willing to take the time to go to a student's home in the evenings to provide instruction. She indicated that it would be particularly difficult in science because of her inability to complete lab experiments at home.

The parents asked if the school could "color outside the lines" and allow the student to be instructed at home in her other subjects but to get the doctor's permission to come to school for science. They reasoned that as her strength returned, she probably would benefit from some involvement at school as long as she didn't get overtired. The administrator said, "No." The rules were clear: Students took all or none of their courses on homebound instruction.

The parents responded that she herself had said that science courses were very difficult to complete on a homebound basis. The administrator acknowledged her comment but repeated: all homebound or all in school. The parents looked at each other, smiled, shook their heads slowly, and signed the forms. Shortly thereafter, the meeting concluded.

Certainly, the school had good reasons for establishing its rules governing homebound instruction. But the communication of those rules alienated two parents and failed to focus on the needs of the student. Thinking about the meeting on the way home that night, I was reminded of a tongue-in-cheek guide for administrator evaluation. It says of outstanding administrators that they "Talk with God." It says of highly satisfactory administrators that they "Talk with angels," of satisfactory administrators that they "Talk to themselves," of low satisfactory that they "Argue with themselves," and of the unsatisfactory that they "Lose the arguments."

I had just experienced a "lost argument." The administrator may have left the meeting feeling that she had won a battle regarding the sanctity of homebound instruction, but enough such victories would lead inevitably to a significant defeat, probably at the polls when the school or district needed a referendum. A continuing focus on the normative values of the department may not effect a change in homebound instruction, but it will influence the quality of communication regarding the inflexibility of the program. It is this quality which suggests the first of five principles that influence effective communication.

Recognizing the Importance of Good Communication

You will avoid a lot of problems if you are perceived by others in your department as someone who believes in good communication. Model your belief that communication is a two-way proposition. Listen as well as you talk to others. Be alert to body language, your own as well as the other person's. Paraphrase the other person's position frequently. It assures your understanding of his or her position and establishes rapport by showing that you are listening. Don't judge and don't be quick to volunteer advice. Whatever benefits you expect, invariably they come at the expense of trust. And don't compare the person's situation to someone else's. It detracts from the importance of his or her issue.

Make "I" statements. "I am angry." "I would appreciate some help with this." "I disagree." Avoid the flipside of each statement: "You make me mad." "Why don't you ever help out in the department?" "You're wrong." "I" statements explain your feelings about an issue without personalizing it. Even with substantial disagreements, "I" statements permit healthy arguments. Once personalized, they become little more than quarreling and bickering.

Communicating Through the Monthly or Annual Report

Engage your staff in planning meetings, small- and large-group discussions, informal get-togethers, and personal meetings. We've already discussed much of this in other sections of the book. You will likely have the responsibility of writing an annual report at the end of the year, maybe even monthly. It should include reference to the planning and the other significant activities that have taken place within your department during the year.

A good annual report format should include the following elements:

- *Program Highlights.* Include in this section reference to new courses; achievements of students, such as National Merit winners, writing contest awards, winners of contests, et al.; community partnerships; club activities; field trips, and guest speakers.

- *Status of School and District Priorities.* The school and/or building administration will develop yearly priorities and will want to receive feedback regarding their relative accomplishment.

- *Needs.* You should have a considerable amount of information to include in the report if you heed suggestions within earlier sections of this book about needs assessments.

- *In-service and staff development.* This section may include reference to the total number of observations you have made throughout the year, but it should include no reference to specific teacher evaluations. Instead, it should refer to the topics, speakers, and activities involved in in-service days, staff workshops attended, staff presentations at workshops or conventions, publications, meetings, and relevant committee activities.

- *Curriculum.* This section involves reference to the selection of new textbooks, likely future proposals, the status of new or experimental courses, adjustments in existing courses, upcoming summer workshops, state or federal mandates that have been accommodated, and such specifics as projects to promote critical thinking.

- *Goals and Objectives for the coming year.* This final section should be an outgrowth of the planning that has taken place during the year in the department.

Once completed, the final report should be shared with the department. Put a routing slip on one copy and circulate it among members of the department.

Don't provide copies for everyone. You may not want some of them lying around the school. The document is an affirmation of your honest communication with your staff, and it acknowledges the important work they did during the school year, another very important way to improve communication.

Acknowledging Good Communication from Teachers

Encourage and reward effective communication. Encourage it by providing **Contact Records** like the one in Figure 9–1. It is offered here as a reproducible, but you probably will want to develop a form that makes at least one copy. The form is useful to document sensitive conversations with students or parents, important discussions with teachers, and information from phone calls that is relevant for others in the building, such as counselors, special education case managers, and administrators.

Persons appreciate such information when they are working with certain students or are planning upcoming meetings with parents or teachers. Reward the use of the form by acknowledging specific teachers in end-of-the-year evaluations. Also mention the input received from specific teachers regarding the use of the **Parent-Teacher Night** form in Figure 9–2.

This form focuses departmental attention on the issues and information that must be shared with parents during presentations at events such as PTO or PTA nights at school. General topics such as new courses, new programs, requests for parent volunteers, priorities for the current school year, and specifics such as your course outline, homework expectations, special classroom activities, attendance and tardiness policies, grading procedures, and promised communication with parents are just a few examples of the issues that should be shared. Not only does the form identify special topics that should be addressed, but it assures a uniformity of information in all classes.

Involving Parents in the Communication Process

Decisions are not isolated entities. Generally, they exist in a series, one affecting another, often reaching beyond the immediate circumstance to influence other situations and people, sometimes unpredictably. Effective communication influences the decisions themselves and increases the predictability of their effects on others. That's why many department chairs organize Parent Advisory Councils to provide a parental perspective to a range of departmental issues.

Such councils do not have the authority to make decisions. They are strictly advisory, encouraged to identify and bring issues to each meeting and to respond to items on the agenda. In fact, their responsibilities should be discussed at the first meeting, and each member should receive a handout like the reproducible **Parent Advisory Council**, in Figure 9–3. Notice that it discourages comments about individual teachers. Parental involvement on such councils should result in ideas flowing, not axes grinding. An occasional compliment may be acceptable, but the fundamental purpose of parental involvement should be input into departmental decisions, not teacher performance.

Consider as well that a by-product of such parental involvement could be increased political power. Former members of the board of education and other politically active parents are excellent people to have on a Parent Advisory Council. They tend to be knowledgeable, dedicated to the school, and influential. Any recommendations or needs statements coming from your department that include the names of such persons will get the attention of the building and district administration.

Handling Confidential Student Information

Will Rogers once said: "It isn't what we don't know that gives us trouble, it's what we know that ain't so." Well-communicated information avoids both kinds of trouble. It promotes accuracy and dispels misconceptions. Consider the ***Confidential Student Checklist*** form in Figure 9–4. A guidance department chair with whom I work has used it for several years with his feeder junior high schools. He asks the schools' guidance and administrative personnel to complete the form to identify students who will need special attention in high school.

He praises the form because it has helped identify special needs students immediately and enables his school to provide important services to them and their parents as soon as the student starts school. He uses it during visits to each school in the spring, when special education and other special needs students are being registered for their freshman classes. During discussions with junior high personnel, he completes individual forms and then, at some future time, discusses each student with counseling, special education, and instructional personnel in his school.

Obviously, confidentiality is an issue, so the form itself is shared with no one. The information is shared in meetings, so that colleagues can take their own notes and discuss the information. The process for sharing such information is almost as important as the information itself.

Communicating Criteria for Effective Teaching

The same is true of the reproducible, ***Criteria for Effective Teaching***, in Figure 9–5. This form should be shared with teachers early in the school year, probably distributed to them in a departmental meeting discussed along with the information in Figures 2–1 and 2–8. Any discussion of the professional growth alternatives should include a look at the criteria that determine effective teaching.

I could have shared this reproducible in Section Two, but I saved it for this section to emphasize the importance of communication regarding the use of evaluative criteria. We have already discussed the importance of expert power in helping teachers grow professionally. Your position in the hierarchy alone does not provide an understanding of these criteria. The title "Department Chair" does not include the transcendental knowledge of how to be one.

You must know how to apply these criteria in an evaluative situation and when and how to use them in supervisory activities. And, most importantly, they must be communicated to every teacher clearly, particularly before a teacher is recommended for remediation or dismissal. The absence of such communication violates the principles of substantive due process and makes your recommendation for teacher dismissal legally indefensible. We will discuss this process later in this section.

So make sure teachers understand the information in Figure 9–5. More importantly, make sure *you* understand it and can discuss it with each of your teachers intelligently. These criteria represent the target that each teacher shoots for each year, and you represent the steady hand that helps them realize their goals.

Communicating with the Custodial Staff

Finally, to assure the custodial staff that we're all in this together, communicate with them routinely and, just as routinely, praise their work. Use the forms in Figures 9–6, *Use of Facilities*, and 9–7, *Work Request*, to request and document their services, then send a note like the one in the following memo to thank them and to share your respect for their work with the principal and superintendent. If you provide specific praise for work that's well done, you'll be surprised how quickly and efficiently they respond to your requests for help.

Preparing Communications for School-Related Trips

Finally, the reproducibles in Figures 9–8, *Parental Permission* and *Waiver of Liability*, and 9–9, *Medical Information*, anticipate the special needs of students on school-related trips. You may or may not want to use them, depending upon the procedures already used in your school.

Many schools, for whatever reason, fail to use such forms and find themselves in trouble periodically. If these forms, therefore, fail to specify the concerns of your school, modify them accordingly, but be sure to use something like them. The anticipation of potential problems can prevent a lot of trouble later on.

Consensus Building

Bernard Bass, in his book *Leadership Psychology and Organizational Behavior,* indicates that collections of individuals about the same age, the same degree of educational attainment, and the same interests have a high degree of interaction potential. School systems should be ripe for team and consensus building. Most of them are; teachers have little difficulty developing a sense of belonging in schools. If they don't identify strongly with the school itself, they identify with a group of cronies that share a table in the faculty cafeteria or grab a quick cigarette in the boilerroom.

"Belonging," therefore, isn't the only issue. Identifying with the normative values of the school and focusing on its goals and objectives is essential if teachers are to have a sense of shared purpose. We have indicated in another section that morale in a school is highest when teachers satisfy their individual needs simultaneously while they contribute to the realization of the school's goals. In essence, consensus is most possible when teachers feel satisfied *and* competent, when they feel good about themselves personally and professionally.

Because we have covered much of this in previous sections, let's look at it now from a different perspective. It's important for department chairs to recognize that teacher needs change as they grow older in their jobs. Midcareer teachers, like their younger counterparts, need a sense of achievement and recognition; they also need revitalization, a change of pace, and renewed enthusiasm.

Consensus building within the department is a function of establishing not only a sense of shared purpose but the ability to work hard to accomplish those purposes. Veteran teachers are occasionally unable to find the energy to make such commitments. They agree with the purposes and value them as professionals, but they sometimes lack the drive to do much about them. Seeking to light the fires of their students, they require a periodic rekindling of their own.

Department chairs, then, alternate between lighting fires and putting them out. Fortunately, rekindling the enthusiasm in a good teacher is a whole lot easier than putting out the numerous brush fires started by bad ones. The following are a few successful strategies:

- Provide occasional released time to work on a special project, one that capitalizes on his or her experience and training.

- Provide frequent recognition for jobs well done.

- Team veteran teachers with first-year or nontenured teachers to provide collegial supervision.

- Engage veteran staff members in discussions of budget, curriculum, and other departmental planning activities. Seek their advice often on subjects with which they have had considerable experience.

- Encourage them to attend workshops and conferences to recharge their batteries.

- Provide the time and the financial resources for teachers to retrain in a different specialty or to assume a different responsibility in the district.

- Make veteran teachers responsible for the orientation of new staff.

Creative department chairs will devise more strategies, some much better than these. They will devise them because they recognize the intrinsic need of every teacher to grow, not just to refine current skills but to develop new ones, the kind that introduce vitality to the job and enhance the teacher's sense of competency and self-esteem. Good department chairs realize that only some teachers get burned out; most get *turned* out—to pasture, like aging thoroughbreds.

The search for new blood and fresh thinking inadvertently disenfranchises some of the most knowledgeable people in the building. The loss is two-fold. The teachers lose some of their vitality and enthusiasm for the job, and the school loses some of its ability to introspect, to see itself through the eyes of teachers who share a perspective acquired only from experience. Given education's current problems, we can't afford to disregard such an accessible and valuable resource.

Parents provide a similar resource. Consensus building involves them as well. Figure 9–10, **Achieving Consensus**, provides a modification of the form provided in Figure 7–1. It uses the same objectives but requests a parental reaction to them. It is just one way to secure input from parents and to assure a sense of common purpose between parents and the school. Once achieved, it can avoid a great deal of unnecessary litigation.

It is interesting to observe that the problems with litigation have introduced other kinds of "conflict." Many schools are wondering why litigation seems to have leveled off but premiums for liability insurance continue to rise. A doctoral study reports that within a recent four-year period in Indiana the cost of court awards and settlements has increased by just 25% but that insurance premiums went up 229%. It would seem that conflicts in education are waged on many different fronts.

Finally, once a sense of common purpose is achieved, department chairs must maintain it by being the buffer between the faculty and outside influences, even influences like the administration. School and district administrators mandate certain expectations. The department chair is the buffer between such mandates and their implementation within the department. The skillful department chair colors most mandates with his or her own personal style and implements them in a way that is consistent with the philosophy of the department.

This requires a great deal of skill, and even then some administrative expectations may be inconsistent with the department's philosophy but must be implemented anyway. Department chairs must simply acknowledge the reality of the expectation and implement it. The real world often confronts us with such situations. At such times, we are well-advised to remember that we are members not only of our department's team but of the school's administrative team, and team membership often requires us to do things we disagree with.

Promoting Team Membership

Having achieved a sense of common purpose among teachers, the department can become a team to work together to achieve these purposes. As any coach knows, effective coordination is critical to a team's success. Every team consists of different kinds of players; some who are more talented, some more headstrong. Some work too hard, others not hard enough; a few even challenge the coach's authority. Coordination may not accommodate all these issues, but will handle most of them.

Members of any team must know the when, why, where, and how of the roles they perform. That's why the calendar that was mentioned in the previous section is such a good idea. Consider just the references to teacher goals. The calendar can mention when the goals are due, the dates of follow-up meetings, and the date and time of the wrap-up at the end of the year.

The use of the calendar, then, makes the goals more immediate, more real. With clear indications of meeting dates on the calendar, goals become more than perfunctory tasks to be completed each year. The calendar also becomes a reminder to you to make classroom observations, to complete monthly and annual reports, and to prepare for meetings with teachers.

We often get buried in paperwork, the immediacy of which seems to make it more important. Without a calendar to remind us of really substantive responsibilities, the due dates on the paperwork would dictate much of what we do each day. The calendar enables us to develop for ourselves and our teachers a format that sustains a focus on what is important to us as a department. Then it reminds us of important upcoming activities.

Coordination, however, is not the only prerequisite for successful teamwork. Members of the team must also feel that their contributions are important. Most teams enjoy the talents of only a limited number of superstars. A relatively few college football players become All-Americans, and only one teacher can be

Teacher of the Year. But everyone makes a contribution, perhaps not as newsworthy as the superstar but every bit as important to the team's success.

- The department chair's job is to recognize every contribution, no matter how small. "Catch 'em being good!" Always find something positive to say after every classroom observation. Visit classes informally for five minutes at a time and then write a note to the teacher praising something you saw. Tell the teacher in such notes how pleased you are to be working with such dedicated professionals. These compliments have a way of becoming self-fulfilling prophecies.

- Celebrate birthdays in the department office. Before each school year, identify all the birthdays in the department, including the secretaries and aides, if you have them. Put the names and the birthdates in a hat and have staff members draw one to find the name of the person for whom they will provide a cake and appropriate decorations. Put the cakes in the department office so everyone can have a piece. Then you give each person a card, and you and the department have gone a long way in establishing the togetherness that promotes teamwork.

- Put up a "Toot Our Own Horns" wall in the department office. Use it to post award notices, copies of published articles, newspaper clippings, commendatory letters from parents, memos from administrators, and other evidence of teacher accomplishment. Ask teachers periodically to share information for the wall. Many are disinclined to toot their own horns and need occasional prompting.

Department Chair as Team Leader

Obviously, the department chair is focal within this process. Teams need leaders. If, for whatever reason, they don't accept their formal leader, they'll find another one. When they do, the potential for conflict is further complicated because of the increased likelihood of their activities being inconsistent with the goals of the department. Fortunately, department chairs don't have to earn a leadership position. Schools grant it along with the title, and teachers are usually willing to go along with it, as long as they continue to trust the department chair.

An important question for you, however, is "Trust what?" Do they need to trust your ability to intervene on their behalf with the administration? To provide the kind of conceptual leadership that satisfies their need to gain insights into what they do? To provide stimulating and fulfilling professional growth relationships? To be the resident expert about guiding them toward the kinds of decisions that improve the program?

To be perceived as an accessible helpmate throughout most of the school year? To be supportive of their need to take risks in order to grow? To provide an atmosphere of honesty that touches much of what happens in the department? The obvious answer to all these questions is a resounding *Yes,* but the last question is perhaps the most important. We can be only moderately intelligent and minimally charismatic as leaders, but if we are completely honest, we have a good chance of being acceptable to those we seek to lead.

Brutal honesty is not the answer; the answer involves a combination of honesty and caring, *sensitive* truth. When people know we care about them, they can accept most anything else in us. Consider Abraham Maslow's claim that the absence of what he called life's metavalues is pathogenic. He believed that people who are routinely denied beauty, honesty, and justice become physically or mentally ill.

People confined to our nation's inner cities suffer a unique depression that only trees and blue skies can cure. Their lives involve a numbing gray sameness that forges successive days into an ever-tightening chain. The effects of poverty are far-reaching. Too often the disadvantaged are also denied justice; the illness that results finds expression in thoughtless violence that affirms their sense of control. The absence of honesty, therefore, affects all of us. The continued absence of sun in midwinter colors our outlook on life, just as the continued absence of honesty colors our relationships with others.

To avoid *any kind* of paranoia in your department, then, be sure to share information routinely. Figure 9–11, **This and That**, provides a form that I used for a few years. I distributed it once a quarter to provide updates on relevant personal issues of members of the department, budgetary information, mention of awards that teachers or groups of teachers may have received, workshops attended or presentations made, significant minutes from building administrator's meetings, board of education decisions, and any other information that should be shared with the department. With a few modifications, it can also become the substance of a newsletter you might share with the parent community.

Finally, it is difficult to separate professional from personal relationships. People who dislike each other can still work together, but if they enjoy a personal as well as a professional relationship, the synergy they create will make their work output that much better. Invite the department, as well as teacher aides and custodial personnel, over to your house for a cookout in the spring and fall of the year. Encourage others in the department to have informal get-togethers or to meet periodically at a local eatery. People reach out more quickly when they like each other.

Planning—The Ounce of Prevention

If conflict resolution is the pound of cure, planning is the ounce of prevention. Section Eight discussed planning in considerable detail, so I will add only a few more thoughts here. I saved the **Curriculum Articulation** form in Figure 9–12 for this section to emphasize how good planning avoids potential conflicts or an unnecessary duplication of effort. Use the form with the other materials in Section One when you revise your curriculum.

The form highlights the fact that the principles of sequence, continuity, and integration are applicable inside and *outside* the school/department. They apply to transitions from junior to senior high as well as from one year to the next. Because they are often complicated by the developmental readiness of incoming freshmen, it is essential for high school personnel to plan collaboratively with junior high personnel to guarantee well-sequenced and cognitively appropriate academic experiences for all freshmen.

This form and the process it involves are steps in the right direction. The **Summer School** form in Figure 9–13, though unrelated to the curriculum development process, is also important for establishing appropriate summer school offerings and experiences for students. Summer school can be very critical for some students. It provides not only enrichment courses but prerequisites, graduation requirements, and make-up opportunities. That students have the right teachers and courses in summer school can prevent lots of problems for them as well as the school.

The Problem Teacher

The crucial question involving the problem teacher is, "Whose problem is it?" If department chairs depend on hierarchical power to resolve issues with problem teachers, they will find themselves up to their necks in problem teachers. Because of their lack of expert power, department chairs will discover that the "problem" belongs to them. Our job is to make sure the problem belongs to the *teacher*.

The information in Figure 9–5, *Criteria for Effective Teaching* is critical. Substantive due process demands that such information be communicated clearly to all teachers, particularly if one or more are to be involved in remediation or dismissal. In addition, the department chair must be an expert in each category, use the criteria to assist teachers with their professional growth, and apply them to determine the need for remediation.

Learned skills require little consciousness of application; they occur routinely. Any of the skills in Figure 9–5 that are new to teachers require conscious application. That's where the department chair comes in, to raise consciousness by reminding them of the criteria and helping them to incorporate them into their teaching repertoires. If teachers simply are unable to learn such teaching skills, then remediation and, ultimately, dismissal become the only alternatives.

The Dismissal Process

The road to teacher dismissal is costly, time-consuming, and riddled with legal potholes. Accidents can occur at any time if key persons fail to accommodate the legal requirements that protect the rights of teachers. Again, the expert power of decision makers is essential if the reasons for intensive evaluation or remediation are to be defensible legally. Unsubstantiated claims of incompetence usually cause more problems for the school than the teacher if the teacher chooses to hire a lawyer.

Administrative dependence on hierarchical power is perhaps the biggest reason why so many poor teachers continue to hide behind tenure in our schools. Many department chairs lack the knowledge to promote professional growth among their colleagues, let alone to fire one for incompetence in the classroom. For those who do have the knowledge, their efforts to dismiss intransigent teachers are complicated further by a range of legal considerations.

Common sense would suggest that department chairs develop acceptable professional growth programs that provide the help teachers need to master the teaching skills expected of them. Such programs make life a whole lot easier for them and the teachers. My experience indicates that it's better to work closely with a teacher during the year to rekindle his enthusiasm for teaching than to grope through the maze of documentation, lawyers, and unions to dismiss him.

The process of dismissing a teacher can take up to two and a half years and cost a school $100,000. Figure 9–14, ***Unsatisfactory Performance,*** serves two purposes. It reminds administrators about the process of dismissal and why it is so time-consuming and expensive, and it informs teachers of the school's procedures. It should be included in the packet of information that is given to the staff early in the year during discussions of the supervisory and evaluative processes. The other materials for the packet can be found in Sections Two and Three of this book.

Finally, remediation and dismissal are last resorts. Experience indicates that they rarely improve performance; they tend to be too adversarial to create the trust required for a productive supervisory relationship. So avoid such alternatives by working closely with each of your teachers to promote the professional growth they require to do the job to everyone's satisfaction, including their own. After all, someone saw something good at one time in even the most unwilling and unable veteran. Remind yourself of what this was and use it as the starting point to recapture the teacher's enthusiasm for learning.

If dismissal becomes the only alternative, however, follow the provisions in Figure 9–14 to provide due process requirements. These relate to the School Code in Illinois. Be sure to check your own state. In addition, go to a local university to bring in teaching experts to document the performance of the problem teacher. Undoubtedly, you already have your expert appraisals and additional validation from other administrators in your school. You'll be on solid ground legally if you supplement those appraisals with the opinions of *other* experts in the field. Then meet with the district's lawyers to discuss necessary steps.

The Steps in Teacher Dismissal

Statutes may vary from state to state regarding teacher dismissal, but the five general areas that warrant dismissal are constant:

- *Insubordination.* Teachers can be expected to follow school and district policies and reasonable directives from school authorities.

- *Neglect of duty.* Teachers sign on to perform prescribed responsibilities. Failure to perform them within a framework of reasonable expectations constitutes neglect of duty.

- *Improper performance of duties.* Teachers may perform duties but are subject to dismissal if such duties are performed in a manner that is negligent or falls short of minimum standards.

- *Improper conduct.* Teachers are expected to behave within a professional code of ethics. Deviations from this code in dealings with students, parents, and colleagues constitute a violation of trust and may result in dismissal.

- *Incompetence.* Teachers can be expected to have reasonable knowledge of their subject areas and of the teaching/learning process. The persistent inability to acquire such knowledge may constitute incompetence and result in dismissal.

Each of these areas is purposely general in order to accommodate a variety of teacher behaviors. Much less general are the processes that validate one or more of these areas during the dismissal of a teacher. An accusation of improper conduct is one thing; proving it is another. The requirements of substantive due process, for example, require the school to:

- Have evaluative criteria.
- Assure that such criteria are reasonable.
- Eliminate vagueness from the criteria.
- Communicate the criteria.
- Administer the criteria reasonably.

Substantive due process means that the reasons for dismissal must relate to the competence of the individual to perform the responsibilities of his or her position. In addition, the school must communicate its expectations of such performance so that teachers are not affected by criteria of which they have no knowledge. In specific terms, this means that the school/district must:

- Develop and adequately communicate its expectations of teacher performance.
- Adhere to all policies, such as the minimum number of classroom observations, expected recommendations for improved performance, follow-up conferences, reasonable time and assistance to improve performance, and written records of observation results and conferences placed in the teacher's file and given to the teacher for his or her personal record.
- Inform staff of the procedure for inspecting its personnel files.
- Establish a procedure for the dismissal of staff and communicate it to the staff.

The requirements of procedural due process assure the constitutional safeguards that guarantee teachers the right to face their accusers, respond to charges, and refute evidence against them. Once the requirements of substantive due process have been guaranteed, for example, and a teacher has been recommended for dismissal, procedural due process principles must be assured. Specifically, they provide for:

- Reasonable advance notice of dismissal.
- The opportunity to explain a contrary position.
- An opportunity to confront accusers.
- The right to appeal.
- Assurance against capriciousness.

Schools assuring procedural due process usually guarantee the following steps:

- Notify the teacher of pending dismissal both orally and in writing.
- Inform the teacher of the specific reasons for dismissal and of his or her right to due process.

- Identify the persons who have made charges against the teacher in writing.
- Provide time for the teacher to refute the charges.
- Organize a conference with the superintendent, board attorney, and appropriate supervisors and administrators.
- Notify the teacher by certified mail of the Board hearing, reminding him or her of due process rights as explained in the district policy book or state school codes and assuring him or her of the right to legal counsel.
- Provide a written record of the proceedings.
- Remind the teacher of his or her right to appeal any decision within the framework of the legal system.

Be sure to maintain good records throughout the process. This includes records of meetings with lawyers, records of discussions with the teacher, written opinions of the experts who have observed the teacher, minutes of administrative meetings, copies of your evaluative reports, and any written responses from the teacher. As indicated, this is a tedious procedure and best avoided by establishing trusting relationships with your staff, the kind that result in growth for them and satisfaction for you.

Let's Wrap It Up

Occasional conflict is disruptive, but continuing conflict is destructive. Any system that experiences continued disequilibrium faces its own destruction. If your body's temperature remains abnormally high, you die. If the air/fuel mixture in your car remains poor, it eventually stops running. If you fail repeatedly to pay your electric bill, someone eventually turns off your lights. Major conflicts, therefore, must be resolved quickly but effectively. The information in this section will help.

On the other hand, conflict is inevitable in schools and sometimes desirable. It reflects change. If the change is purposeful and well-planned, the conflict may suggest that the changes are working. Schools without conflict may be lacking the energy that results in substantive improvements in student learning and teacher growth.

However inevitable or desirable, conflicts must be resolved, or they will continue to provoke bad feelings and ultimately impair the effectiveness of the department. In addition to the strategies mentioned in this section, a few additional words of advice will help you resolve such conflicts. The advice is best summed up with this principle: Be aware of your own behavior when dealing with conflict.

First of all, know what pushes your buttons. Don't allow yourself to be drawn into a conflict for all the wrong reasons. When involved in a discussion with the other person(s), depersonalize the situation. Talk about behaviors, not people. Know when to walk away, when to call "Time out." A wise father once told his son, "Never pass up the opportunity to keep your mouth shut." There comes a time in a "discussion" when such advice is especially appropriate.

Pay attention to the tone and speed of your own language, to your body language as well. Sometimes our actions are so loud, no one can hear what we say. Don't allow past circumstances to influence the current situation. Focus on the issue(s) at hand. Make sure you expect from the situation only what is realistic. And, above all, be realistic about what you can and cannot resolve.

A friend of mine, a professor of administration in a very prestigious school, once told me to distinguish between problems and dilemmas. He believed that problems could be resolved; dilemmas couldn't. Dilemmas required that the situation simply be made more comfortable for everyone involved. Making such a distinction has helped me considerably over the years.

Finally, remember that it's easier to avoid a conflict than to resolve one. The time and effort devoted to establishing trusting relationships provides immediate and long-range benefits. You will find yourself enmeshed in fewer conflicts, and you will be the person your teachers turn to when they are in conflict with each other or the school.

Figure 9–1

CONTACT RECORD

To: _____ _____ _____
        Last Name   *First Name*   *Counselor*   *Date*

CONFERENCE WITH: _____

_____

Phone: _____

Other: _____   **Signed** _____

Figure 9–2

PARENT-TEACHER NIGHT

Just a quick reminder about the few specifics we must remember to share at the upcoming Parent-Teacher Night at school. Be sure to discuss and, if possible, share copies of

- Your course outline,
- Homework expectations,
- Attendance and tardiness policies,
- Grading procedures,
- Field trip procedures,
- Behavior expectations,
- Promised communication with parents, and
- The particulars of any special activities you have planned.

You might then discuss the goals of your course and, perhaps, even engage the parents in a classroom activity or two. That, of course, is up to you. Just remember to have fun with them. They are our allies throughout the school year, and this is one of our best chances to establish a relationship with them. It's also a great opportunity to show the community just how good this department is. I certainly plan to tell everyone!

Because I will have this opportunity to talk with many of the parents, I would appreciate some feedback from you regarding the topics and issues I must remember to discuss with them. Remind me about special programs and plans for the future, some of which you might mention, too. Thanks for your help.

Figure 9–3

PARENT ADVISORY COUNCIL

Welcome to our Parent Advisory Council. I am pleased that you have decided to join us for this very important advisory committee. I discovered a long time ago that a continuing dialogue between the school and its parent community is critical if we are to provide an educational program that will meet the changing needs of our student body. Our department's program must be aware of parental expectations, if not to satisfy them, at least to discuss them openly and honestly. Parents possess a unique and important perspective for school systems, and they provide a valuable resource for departmental activities. We are about to share a wonderful opportunity to influence the learning experiences of our students and to establish an even more positive relationship between the school and community.

To make the most of this relationship, I recommend the following ground rules:

1. Because we will be focusing on program considerations exclusively, I suggest that we allow no discussions of individual teachers.

2. I will provide my agenda of the items to be discussed at each meeting. Each will be a discussion item, but I will inform you of any and all decisions that result from the discussion.

3. You too will have valuable agenda items. Please share them with me at least three days prior to each meeting.

4. We will meet once a month, unless we have no agenda items, at which point I will notify you that the meeting has been cancelled.

Again, thank you for devoting your time to such an important activity. I look forward to working with you.

Figure 9–4

CONFIDENTIAL STUDENT CHECKLIST

The following checklist has been developed to enable special services personnel to identify the highly symptomatic students who may require special attention in high school. Early intervention is our school's most successful way to introduce such students to the demands of a new school environment. For that reason, we would appreciate a few moments of your time to check the characteristics that apply to students you suspect of being "highly symptomatic."

We recognize that no one characteristic is determinative; several in combination may not identify a student in need of special attention or placement in high school. The information you provide, however, will engage the professionals who can make such determinations. The result will be a plan that promotes a more successful high school experience for the student. In advance, thanks for your help.

Student's name: _____

Jr. High contact person: _____

High Priority—Call me: _____

Has this student evidenced any of the following behaviors?

Please indicate if they are past or current behaviors.

1. Difficulty with Academic Performance

   _____ Incompletion of homework or other assignments

   _____ Grades are inconsistent with tested aptitude

   _____ Inability to work independently

   _____ Poor study skills

   _____ Difficulty with comprehension

   _____ Poor memorization

   _____ Difficulty following directions

   _____ Has repeated a grade

   _____ Receiving outside tutorial assistance

2. Problems with Social/Behavioral Adjustment

   _____ Excessive absenteeism

   _____ Inappropriate self-management and behavior

   _____ Poor peer relationships

   _____ In need of structure

   _____ Issues involving police

   _____ Otherwise immature (Please describe behavior.)

Figure 9–4, continued

Has the student ever received any of these services? Please indicate when:

3. Involvement with Related Services

 _____ Case Study Evaluation—approximate date, please:

 _____ Frequent counselor contact

 _____ Social work intervention

 _____ Known referral to resource outside school

 _____ Hospitalization(s): Emotional/chemical/eating disorder?

4. Family Factors

 _____ Adoption

 _____ Family issues such as divorce, death, alcoholism, or other dysfunction

 _____ Other (Please describe.)

5. Additional Comments (*Confidential*):

Figure 9–5

CRITERIA FOR EFFECTIVE TEACHING

Clarity

Concepts, ideas, and directions are presented logically, rationally, clearly.

Proper materials selected for students.

Objective and rationale are given, and students understand expectations and standards.

Opening activity is meaningful and motivating.

Flexibility

The ability to use a variety of appropriate techniques.

The teacher matches the method to content for the students.

Appropriate right and left brain techniques are used.

Questions are rephrased or concept broken into smaller steps when necessary.

Evaluation

Concurrently with clarity and flexibility, the teacher monitors the cues (feedback) from the students so that methods or techniques are changed.

The teacher makes sure the problems in mastery are not teacher-caused.

Checks for understanding, formal and informal, are made frequently, and at the end of the class especially.

Enthusiasm

The teacher exhibits enthusiasm for the material, the students, and the activity through movement, voice, gesture, facial expression, and responses to student contributions.

Task-Orientation

The students are able to focus on a particular task (Objective, goal, purpose).

The class is engaged in meaningful activity.

All students participate actively.

Use of Student Ideas

Teacher acknowledges, modifies, applies, summarizes student contributions to build rapport and to show mutual respect (positive reinforcement).

Student contributions are used to develop concepts or process.

Induction helps students discover generalizations, rules, processes.

Figure 9–5, continued

Criticism

Evaluative or critical comments have no negative behavior or tone that discourages participation. Students take risks willingly.

Critical (strategic, logical) thinking is encouraged to correct erroneous response.

Classroom management is handled without disruption to instruction. Preventative rather than punitive measures are employed.

A strong, positive feeling tone is created through teacher's management and behavior.

Questioning

Lower order questions (who, what, when) that do not prompt discussion are avoided in favor of higher order questions (why, how).

Questions lead students to think, to form valid conclusions from evidence, to master processes.

Higher levels of the thinking skills taxonomy are reached.

Teacher practices adequate "wait" time between questions.

Use of Structuring

From a stated objective, activities designed for students to master the objectives and appropriate evaluation techniques, a structured lesson is designed.

Sequence of instruction moves smoothly and logically from concept/skill to concept/skill, from known to unknown, from simple to complex, from concrete to abstract.

Instructional session has a definite beginning, middle, and end.

Process is developed clearly, and students demonstrate mastery because of organization and practice.

Through organization of instruction and adequate practice, students are able to summarize (reiterate, paraphrase) the sessions' essential points; i.e., present closure.

Figure 9–6

USE OF FACILITIES

_____
Date of Request

Date of Event _____

Time of Event _____

Location _____

Event _____

Organization _____ **Sponsor** _____

List all equipment needed for your event. We will notify the person(s) in charge to have it ready for you. *Last minute requests for additional equipment may not be honored.*

Rehearsal, Decorating and Clean-Up Arrangements: If you will need access to the room or area you are reserving prior to the time listed above, please indicate what time _____. What time will your event be over? _____

Audio-Visual Equipment:

of microphones _____   # of floor stands _____   # of desk stands _____

portable P.A. _____   overhead projector _____   16 mm. projector _____

carousel slide projector _____   carousel remote control _____   screen _____

TV _____   VCR _____   other _____

Maintenance/Custodial Service:

of tables _____   # of chairs _____   other _____

Please diagram any special room or area arrangement that you will need for your program. (Catering/refreshment arrangements are the responsibility of the sponsor.)

Approved/Date _____

Figure 9–7

WORK REQUEST

Request Date _____

Job Location _____

Event Date _____ **Time** _____

Reason for Request _____

_____

Office Use Only
Assigned to _____
Date Assigned _____
Date Completed _____
Time Spent _____
Reason for Delay _____

Work Needed
(check one)

☐ When you have time
☐ Place on work schedule

Description of Work Needed

_____

_____

_____

Requested by _____

Department Chairperson _____

Approved by _____
           (Assistant Principal)

Figure 9–8

PARENTAL PERMISSION TO PARTICIPATE IN SCHOOL ACTIVITY AND WAIVER OF LIABILITY

Students have many opportunities to participate in various extracurricular activities at school as an outgrowth of classroom interests or special interest clubs. On occasion it will be to their advantage to attend activities away from school on an optional basis. However, the Board of Education of the School District cannot assume responsibility for the safety and welfare of students while they are off campus beyond making reasonable provision for their supervision by representatives of the School District designated to supervise the activity.

Your signature on page 2 constitutes and is evidence of 1. Your consent to permit your child to participate in the school activity; 2. Your agreement to accept general liability for the participation of your child in the school activity; and 3. Your agreement to waive, release, indemnify and hold harmless the Board of Education of School District _____, its members, agents and employees, from any and all claims and liability arising out of your child's participation in the school activity and transportation thereto and therefrom as described below.

- -

My child, _____, has my permission to participate in the following school activity:

_____,

taking place on _____, on the terms and conditions stated above.

I understand that my child will travel by _____, leaving at

approximately _____, on _____, and

returning at approximately _____, on _____.

THIS IS A SCHOOL-SPONSORED EVENT AND ALL SCHOOL RULES WILL BE ENFORCED. IF THERE IS ANY UNAUTHORIZED USAGE OF DRUGS, ANY USAGE OF ALCOHOLIC BEVERAGES, OR OTHER VIOLATIONS OF SCHOOL RULES, PARENTS WILL BE NOTIFIED AND THE CONSEQUENCES WILL BE IMPLEMENTED BY THE DEANS.

Loco Parentis

From _____, 19___ to _____, 19___, should our child require medical attention as a result of accident or serious illness,

we do hereby grant and bestow upon _____ permission and authority for and on our behalf to authorize any licensed medical practitioner to render medical aid and treatment to the above-named person.

Figure 9–9

MEDICAL INFORMATION

List any medicines your child might take on the trip. Also list allergies your son/ daughter has to drugs or medicines.

_____

_____

Any other relevant medical conditions:

_____

_____

Consent   **Phone**

_____   _Residence:_ _____
(Parent or Guardian)

Date: _____   _Work:_ _____

Emergency phone numbers where parents might be reached if not at home:

_____

Person to contact if parents cannot be reached:

_____   Phone #: _____

Figure 9–10

ACHIEVING CONSENSUS

To the parents of DHS students:

The Guidance Department, in an attempt to achieve consensus with our parent community, is asking selected parents to respond to the following checklist. Please identify the five most important educational objectives for our students requiring the mutual efforts of parents and school. Identify the most important with a 1, the remaining four in descending order.

We must help our students:

_____ Develop social skills.

_____ Value the processes of education (learning how to learn).

_____ Analyze experiences and relationships which have brought them the greatest happiness.

_____ Identify strategies for relating to society's institutions.

_____ Explore experiences that lead to lifestyle and vocational choices.

_____ Explore their personal strengths and weaknesses.

_____ Understand the increasing interdependence among segments of society.

_____ Experience and study democratic principles in action.

_____ Develop a positive self-concept.

_____ Explore people, relationships, interests, goals, et al. in relation to the basic values of the students.

_____ Discuss the what and why of their responsibilities to other people.

_____ Explore and understand the difference between needs and wants.

_____ Learn positive ways to assert their influence on society.

_____ Explore family roles and determine the appropriateness of their own role.

_____ Practice decision making as it relates to values, attitudes, and reasoning.

_____ View other people in a cooperative, not a competitive way.

_____ Develop a willingness to take risks in the face of uncertainty.

_____ Practice good physical health.

_____ Appreciate beauty.

_____ Learn to appreciate the moral and social value of hard work.

_____ Experience the satisfaction of a job well done.

Our department may require assistance from others in the school to accommodate your preferences. Be assured that we will seek it and publicize our suggested activities for responding to your recommendations. Thanks for your continuing help and interest in our school.

Figure 9–11

THIS AND THAT
(Informal Department Update)

It's time for another update on the goings-on in and around the department. I thought you might like to know:

Figure 9–12

CURRICULUM ARTICULATION

Our department is considering some important changes in its freshman curriculum. We have nothing finalized yet but have developed a list of tentative recommendations. The following are some of the specifics. Please look them over and give me some feedback within the following framework:

Type of Change

_____ Addition of new course

_____ Deletion of existing course

_____ Name change

_____ Sequence adjustment

_____ Other

Description of Student Need

Relationship to Upper Level Courses in Curriculum

Support for the Course Based on Best Practice or Current Research

Course Objectives, Possible Content, and Suggested Textbook

On a separate sheet of paper, please provide whatever feedback you feel is appropriate. We are interested particularly in your reactions to the content of the textbook, the continuity and sequencing the course may have with your eighth grade curriculum, and the possible duplication of elements within one or more of your courses. We also would appreciate your expert opinion on the cognitive demands the course(s) will place on students. As entering freshmen, are they ready for such a course? In advance, thanks for your time and expertise.

Figure 9–13

SUMMER SCHOOL

It's time for summer school planning again. If you are interested in teaching one or more courses in summer school, please indicate your interest on the bottom of this form. Also please identify the course or courses you are interested in teaching. Please remember that courses offered in summer school may or may not be offered, depending upon enrollment. The summer school program must pay for itself. If interested, fill out this form and get it back to me by _____. Thanks.

Your Name: _____

The Course(s) you are interested in teaching: _____

_____

_____

If the course is not in our curriculum already, please provide the following additional information (attach additional sheets for each item as needed):

1. The perceived student need for the course:

2. The relationship of the proposed course to others in the curriculum:

3. The place of the course in the curriculum sequence:

4. Course description (as in curriculum book):

5. Course objectives:

6. Possible course content:

Figure 9–14

UNSATISFACTORY PERFORMANCE

If a tenured teacher's performance is judged unsatisfactory or does not meet district expectations, evidence will appear, both informative and summative documents written by supervisors. The first step in improving the teacher's performance is Intensive Supervision. Putting a teacher in this category is a consensus decision by the department chair, assistant principal, and principal who evaluate the teacher.

The minimal supervisory calendar for teachers on Intensive Supervision is the same as for first and second year probationary teachers. Supervisors will provide the teacher with specific points for improvement, suggestions for making the improvement, and the outcome that will indicate the improvement has been made. This process hopes to develop the teacher's performance to an acceptable level. Intensive Supervision may also involve disciplinary measures, such as being held on a salary step for the year. Through cooperative efforts on the part of everyone involved, it is hoped that the teacher's performance will improve and the teacher will return to the regular supervisory program.

Should the Intensive Supervision specifications not be met, the supervisors may recommend that the period of this stage be extended or that the teacher be placed on formal Remediation. The process of Remediation is governed by *The School Code* and requires legal counsel to prepare a Bill of Particulars, a Board resolution, and other guidance. Again, the purpose of the process is to improve the teacher's performance to an acceptable level and to return the teacher to the regular supervisory program.

During the Remediation process, the teacher is entitled to the services of a Consulting Teacher who has been selected by the following criteria:

1. Recognized as an excellent classroom teacher;
2. Has at least five years experience;
3. Demonstrated knowledge relevant to the assignment of the remediating teacher;
4. Selected from a list created by the District and the DEA, or supplied by ISBE from another district, as needed.

and who functions as:

1. Resource to the remediating teacher;
2. Receiver of information on the teacher's progress;
3. Nonparticipant in evaluating the teacher's performance.

The role of the Consulting Teacher is also set by *The School Code* (as amended by Senate Bill 730).

Everyone involved in the Remediation works to bring the teacher's performance to a level that meets district expectations. If the process does not effect an improvement in performance, a recommendation for dismissal will be sent to the Board of Education.

At this time, the teacher has a right, upon request, for a hearing first with the Board of Education, and subsequently to the legal system, if necessary, for appeal.

A FINAL REMINDER

Classroom teachers have the most important jobs in the building. Their behavior in and out of the classroom has the most immediate and lasting influence on what and how kids learn. Because department chairs have a similar influence on what and how teachers *teach,* their jobs are as important. In fact, no one else in the school can be expected to have a more complete understanding of curriculum and instruction than department chairs.

The tools of the principal and other administrators are budget documents, staffing considerations, state and federal mandates, legal requirements, student behavior, planning activities, and other significant managerial functions. The tools of teachers and department chairs are curriculum and instruction, both of which are so intricate in their operation that only experts can be expected to use them effectively. Department chairs are those experts.

ON BEING A GOOD DEPARTMENT CHAIR

To provide an initial framework, let's take a tongue-in-cheek look at some principles that have sustained some administrators over the years. These are more than well-researched hypotheses; they are apriori truths, forged by several disagreeable career experiences:

1. Keep teachers in their classrooms, isolated from their colleagues effectively. Associate them with authority and ongoing evaluation closely; affiliate them with each other marginally. Teachers working in close collaboration create a positive synergy, which tends to be threatening to some administrators.

2. Affirm hierarchical relationships whenever possible. Force teachers to struggle through the chain of command. The experience is even more exhausting than it is demeaning.

301

3. Sustain deference in all relationships. Expect to be treated by teachers as not only hierarchically but personally superior.

4. Make sure your department operates independently of others in the building. Applaud administrators who rarely promote close collaboration.

5. Rely on positional authority in the face of decisions and relationships. Disregard the need for expert authority. You'll find that few teachers expect it anyway.

6. Observe teacher performance only to evaluate and control, not to encourage and help. Teachers who receive encouragement become autonomous, not dependent.

7. Maintain a disjointed flow of information, always, for example, separating in-service training from *practice* in the classroom. Provide in-service training information and then evaluate quickly how teachers use it. That will keep them confused sufficiently.

8. Finally, be sure to restrict teacher involvement in the decisional processes that most affect them—their classroom activities. Teachers don't make good decisions anyway; they haven't had much practice.

You and I must never forget that people who espouse such principles have tradition on their side, an inexhaustible constancy that defies change, no matter how desirable. To break tradition's grip, we must deny these principles vigorously and do what we can to engage teachers in departmental decision-making and planning, particularly in areas that involve curriculum and instruction.

TEACHER BURNOUT

Department chairs who fail to deny these principles risk not only a disregard for the goals and objectives of the department and school but the dissatisfaction of teachers. "Burnout" is a reality in every profession, but especially in education, where prestige is traditionally in short supply. Social usefulness and dedication are at the core of the teaching profession, but they usually take a back seat to the fascination of law, medicine, and business, where closing a six-figure deal is considered more glamorous than influencing a six-year old's life.

Good department chairs help teachers face the frustration of having less prestige than other professions. By so doing, they reinforce the inherent "prestige" of teaching. Sharing such frustrations openly with a trusted department chair or with a formal colleague group is much more effective than the periodic catharsis of a cafeteria gripe session. Beyond such a sharing, department chairs must also acknowledge and try to eliminate those elements in the teacher's life that *cause* such frustration.

Playground duty, cafeteria and hall supervision, and a variety of clerical tasks may be essentials within schools, but they don't have to be the exclusive responsibility of teachers. Creative administrators across the country are hiring the elderly or seeking the services of volunteers within the community to perform such tasks. Obviously, adequate and *legal* supervision of students must be guaranteed, but the fear of litigation must not be the sole determinant of *who* watches the hallways.

Also, try to find a place for teachers to relax—their own place, a faculty lounge, or a room removed from the ebb and flow of daily activity. Work with other department chairs to develop such a facility for all staff; perhaps include a professional library, a stereo from the school's AV department, a bulletin board that proclaims teacher accomplishments, comfortable furniture, and individual workplaces.

Such a facility also provides a place during the day to find the time to complete the array of tasks that befall teachers. Sometimes the scope of these tasks is enormous, and whatever you do to relieve the pressure associated with them makes the tasks that much easier for teachers. In addition, work with teachers to find ways to change the tasks. You may not be able to eliminate many of them, maybe only one or two, but the attempt will do much to improve the morale of the staff.

Recognize as well that department chairs can reduce teacher burnout by assisting teachers with their reputations. As indicated in other sections of this resource, publicize their accomplishments and proclaim them to the community and the rest of the school as experts in their fields. The respect they receive from the community and their colleagues is one of the surest ways to promote prestige. People with a sense of prestige are disinclined to burn out.

Perhaps most importantly, when working with teachers on their classroom instruction, don't allow the research and theory surrounding methodology to dominate teaching behaviors. Remember, for example, that **Madeline Hunter's 7-step lesson design**, a copy of which is included in Figure 10–1, is not a *menu*. She is the first to deny its use as a prescription for teaching.

The principles contained in her seven steps result from decades, maybe centuries, of learning and teaching theory. As such, they provide a framework within which lessons can be developed. They are not designed to tie the hands of teachers and to stifle the spontaneity of the teaching/learning experience. Methodology is not a straitjacket, tailored to fit comfortably but restrictively by short-sighted department chairs.

More appropriately, it is a well-designed but comfortable item of apparel that complements the teacher's appearance and promotes rather than restrains the teacher's individuality and artistic expression. It may be true that nothing teaches more effectively than the spontaneous enthusiasm of a well-educated person, particularly if that enthusiasm is complemented by an understanding of teaching and learning theory. Such theory, however, is invariably less important than the teacher's love of what he or she is doing.

Finally, we might sum up this section on teacher burnout with the three basic principles found in job enrichment theory. It tells us that all teachers, to feel satisfaction in their jobs and to reduce the sometimes inevitable effects of burnout, must experience:

- *Meaningfulness.* They must sense that what they are doing *matters*. Such an awareness promotes self-esteem and a sense of prestige, the absence of which contribute to teacher burnout.

- *Responsibility.* They must be able to influence their work environment. They must feel valued and respected.
- *Knowledge of results.* They must see that what they do produces results. Department chairs must help them see these results. Such results involve not only student learning but program revision, administrator respect, parental appreciation, and personal growth.

Department chairs promote these principles in a variety of ways, but one of the most obvious is by delegating responsibility.

Delegation as a Key to Sanity

To the shortsighted, delegation involves distributing distasteful tasks to disinterested teachers. To the effective department chair, however, it is a miracle of organizational efficiency. We've already accepted the premise that teachers enjoy being recognized for their expertise. Delegation is one of the quickest ways to reengage "tuned-out" teachers and to provide for others the circumstances that promote motivation.

Delegation is also a way to maintain your sanity; it involves one of our organizational world's truly symbiotic relationships. What provides pleasure for one relieves pain for another. The cascade of paperwork that threatens your sanity can be used to engage selected staff members in significant departmental activities. Obviously, the tasks have to be meaningful, and the staff members usually have to be competent—but not always.

The unable and unwilling teacher may not contribute individually, but he or she can be teamed with someone else in the department who will model the right kinds of behaviors. Unable or unwilling teachers generally need to be "told" what is expected of them. Such a "telling" can be accomplished in a variety of ways, not the least of which is through association with a positive role model.

Similarly, the unable but willing teacher can benefit from delegation by working on a committee that responds to the task as well as trains the teacher. The unable but willing teacher generally needs to be "sold" on expected behaviors. The "selling" tends to be a function of working with people in the department who reflect such behaviors routinely. For this and other reasons, significant committee activities are excellent training grounds for inexperienced teachers.

Finally, and to extend the rhyming analogy, the able and willing teacher is "gold:" valuable, bright, usually malleable, a departmental resource to be displayed proudly. Whereas the needs of the unwilling and unable teachers involve the security and psychological levels on Maslow's hierarchy, and the willing but unable involve social and esteem needs, the able and willing teachers need frequent opportunities to self-actualize. Delegation provides such opportunities.

Theorists and researchers from Maslow to Herzberg have indicated for decades that recognition and achievement are higher order motivators than money or fringe benefits. Experience has taught me the same thing. Some of the highest paid teachers in schools are the first out the door when the bell rings. Involvement and recognition for their efforts, not money, revitalize worn-out and disenfranchised teachers. The same involvement and sense of achievement satisfy the self-actualization needs of the active, capable teachers. Money really doesn't do a whole lot for a sense of *self*-worth.

Look at it this way. Sickness caused by the desire for money plagued amateurism for so many years and altered its appearance so imperceptibly that its death has gone virtually unnoticed in this country. Money entered the sports picture so insidiously that many amateur track athletes were professionals before even *they* knew it. Now we have professional basketball and tennis players pocketing as well as wearing the gold in the Olympics.

Payment to me when I was playing football in college, although probably desirable at the time, would have severed my link with an idealized world of sport, where all players, not just the great ones, sacrificed their time and energy for a sense of personal and team accomplishment. It was something money couldn't buy. The same sacrifice, focused on money instead of achievement, robs athletes of one of the few times in their lives when simple self-satisfaction is free from the need to win or unencumbered by the clutter of "things."

All of us feel the same way, especially teachers, who admit readily that they didn't go into education for the money. They want their fair share, but they want and need much more. And you can give it to them by acknowledging their needs to contribute, achieve, and be recognized. In this sense, delegation is a valuable motivational tool, while it liberates you from some of that paper on your desk.

You and the Job

The role of department chair is not an organizational destination but a journey. Like your teachers, you must continue to grow in the job, to refine the expert knowledge that is so critical to the improvement of curriculum and instruction in your department. One way to accommodate that is to secure feedback from your staff regarding your performance. Figure 10–2, *I Need Your Help*, provides a reproducible of a form that I used for several years.

The use of the form provides two important benefits. One, it enabled me to reflect on my performance and to adjust my behavior as needed. Two, it told my staff that I believe in feedback from others to modify my professional behavior. In essence, it reaffirms that we're in this together, that we can help each other to improve as professionals.

Finally, this characteristic of good department chairs to collaborate with their teachers suggests additional principles to keep in mind if you want to survive in the job. These principles provide an overview of key elements in this book. I have provided them as a reproducible in Figure 10–3, *The Ten Suggestions, Reminders for Department Chairs*, in case you want to display them in your office as evidence of your good intentions! You'll notice that certain elements have been omitted from the figure because of their possible misinterpretation.

THE TEN SUGGESTIONS

1. As indicated in the title, rarely give a command. Progress in schools, as in society, often results from the rejection of someone's "command." True leaders engender a sense of common purpose, a will to carry on, both of which make commands unnecessary.

2. When you first get a job, don't say or do anything for the first 6 months. Stop, look, and listen. Oscar Wilde once said, "To do nothing at all is the most difficult thing in the world, the most difficult and the most intellectual."

3. Don't expect to have all the answers. Fight the need to prove yourself, to show how smart you are. Instead, ask the right questions. Give everyone else the chance to show how smart *they* are.

4. Establish processes to handle job responsibilities; then trust the processes. Groups of dedicated people create synergy. Margaret Mead once said, "Never doubt that a small group of thoughtful, committed citizens can change the world; indeed it's the only thing that ever does."

5. Be true to Woodrow Wilson's advice that evaluation should provide light, not heat. Evaluation should improve teaching, not your position or status in the department. Also remember that evaluation is a form of measurement and that measurement by itself cannot make anything grow.

6. Sustain a focus on your department's normative values. You will never be wrong. You may, perhaps, be misunderstood at times—but never wrong. And never lose your enthusiasm. Little significance will be achieved in your department without it.

7. Don't worry about authority. The more you want authority, the more you seek security, not progress. Invest in others, and you'll have power. They will give it to you. That's the only way to get it.

8. Master your craft; continue to study, to grow professionally. Authority without knowledge is a car without a driver, a force without purpose or direction.

9. Revolutions of the intelligent, not riots of the ignorant, lead to genuine change. Always seek the counsel and involvement of your most intelligent and committed department members.

10. Finally, never to try to make yourself look good. Your job is to make everyone else look good. Make the administration look good, and they'll give you authority. Make your teachers look good, and they'll give you power. Then, *you'll* look good.

Let's Wrap It Up

A friend of mine, a long-time department chair in a prestigious high school just outside Chicago, once said, "I remember my first year on the job, trying to convince everyone of how worthy I was to be the department chair. Someone should have slapped me. I had a group of teachers who were more than capable of self-reflection, and I kept getting in the way because of my desire to be needed."

His words suggest a final bit of advice. Establish the proper mix of personal needs and professional responsibilities. Accept the job for the right reasons, to advance the cause of education for your students and to be a "teacher aide" for your staff. If you seek the job to advance your own causes, I remind you of these oft-quoted words: "The man who lives for himself is likely to be corrupted by the company he keeps."

Two final quotes: If you seek the job to enhance your personal power within the organization, consider this quote: "I have never been able to conceive how any rational being could propose happiness to himself from the exercise of power over others." The speaker? Thomas Jefferson. And finally, remember the words of Kahlil Gibran, from "On Teaching," in *The Prophet:*

> The teacher who walks in the shadow
> of the temple, among his followers,
> gives not his wisdom, but rather of
> his faith and his lovingness.
> If he is indeed wise, he does not bid
> you enter the house of his wisdom, but
> rather leads you to the threshold of
> your own mind.

Such is the ultimate responsibility of any teacher, and department chairs must be among the school's best teachers. If you are currently a department chair or plan to become one, you will influence the lives of students and teachers every day, in ways that have far-reaching effects on their lives. No influence in our society, therefore, is more important or requires greater sensitivity and understanding. I wish you well with your job and hope that, in some small way, this resource helps you with it.

Figure 10–1

MADELINE HUNTER'S 7-STEP LESSON DESIGN

1. *Anticipatory Set*

    Are my students ready for what is to come?

2. *Objective*

    What am I going to teach and why?

3. *Input*

    How can I best teach the new information?

4. *Modeling*

    How can I help my students visualize what I am presenting?

5. *Checking for Understanding*

    Are my students comprehending what is being presented?

6. *Guided Practice*

    What kind of practice do my students need to reinforce their learning?

7. *Independent Practice*

    What kind of extended practice will reinforce learning?

Figure 10–2

I NEED YOUR HELP

As we approach the end of the school year, I find myself once again seeking your help. This time, I am interested in some feedback regarding my performance this year. Hopefully, you and I have discovered the benefits of working together on your classroom observations; now help me benefit from *your* input. I have provided several different categories requiring your feedback. Please provide your *specific* perceptions of my performance in each area. In other words, don't say "Nice job" or "Better luck next time;" tell me specifically or anecdotally what I might do to maintain or improve my performance in each area. In advance, thanks for your help.

Classroom Observations (Supervisory):

Classroom Observations (Evaluative):

Information Flow:

Organizing and Conducting Department Meetings:

Availability:

Coordination of Planning Activities:

Representing the Department (to administration, parents, school, et al.):

Other:

- What *one* thing do you most need from me?

- What else would you like to add?

Figure 10-3

THE TEN "SUGGESTIONS"
(Reminders for Department Chairs)

1. Rarely give a command. Progress in schools, as in society, often results from the rejection of someone's "command." True leaders engender a sense of common purpose, a will to carry on, both of which make commands unnecessary.

2. Don't be doing something all the time. Stop, look, and listen. Oscar Wilde once said, "To do nothing at all is the most difficult thing in the world, the most difficult and the most intellectual."

3. Don't expect to have all the answers. Instead, ask the right questions. Give everyone else the chance to show how smart *they* are.

4. Establish processes to handle job responsibilities; then trust the processes. Margaret Mead once said, "Never doubt that a small group of thoughtful, committed citizens can change the world; indeed it's the only thing that ever does."

5. Evaluation should provide light, not heat. It should improve teaching, not your position or status in the department. Also remember that evaluation is a form of measurement and that measurement by itself never made anything grow.

6. Sustain a focus on your department's normative values. You will never be wrong. And never lose your enthusiasm. Little significance will be achieved in your department without it.

7. Don't worry about authority. The more you want authority, the more you seek security, not progress.

8. Master your craft; continue to study, to grow professionally. Authority without knowledge is a car without a driver, a force without purpose or direction.

9. Revolutions of the intelligent, not riots of the ignorant, lead to genuine change. Always seek the counsel and involvement of your most committed department members.

10. Finally, never to try to make yourself look good. Your job is to make everyone else look good.

NOTES

NOTES

NOTES

NOTES

NOTES

NOTES